Praise for this book, pre
The Art of Urb

D1025866

"This empowering cycling book .... come in the glove
box of every new car sold."
—Marla Streb, World Champion Downhill Mountain
Bike Racer

"While it's hard to imagine a book about [urban] cycling
could fill over 250 pages, let alone strive to be a near
masterpiece, that's just what *The Art of Urban Cycling:
Lessons from the Street,* an all-encompassing how-to
book by veteran bicycling messenger Robert Hurst, has
accomplished.
    "With a spot-on foreword written by Luna downhiller
Marla Streb and a detailed index of footnotes and bibliography, Hurst has compiled a cerebral but hip manifesto for
[urban] cyclists looking to coexist in a system that has left
them to fend for their lives."
—*VeloNews,* Journal of Competitive Cycling

"This book goes beyond the basics and the tips to explore
in greater depth the issues and situations that explain why
good bicycling is an art more than a science."
—*League of American Bicyclists*

"Hurst offers many useful insights and plenty of food for
thought that you'd be wise to consider before pedaling
your way through rush hour traffic again."
—Bob Walch, *Adventure Sports Journal*

the Art of Cycling

A Guide to Bicycling in 21st-Century America

ROBERT HURST
Foreword by Marla Streb

FALCONGUIDES ®

GUILFORD, CONNECTICUT
HELENA, MONTANA
AN IMPRINT OF THE GLOBE PEQUOT PRESS

Photo montages by Casey Shain
Spot photographs and photos used in montages by Meghan L. Miller, Robert Reid, David Singleton, photos.com, and the author: pages iii, v–xii, xx–2, 10, 13, 29, 38, 40, 55, 60–62, 69, 150, 158, 162, 186, 197, 198–200, 216–18, 231, and 238–40 by Meghan L. Miller; photographs of cyclists pages x–xi, 41–42, 60–62, 135, 156–57, 184–85, 198–99, and 238–40 by Robert Reid; photographs page 135 by David Singleton; photograph of ambulance pages 156 and 158, photograph of bicycle wheels page 198 and 218, courtesy photos.com; photographs of tools pages 216 and 231 by Robert Hurst.
Traffic diagrams by Robert Hurst
All illustrations by Sam Turner, except illustration on page 5 by Diane Blasius
Text design by Casey Shain
Cover design by Todd Grosser

Library of Congress Cataloging-in-Publication Data

Hurst, Robert (Robert J.)
 [Art of urban cycling]
 The art of cycling : a guide to bicycling in 21st-century America / Robert Hurst ; foreword by Marla Streb. — 1st ed.
   p. cm.
 Originally published: The art of urban cycling. c2004.
 Includes bibliographical references (p. 253) and index.
 ISBN 978-0-7627-4316-2
 1. Cycling—Handbooks, manuals, etc. 2. City traffic—Handbooks, manuals, etc. I. Title.
 GV1043.7.H87 2007
 796.6—dc22

                                                                        2006021484

Manufactured in the United States of America
First Edition/Second Printing

For my beloved grandmothers, Emma Kinner
and Paula Keene
Laugh, love, and give encouragement.

contents

Foreword   *xiii*

Acknowledgments   *xv*

Introduction   *xvii*

ONE: *Frankenstein's Monster*

Continuum   2

Bicycles in the Age of Manure: Leonardo to Starley   3

The Bicycle Craze of the 1890s   10

Chumps of the Road   12

From Bicycles to Automobiles in Sixty Seconds   14

Speed and Greed   15

Barney Oldfield and the Arena of Death   17

A Dark Wave Cometh   20

Fake Gas Tanks   22

Transportation and the Shape of Cities   23

Automobile Suburbs   24

The Great Streetcar Massacre   26

Congestion   28

Enclosure   33

Rage   35

Cycling the New American City   35

Invocation   39

TWO: *The City Surface*

Pavement: Get Over It   42

Responsibility and Surface Hazards   43

The Great American Pothole   45

Cracks and Seams   47

Waves   49

Lane Markers   49

Wet Metal   50

Drainage   51

Railroad Tracks   53

Toppings   54

Plazas   56

Curbs   57

THREE: *In Traffic*

Beyond Vehicular Cycling   62

Blame Versus Responsibility   66

Vigilance   69

Route Choice   72

Road Position and Location   76

The Invisible Cyclist   79

Space Versus Visibility   80

The Myth of Lane Ownership   81

Running Green Lights   84

Eye Contact, Stop Signs, and Fake Right Turns   86

The Gap Effect   *89*

Four-way Stops   *92*

Momentum   *93*

Notes on Traffic Lights   *95*

Waiting at Traffic Lights   *97*

Running Red Lights   *101*

Left Turns   *103*

Corner Cutters   *104*

Looking Back   *105*

Seeing without Looking   *107*

Instinct Unveiled   *109*

Turn Signals   *111*

Hand Signals   *112*

In Defense of Gutters   *113*

The Door Zone   *116*

Reading Parked Vehicles   *118*

Close Combat: Positioning in Heavy Traffic   *121*

Riding a Straight Line   *123*

Track Stands   *125*

Turning and Cornering   *128*

Panic Stops   *130*

Bicycle Lanes and Paths: Good or Evil?   *134*

On the Bike Path   *141*

Sidewalks and the Law   *143*

Riding in Suburbia   *147*

Riding at Night   *149*

Riding with Others   *153*

FOUR: *Bicycle Accidents and Injuries*

The Statistical Quagmire   *158*

The Stats at a Glance   *161*

Cycling Fatalities   *162*

The Paradox of Experience   *164*

The Accident Immune System   *165*

Road Rash   *166*

Collarbones   *168*

How to Fall   *171*

Facial Injuries   *173*

Head Injuries   *174*

Other Injuries   *175*

Disclaimer   *176*

The Helmet Controversy   *176*

What Are Helmets Built For?   *179*

Torsion Injuries   *181*

The Helmet Verdict   *182*

FIVE: *Air Pollution and the Cyclist*

A Historical Reality Check   *186*

The Good News about Air Pollution   *188*

What Am I Breathing and What Does It Do to Me?   *190*

Breathing Strategies for the Cyclist   *193*

Does Air Pollution Cancel the Health Benefit of Cycling?   *196*

SIX: *Punctures and Flat Tires*

Flat Repair Equipment   200
Fixing Flats: A Primer   201
Broken Glass   204
Tire Wiping   205
Glassphalt   207
Tribulus Terrestris   208
A Thorny Dilemma   211
Random Sharpies   212
Pinch Flats   213
Blowouts   214

SEVEN: *Equipment*

The Cult of Equipment   218
Bike Choice   221
Track Bikes   223
Bike Fit   225
Tools   227
Clothing   232
Messenger Bags, Backpacks, and Panniers   234
Drivetrain Maintenance   236

EPILOGUE: *Of Bicycles and Cities*   239

Chapter Notes   243
Bibliography   253
Index   257
About the Author   265

foreword

It's about time that this book was written.

Robert Hurst succeeds in writing about cycling the way that Rachel Carson triumphed with *Silent Spring*, the seminal work whose publication spawned Earth Day, the Environmental Protection Agency, consumer recycling, and how we look at the world. *The Art of Cycling* is a clarion call not only for cyclists and those with whom we share the road, car drivers, but also for our elected representatives and urban planners who imagine and build the communities where we live.

Hurst is illustrative and inspiring without sounding preachy or depressing, even during the passages where he is righteously angry. His insightful humor ensures that this book is more than just a droll "how-to" guide.

As a professional bike racer myself, as well as a century rider, and daily bike commuter, the almost perfect utility of the bicycle is reaffirmed in my mind with each pedal stroke on every ride, whether to the finish line or to the video store. I have bombed down the Kamikaze course at 60 miles per hour. I've won a Winter X Games gold medal skidding on snow. On my downhill bike, I've flown more than 40 feet through the air and landed with a fair share of broken bones. During the last ten years, while on the pro tour, I've ridden through Tokyo at rush hour, across Paris amid a general strike, and around Rome when it seemed that every Fiat's horn was signaling in Morse code.

Yet, sometimes it's more dangerous just riding across town to pick up my mail.

In this book, Hurst has expressed all the emotion and logic for cycling as a means of transportation and as a way of life, which I sadly suppress. After a day of defending my right to Mount Tam's fire roads or chasing a morning's skinny tire group ride through Marin County's dairy valleys, or when I am coasting along to the grocery store, too often there occurs a moment. A super-sized SUV roars past almost clipping me with a passenger door mirror. I am speechless—too tired to reserve my right to ride a bicycle on a public street. The tailpipe speeds away, and the moment passes, even more likely to happen again tomorrow.

The sad irony is that Marin County, California, is supposed to be a "bike friendly" community. During this last off-season, I rode my bike from Fort Lauderdale to Baltimore and I can attest that "sharing the road" is more a concept than a reality.

But it doesn't have to be this way. Robert shares his strategic and tactical lessons for riding safer and faster through the urban landscape, sometimes even skirting the edges of the law more as a practical measure than as an act of civil disobedience. And I applaud.

Robert Hurst reminds us that if we cyclists don't skillfully exercise our right to the road, we lose our right to the road. This empowering urban cycling book should come in the glove box of every new car sold.

— MARLA STREB

Marla Streb is a world champion mountain bike racer, has starred in the Imax film *Top Speed,* and is the author of *Downhill: The Life Story of a Gravity Goddess* published by Penguin Putnam. Before she joined the World Cup mountain biking circuit, she was a research biologist at the Scripps Research Institute, devoted to finding a cure for AIDS. Marla began riding a bike on a daily basis in 1990, when she took an extra job as a bike messenger. Soon, however, it became her life's passion and she is now one of the fastest (and bravest!) bicyclists in the world. Check her out at www.marlastreb.com.

acknowledgments

Although the gaffes and screwups in these pages are solely the responsibility of the author, who begs your pardon for them, the good stuff comes from many people.

Thanks first to the forward-thinking editors at Globe Pequot, Scott Adams and Dave Singleton, who showed great patience as they waited for me to finish this and that.

Deepest gratitude also to the incomparable Marla Streb for writing the foreword, and to Sam Turner for his illustrations.

Heartfelt thank-yous go to the several dozen urban cycling maniacs that I am blessed with knowing, many of whom are close friends. For years I watched them negotiate the city streets with style, grace, and intelligence. The cumulative riding experience among them is mind-boggling. The advice they give comes from millions of miles and a sprinkling of near-death experiences, and does not always correspond to the conventional wisdom. Especially among this group I must thank Robert Reid, Christie Martin, Mike McGranahan, Steve Campana, and Joe Dillon; their comments were instrumental in the book's completion.

I received free help smoothing out the manuscript from Kamla Hurst and Steve Campana, and gave my dad, Jerry Hurst, a fat target for his grammatical acuity. (Dad is a retired high school English teacher.)

Sincere thanks to John Forester. Although much of what I say here is at odds with his instructions about riding in traffic, and this book in your hand is on some level an answer to his own books, that I feel so obliged to address his "vehicular-cycling principle" right away and then so often afterward is a testament to its power: vehicular cycling is a functional style that serves many cyclists very well. Forester is quick to point out that vehicular-style cycling is a very old style that came to the United States by way of England in the 1930s, but the articulation of the vehicular-cycling principle was an original Forester project, and he has been defending it (with gusto) for more than a quarter century. And you won't have to look too hard to find loads of statistics and ideas that I, like many other cyclists, first came across in Forester's books, *Effective Cycling* and *Bicycle Transportation: A Handbook for Cycling Transportation Engineers*. These stats are referred to copiously herein, an example of how the same numbers can support different conclusions.

Jobst Brandt, author of a guide that hopeless bikeophiles call "The Book" (*The Bicycle Wheel*), cheerfully skewered my section on tire wiping, and his presence in these pages lends a brief flash of wisdom, and I am grateful for that.

Finally, thanks to all the cyclists out there who ride every day, snow or shine, in a way that makes it easier for others to do the same.

introduction

Any book about cycling in America would necessarily have to be about lots of different things. So here is a book about lots of things. It's a book about history—the history of bicycles and the history of cities and the unlikely effect that one had on the other. It's a book about streets, about pavement and potholes and cracks. A book about helmets and wrecks and injuries. A book about air pollution, flat tires, and various other misunderstood issues. Perhaps most important, here is a book about riding a bicycle in traffic. And not just any traffic, but the industrial-strength traffic of the modern American metroplex, where cyclists are sometimes made to feel like tiny prey animals on the run.

In the making of a book with so much different stuff, many a fine line has been walked in addition to the many that have been crossed. Maybe the most precarious tightrope walk of them all was the attempt at creating a book that would somehow be accessible to beginning riders while not boring experienced riders to tears. There are a few places where one group or the other might feel abandoned, but if you'll just hang in there the author will climb back onto the high wire and the book will come back into range.

No doubt many readers who are beginning cyclists would benefit from information that they won't be able to find in here. To these readers, a friendly word of warning: This may not be the basic guidebook you're looking for. For instance, this book doesn't delve into basic mechanical issues except where they directly impact safety or are particular to the urban arena. It avoids dealing with many of the most frequently asked questions, especially those about proper clothing, and those about the physiology of cycling, although there will be brief and occasional touches on these. This should be a useful book for commuters, but it is not a handbook for commuting. We have different, if not bigger, fish to fry.

There are a huge number of books already in existence that tackle the nuts-and-bolts subjects with great effectiveness. But, on the more esoteric subject of riding in traffic, the offerings have been notably few. For decades, the topic has been dominated by one book, one way of thinking. John Forester's *Effective Cycling,* with its centerpiece vehicular-cycling principle ("cyclists fare best when they act and are treated as drivers of vehicles"), has been pretty much the only game in town. Forester's whole deal began as a scathing indictment of the primitive bicycle paths and lanes of the 1970s and grew into a comprehensive system of riding in traffic. Forester's huge shadow falls across everything that has been written on urban cycling since, and this book right here is another prime example of that. But, while most of the others use Forester's advice as their model, we will take things down a different road.

A large number of cyclists around the world subscribe to Forester's views or similar views. At least, that is their stated position. It is a proud position. Out on the street, however, things aren't so simple. For instance, experienced vehicular-style riders tend naturally to adjust their proud, legalistic technique at certain times to anticipate the possible mistakes of motorists. In doing so, this takes them, at least momentarily, out of the realm of strict vehicular cycling. In addition, many vehicular cyclists are not above doing very nonvehicular things like busting stop signs and squeezing through traffic jams.

At the other end of the spectrum are cyclists who have rejected the vehicular-cycling code, in word and deed. These blasphemers might call themselves, as some of them do, the "invisible cyclists." They ride under the theoretical assumption that they are unnoticed and invisible, but still vulnerable, to all the drivers they encounter. The invisible cyclist tries never to depend on the vision of motorists or pedestrians. This style is philosophically divorced from the traffic laws, although those who practice it will claim their style follows an obvious, conservative logic nonetheless. While this philosophy is admirably cynical and vigilant, it is also impractical. Because, to the vast majority of other road users, the cyclist is, in fact, visible. And there will be situations where the cyclist who is trying to get somewhere in a reasonable hurry will not be able to avoid dependence on the vision of others.

It becomes apparent that the invisible cyclists don't ride completely as if they are invisible, nor do the vehicularists ride in a strictly vehicular fashion. Both styles have their strong points, but neither one is wholly adequate on its own. Both philosophies are terminally simplistic. Neither extreme is a match for the complexity (chaos) of traffic.

Being more than a little obsessed with the subject, I have had countless conversations throughout the years with devoted cyclists about their preferred methods, habits, and superstitions of riding in traffic. Most of these riders were veteran professional drivers like myself—bicycle messengers. Some were/are long-distance commuters, some everyday transportational cyclists, some hard-core racers, and some all of the above. The collective experience in this group, the total miles, the hours in heavy traffic, is staggering. Through all of these miles and hours in traffic, a common thread between each of these types of riders emerged. These highly experienced cyclists practice an advanced style that borrows heavily from both the vehicular and the invisible styles, but is hooked on neither. The rider slides over to one extreme, the ultra-predictability of vehicular cycling, or to the other extreme, the take-no-chances invisible style, or to one of an infinite number of combinations and compromises along the continuum between these two poles, depending on the moment at hand.

Those who practice this style of riding have a hard time putting it into words. But when they try, something that comes up again and again is the theme of flexibility. Constant subtle adjustments to an ever-changing situation. The fleeting moment cannot be mastered. When you ask these expert riders how they react to a certain situation in traffic, they can't give a straight answer, because everything *depends*. What they are trying to describe is the art of cycling.

You don't have to be a hard-core rider to benefit from the hard cores' knowledge. There are important lessons in this advanced method of the masters for the weekenders and dabblers among us. This is a book about many things, and it is also for many different types of riders. There are those on folding bicycles with 20-inch wheels, those on cruisers, road bikes, recumbents, mountain bikes, and everything in between. Some cyclists consider themselves to be quite serious about cycling in general and are always decked out in Lycra. Others may have that single orange pannier, the long gray beard, and that stern look. Some others may ride only when the car is out of commission and may feel horribly embarrassed while doing so. There are cyclists in the suburbs and cyclists living in row houses near downtown. I hope they will all benefit from the ideas put forth in this book. We're all in this together.

frankenstein's monster

Continuum

Setting out to write a book about cycling, it didn't seem likely that I would be spending too much time explaining the history of the bicycle itself. Since the book's primary concern would be the cyclist's relation to the twenty-first-century city, it figured that the old-timey stuff would provide, at best, colorful side matter . . . but then an undeniable truth was revealed: The birth of the bicycle, the rise of the auto, and the postmodern American sprawled-out city are all lined up along the same continuum.

As cyclists in the new millennium, our situation has strange and ironic roots in the time of hoop skirts, silver panics, and railroad tycoons. The bicycle craze of the late nineteenth century led seamlessly into the automobile craze of the twentieth and twenty-first. Indeed, as you will later read, a strong argument could be made—a correct one, too—that the success of autos was *dependent* on the prior development of the bicycle. The automobile craze, having been coaxed into existence in large measure by the fledgling bicycle community, became a chronic condition that shaped America's "built environment" as drastically as its consciousness;

it poked around the edges of mainstream culture, changed it, then finally became it. The car culture is a version of Frankenstein's monster that, today, every cyclist must face.

And so, because it will do us no good to avoid the wicked truth, let's begin at the beginning. . . .

Bicycles in the Age of Manure:
Leonardo to Starley

The seemingly straightforward task of explaining the history of the bicycle became rather messy in 1974, when Italian scholar Augusto Marinoni announced that Leonardo da Vinci invented the modern bicycle in the fifteenth century. It was stunning news.

Monks from the Grottaferra Abbey near Rome, charged with restoring one of the Vatican's obscure Leonardo da Vinci notebooks in the late 1960s, unwittingly revealed a blockbuster scribble that had been, according to Marinoni, locked away for several hundred years. In the restoration process, the monks separated two sheets that had been glued together since the early 1600s and found out the likely reason why those pages had been sealed up in the first place. On the revealed pages, dated from 1493, were the doodles of one of Leonardo's more restless students: a few obscene cartoons of walking penises—check for yourself if you don't believe—and a nasty, perhaps jealous, caricature of a young man named Salai, who is known to have been Leonardo's prized pupil. But there was also a crude sketch of what is, unmistakably, a *bicycle,* up in the corner away from the cartoons. And not just any bicycle, but a *chain-driven* bicycle, using technology associated with the late nineteenth century. Marinoni contended that the sketch of the bicycle was the anonymous student's rendition of a genuine Leonardo design.[1]

Marinoni's claim was met with are-you-kidding-me skepticism from some historians and other academics, for several reasons. To those who were familiar with the bicycle's slow, almost painful emergence during the nineteenth century, the sudden appearance of this chain-driven design from the 1490s simply did not fit into their worldview. Their skepticism was bolstered when Carlo Pedretti, a da Vinci scholar from UCLA, said he had examined the same pages and saw no bicycle at all, only twin circles along with the obscene cartoons, implying that the bicycle had been filled in later using the circles for wheels. The skeptics concluded that the drawing must be a forgery, a hoax—perpetrated by the monks, some unknown smart-ass, or Marinoni himself.[2]

As it stands today, there is no conclusive proof to solve this debate in favor of either side. Truthfully, though, it is definitely *possible* that Leonardo conceived the bicycle. Examining illustrations from Leonardo's *Codex Madrid,* which he penned at around the same time his student allegedly copied the bicycle design, one can see that Leonardo was heavily engaged with many different kinds of chain and gear combos. On one page of the *Codex Madrid,* there is an intricate drawing of a chain that looks almost exactly like today's bike chains, complete with peanut-shaped links. He even drew designs for coaster brakes. Almost all the elements of the modern bicycle are there in the *Codex Madrid.*[3]

Whether Leonardo da Vinci invented the bicycle or not is essentially irrelevant, because, either way, his version of it never caught on. There is no evidence that such an advanced bicycle was ever built or used before the 1800s. One thing we can say for sure: If Leonardo *did* create that design, it is one of the more interesting twists of world history that it was lost, sealed up, and hidden away, cheating perhaps a dozen generations out of the genius of the bicycle. For almost four centuries after Leonardo, road travel was restricted to the same ol' tired draft animal routine that had been used since, oh, about 3000 B.C.

Whenever we start getting into discussions about inventions and historical events, there is a tendency to boil complex stories down to a manageable list of names and dates, which always turns out to be incomplete. This has been a serious problem with many of the written histories of the bicycle. The reader should know that there are, without a doubt, many more names involved than those found in any book, including this book, names that are long forgotten or were never known—just a word of warning as we embark on our own quick survey of the bicycle's development in the nineteenth century. Keep a watchful eye, as there will be some

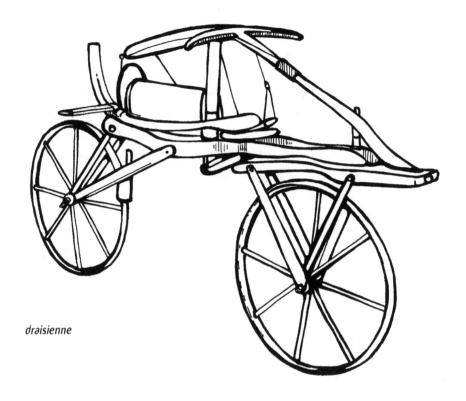

draisienne

name-dropping. Unavoidably, there are some names to remember, and some names to forget.

Before the Leonardo controversy, the invention of the bicycle was most often credited, quite erroneously, to a German fellow named Baron Karl von Drais de Saverbrun, or just Drais. Drais built a wooden, two-wheeled vehicle in 1816 and patented it as the *draisienne*. There were no cranks or pedals; the rider was meant to straddle the "running machine" and propel himself with the tips of his toes. Aside from certain anatomical issues *(ouch!),* images from the period tend to indicate that prancing around on a *draisienne* looked about as ridiculous as one might imagine, with the tights and poofy shirts not helping one bit.

This was no bicycle—it was a scooter with a seat. Furthermore, Drais did not even invent the scooter, as variations on scooterlike contraptions go back to ancient times. So we cannot safely bestow upon Drais the credit for giving the world its first taste of two-wheeled wonderment. Drais's chief contribution was to add a steerable front wheel to a preexisting design. While this was indeed a groundbreaking innovation, it is still a long stretch to say he invented the bicycle.

Let us go further along in time. About twenty years beyond the first *draisienne,* 1836ish, a few Scottish fellows got tired of prancing and managed to rig their scooters with various cranks and levers. The exact nature of their tinkering remains a mystery, but it is believed that their vehicles used a rear-wheel-drive treadle system, sort of like an old sewing machine. These guys (Kirkpatrick MacMillan and Gavin Dalzell are the names that survive) were really on to something.

The attempt at a more elegant self-propulsion was taken up by well-meaning Pierre and Ernest Michaux in the decade following 1855. This Parisian father-son team tweaked and promoted their designs for small,

"Boneshaker" circa 1855

High-wheeler circa 1878

yet heavy, crank-driven vehicles that came to be called "velocipedes" by the hopeful and "boneshakers" by the cynical.

The Michauxs' inspiration was beautiful, but their execution was a flop—*they put the cranks and pedals on the front wheel.* Guys! Here the development of the bicycle took an unfortunate turn down a dead-end street. Cyclists would be shackled to this fouled-up design for the next thirty years. Because of the crank placement, their machines were more Bigwheel than bicycle. The velocipedes' top speed was a Bigwheelish 10 miles per hour. Variations on the boneshaker theme nonetheless enjoyed a flash of popularity around Europe, England, and even in the United States.[4]

Putting cranks on the front hub probably seemed like a genius idea at the time, but it had several major flaws: Most important, it meant that the maximum speed was limited by the size of the front wheel. Essentially, the bike's only gear *was* its front wheel. This is why in 1869 the boneshaker makers began to enlarge the front wheels of their vehicles, modestly at first. English builders were the first to make the wheels as high as possible—as high as allowed by the leg length of the rider. The rear wheels became ever smaller in a desperate attempt to save weight.

These funky high-wheelers became somewhat popular in America after they were introduced at Philadelphia's Centennial Exhibition in 1876. At first the demand was filled by imports from England. After 1878 they were manufactured stateside by Colonel Albert Pope. Pope priced his "Columbia"-brand machines for around $300 each—very expensive Bigwheels—and he had no problem selling them. The high cost of the

Safety Bicycle circa 1890

machine meant that a troubling air of class division was destined to follow the two-wheel phenomenon from the beginning.*

The high-wheeler was received as more of a novelty than a serious utilitarian device. It was a toy, but it was an inspiring toy. Large numbers of affluent Americans joined cycling clubs; some even had the nerve to race these things in road and track events. They called them "bicycles," even though one could argue they hadn't quite figured out what bicycles were yet.[5]

You start to see why the drawing in Leonardo's notebook caused so much disbelief. The process of eeking out a chain drive seems to have been unduly agonizing through the 1800s.

Finally, in 1885, after the front-wheel-drive idea had run its course like a bad flu, J. K. Starley of Coventry, England, invented the "Safety Bicycle." Starley's bicycle was intended as a humble alternative to the dangerous high-wheeler, but the outright superiority of his design soon became obvious. Starley had most of the right parts in the right place. The wheels were of near-equal size, and he had the cranks at the bottom bracket with a direct-drive chain to a sprocket on the rear hub. There was a semblance of a diamond frame. Brakes? Who needs 'em. Starley's bike had a fixed gear, so the ineffectiveness of its primitive friction brake was a nonissue.[6]

Starley's chain drive was adopted by hundreds of different manufacturers, and after a few modifications the safety bicycle became the standard that survives, in the same basic form, through the present day. Sleek-looking safety bicycles were being mass-produced in America by 1887. In a world populated by increasing numbers of *actual bicycles,* the high-wheelers became known as "ordinaries" and were suddenly obsolete.

Maybe he was channeling Leonardo. Maybe he was just a pure, plain genius. Either way, we needed him. Forget about Drais. Starley is the name to remember. John Kemp Starley.**

---

* By comparison, a new Model T could be purchased for less than $300 in 1927. (James Flink, *The Automobile Age* [Cambridge: MIT Press, 1988], p. 38.)

** Not to be confused with *James* Starley, J. K.'s uncle, who designed high-wheelers and tricycles and introduced the tangentially spoked wheel in 1874. (McGurn, *On Your Bicycle,* p. 66.)

Frankenstein's Monster

The Bicycle
Craze of the 1890s

One thing John Kemp Starley didn't have was the *pneumatic tire*. His early safety bicycles were outfitted with solid rubber tires wired to the rims, just like the high-wheelers. Imagine riding rough dirt roads and cobblestones on solid rubber tires. When an Irish veterinarian named Dunlop developed the world's first practical pneumatic tire in 1889, the modern bicycle achieved the efficient, elegant, and almost-perfect form that is still so familiar to all of us. By 1893 the new tires outfitted every new bicycle sold in America. The pneumatic tire—soon to become a critical ingredient in the emergence of auto and airplane transportation—was the catalyst that launched the bicycle craze of the 1890s.[7]

If you think bicycles are great now, imagine them back then, when the chain drive was brand-new, and the very thought of balancing and cruising on two wheels was still a novelty. Riding on air-filled tires must have felt silky smooth after the boneshakers and several thousand years of wagons.

Not surprisingly, hordes of people fell in love with the bicycle in the 1890s.

At the height of the craze, it is estimated that there were as many as four million cyclists in the United States alone. In 1896 America, according to James McGurn, "about 250 major cycle factories produced well over a million bicycles." Augmenting the main factories were about 600 accessory makers. It was reported that more than 120,000 enthusiasts visited a bicycle exposition at Madison Square Garden in 1896.[8]*

Because bicycles were still quite expensive items, beyond the reach of most Americans until market saturation caused a price collapse after 1896, the vast majority of early cyclists in America were affluent, and they were city people. This *connectedness* helped cyclists start molding the environment to their needs. Many of the cyclists massed together into a formidable block of nagging civic agitators. The League of American Wheelmen (LAW), formed by Colonel Pope during the high-wheeler era, swelled in membership and became a feisty bunch after the invention of the safety bicycle. Guided by the savvy industrialist Pope, who understood the connection between the condition of the nation's roads and his huge bicycle business, the LAW's earliest and most important fight was for smooth roads and pavement. The politicians eventually fell over themselves trying to gain favor with the cyclists, and a significant road improvement drive was initiated.[9]

Things were really looking up as the bike craze spawned the world's first bike paths. The 5.5-mile Coney Island bikeway was so well traveled after it opened in 1895 that its surface was in constant need of improvements and repairs. On the other coast, an audacious plan to build an *elevated bicycle highway* between Pasadena and Los Angeles became a tragic symbol

---

* It was inevitable that a machine as progressive as the bicycle would crash into some of the socially backward leftovers of American culture. At the time of the safety bicycle's arrival, the traditional role prescribed for women in Western society was oppressive and untenable. When many women started riding bikes in the 1890s, the silliness was revealed in sharp relief. Many conservatives, perhaps more women than men among them, had a visceral, emotional reaction to the very idea of a woman on a bicycle. How *unladylike*—to actually want to go places and do things, to move and sweat, how dare they! Eventually, folks got used to the idea of female cyclists and became obsessed with their apparel. At a time when proper ladies were expected to be in full-length skirts, corsets, and big-ass hats, many female cyclists chose to ride men's bikes in practical outfits that were also much more revealing. *Ankles!* The bicycling "bloomer girl" became a potent symbol of feminine independence. In 1896 Susan B. Anthony said famously, "Let me tell you what I think of bicycling . . . I think it has done more to emancipate women than anything else in the world . . ." Which is pretty sad if you think about it too hard. (Pryor Dodge, *The Bicycle* [Paris: Flammerion, 1996], pp. 122–30.)

of the bicycle's sudden rise and fall in America. A private company built 9 miles of the fully enclosed wooden bikeway, which was as high as 50 feet off the ground in some spots, before a freaked-out railroad won an injunction to stop the bikeway from crossing over its tracks. The project languished in court for years. As the auto fever engulfed southern California, the bikeway was abandoned and forgotten.[10]

Chumps of the
Road

Bicyclists, I'm sorry to report, have always been the *chumps of the road* in America. Those of us who would like to blame automobiles and the automobile culture for all of the problems that cyclists have ever faced should take a sober look at the situation in the 1890s, when automobiles were still science fiction, and bicyclists swarmed the city streets and country lanes without ever having to worry about getting run over by a truck. Even then there was an atmosphere of conflict, distrust, and outright malice between those who cycled and those who didn't.

Then as now, much of the poisonous atmosphere was derived from traffic blowups. The general attitude of urban pedestrians concerning cyclists was sour at best—the cyclists came upon them swiftly and silently, scared the hell out of them, and were gone before the pedestrians could deliver a proper scolding. And the attitude of the wagon and coach drivers could best be described as seething hatred. The sudden appearance of cyclists disrupted an already delicate, tenuous balance that existed between pedestrians and horse traffic. Horses did not react calmly to bicycles, and the teamsters' task became much more difficult as a result.

Competition for road space was far from the only source of animosity, however. The same affluence and gentility that endowed cyclists with their early civic influence also assured that there would be a healthy dose of urban-rural conflict and an unmistakable whiff of class conflict floating over every ride. In sharp contrast to some other countries around the world, the

American rural population failed to embrace the bicycle. To the average rural American, bicycles were silly contraptions, expensive toys for city dandies who, obviously, had way too much time and money to burn. Until about 1896 or so, when the market was flooded and prices plummeted, the exorbitant price of bicycles ensured that few in the working class would be able to experience and enjoy them. *The typical bicycle cost about the same as the average factory worker's salary for six months.*[11]

And the riders—who were these people? Wannabe cavalrymen, blowing bugles and riding in formation. Clearly delusional. Men in girly costumes, women in manly bloomers, scaring the horses and blocking the roads. There was so much to dislike. When the local clubmen came wheeling single-file through a country town, the residents came out to watch, and to sneer. If the cyclists left their machines unattended, they would frequently find their tires punctured by snickering kids with needles and tacks. Individual cyclists were occasionally besieged by rock-throwing farmboys. No wonder that some cyclists in late-nineteenth-century America took to carrying collapsible "Bicycle Rifles," available from the Sears Roebuck Catalog, along on their rides.[12]

Of course the bicyclists themselves are not blameless and never have been. Bicyclists have always been rather poor at making friends on the roadways. Let's face it: Cyclists suck at resolving conflicts. All of the conflicts that cyclists faced in the nineteenth century are still with us today, and some new ones as well.

From Bicycles to Automobiles in
Sixty Seconds

Rolling onto the horse-dominated scene, the safety bicycle finally heralded the revolution in individualized transport that had been hinted at during the *draisienne,* velocipede, and high-wheeler spasms. To the chagrin of the teamsters and cart drivers, who were now being passed regularly by long lines of smug cyclists, and perhaps to the relief of the horses, the safety bicycle was an obvious improvement over the horse in terms of efficiency and speed. And unlike the rail-bound traveler, the cyclist could go wherever the roads went—basically everywhere. According to John Rae, the bicycle alone created "an awareness of the flexibility and convenience of travel by road" after a long period of myopic reliance on railroads.[13] Now here was an idea—*speed without rails.*

After the safety bicycle blew the mind of the world and exploded its expectations for personal mobility and freedom, it turbocharged industrial technology as well, paving the way for the motorized *Putsch* that would soon follow. Many of the essential elements of early automobiles were developed just a few years earlier in bicycle factories and shops. In addition to Dunlop's pneumatic tire, the bicycle engineers laid at the garage door of the automobile age many crucial advancements, including lighter and stronger metal alloys, durable bearings, a mastery of chains and gears, and the know-how to have it all produced for a commercial market; the most ambitious American bicycle manufacturers pioneered certain factory-testing and mass-production techniques before Henry Ford snagged popular credit for the whole shebang.*

Of the bicycle's monumental impact, automobile historian James Flink wrote that "no preceding technological innovation—not even the internal-combustion engine—was as important to the development of the automobile as the bicycle."[14] Pause for a second to let that one sink in.

The words "former bicycle mechanic" and "former bicycle manufac-

---

* The concept of planned obsolescence is also attributed to bicycle manufacturers. See Smith, *A Social History of the Bicycle,* pp. 18–19.

turer" reverberate powerfully through the halls of history. We teach our kids about the Wright brothers—former bicycle manufacturers—and the pioneering flight of their mechanical bird. But what about the *f.b.m.*s who jump-started the auto industry? The list is long, as the progression to motors seemed quite natural, irresistible, to the bike makers:

> ... among others [former bicycle manufacturers], Opel in Germany; Clément, Darracq, and Peugeot in France; Humber, Morris, and Rover in Great Britain; Pope, Peerless, Rambler, Winton, and Willys in the United States. A substantial proportion of engineering talent as well in the early automobile industry was provided by former bicycle mechanics—including William Morris, who initiated volume production of automobiles in Great Britain; Charles E. and J. Frank Duryea, who built the first successful American gasoline car; and William S. Knudsen, production head first at Ford, then at Chevrolet, and later president of General Motors.[15]

So if you're the type who must always be looking for culprits, look no further than the bicycle lovers, the bicycle riders and racers, the bicycle fixers, and the bicycle makers. They planted the seed, watered the ground, and tended to the seedling that became our unrestrained car culture.

Speed and
Greed

Bicycle racing grew quickly to become the world's fastest, most compelling spectator sport in the late nineteenth century. In the United States, crowds in the tens of thousands flocked to the races on tight, steeply banked wooden tracks. The racers were celebrated for their fearlessness as much as their athleticism. At that time, bicycle track racing was one of the wildest, most dangerous activities that could be attempted by a human being. Crashes were numerous and spectacular. *("I say, Mabel, this beats the hell out of lawn tennis!")* American racers honed their art in the

States, where the competition was most fierce, then went abroad to crush the riders from Europe and Australia. Americans August Zimmerman, Major Taylor,* and Iver Lawson were all crowned world champions before 1905.[16]

Even before the turn of the century, however, many of the most dynamic racers spun off, transferring their tremendous energy to the budding sport of auto racing. Auto racing was the next big thing. It's hard to imagine now, but bike racers around the world became obsessed with race cars—financing, designing, building, driving, and selling. In addition to the riders themselves, many race officials, promoters, and mechanics went over to the dark side, to a new sport they considered to be more thrilling, and more potentially lucrative. Speed and greed, not necessarily in that order.

Many of these budding motorheads hoped to follow in the footsteps of Alexander Winton. Winton was a former bicycle manufacturer from Cleveland who began producing a limited number of autos for a very high-paying clientele; he used the races to advertise his product and found great success. It was recognized that defeating Winton in a race would instantly make any new builder's reputation. With this goal in mind, Tom Cooper, a national champion track sprinter who had already made a mountain of cash from bicycle racing, teamed up with a still-struggling Henry Ford to build two overpowered race vehicles in 1902. The Ford-Cooper racers had cylinders as wide as saucers and sounded like a war. Even then they were considered primitive and crude compared to other motorcars.[17] Instead of steering wheels, there were handlebars.

Cooper intended to drive one of the cars himself; as for the other, Cooper recruited a tough bike-racing friend named Barney Oldfield to drive that one, because, it's been said, Ford was too timid, or too smart, to pilot the beast.

---

* Marshall "Major" Taylor became the first black champion of any professional sport in 1899—almost fifty years before Jackie Robinson's entry into pro baseball. Cyclists probably shouldn't feel too grand about this, as Taylor was treated poorly overall. He was banned from several tracks, and some of the top riders, such as Eddie "Cannon" Bald, refused to race with him. (Peter Nye, *Hearts of Lions* [New York: W. W. Norton & Company, 1988], pp. 42–54.)

Barney Oldfield and
the Arena of Death

There is an exhilaration in driving fast that I cannot resist; it is like intoxication.[18]

— BARNEY OLDFIELD

On the afternoon of October 25, 1902, a high-class crowd gathered outside Detroit to watch a bizarre spectacle called an automobile race. The venue was Grosse Pointe Raceway, which was, like most of the early auto-racing tracks, a dirt horse-racing oval. If the Detroit races were like the other auto races of the era, there were probably about one hundred or so of the spectators' private automobiles parked—displayed, really—between the grandstand and the track. Many of the proto-mobiles would have been very expensive, exotic, and made in France, and there would have been several steamers and electrics among them, as the gasoline engine had not yet emerged as the victor among these competing technologies.[19]

The folks arriving at the track that day weren't ready for it, but they were about to be treated to an event of powerful importance.

Twenty-four-year-old Barney Oldfield found himself in the driver's seat of the Ford-Cooper 999, lined up to race in the 5-mile main event against a field that included one of Winton's cars. Oldfield had turned some practice laps in the 999 before, but this was his first race. He was feeling uncharacteristic jitters.

"I hit the first turn at a rapid clip," he recalled many years later. "The regular procedure on coming to a turn had always been to shut off. I knew that. So I decided not to do it. Instead, I opened my throttle as wide as it would go . . . I slid all the way around the first turn, the 999 trying to jerk away from me and go straight ahead through the outside fence. The rear wheels insisted on getting ahead of the front ones. I used to stop skids on the bicycle by turning the front wheel in the direction of the skid, so I jerked the tiller bar of my racer so as to point the front wheels toward the outer fence."[20]

Oldfield thus spontaneously invented the sliding turn that has been the staple of dirt-track drivers ever since. More importantly, the spectators were enthralled with his on-the-edge driving style and couldn't take their

Frankenstein's Monster

eyes off him. Did this guy have a death wish? Surely, the 999 would go flipping and careening off the track and explode in a ball of flame at any moment. Now *this* was entertainment![21]

Oldfield didn't wreck; quite the opposite, he won the 5-mile race by almost a mile. He continued his automotive reign of terror into the next year, traveling from city to city, cracking his own speed record at each successive track. Amazed fans mobbed him, did the "Hip, Hip, Hooray" thing, and carried him away on their shoulders. His 70-mile-per-hour sliding daredevil turns became the main attraction in American sports through 1903. He dumped the 999 to drive for Alexander Winton in midsummer but didn't slow down a bit (this and subsequent switches show that his success had less to do with any particular car and more to do with his own talent and daring).*

Before long, Oldfield found that his crazy-man image preceded him to each city. He knew how to work the crowd: "Despite the terrific speed, the absolutely fearless and reckless driver, wearing his perpetual good-natured smile, nonchalantly waved his right hand to the crowded grandstand. . . ."[22] This report fails to mention the cigar that was forever clenched in his teeth during the races, even when his face was caked with mud and oil, and the whiskey flask that was probably swinging around his neck.

Oh, Barney. Such a poor example for the children. Barney Oldfield's dream run came to a crashing halt on September 8, 1903, on his return to the Grosse Pointe track. Oldfield lost it in the turn after blowing the right-rear tire of his Winton Baby Bullet. The Bullet shot through the fence and killed a spectator. Oldfield was terribly bothered by the man's death. His first reaction was to quit racing, but his need for speed prevailed and he went on. Less than one year later, in St. Louis, Oldfield crashed through another fence—"I went right into the crowd at that point"—this time killing two spectators and injuring many more.[23] Oldfield went through the fences a lot in those days. "I got so I didn't call going through the fence an

---

* This didn't stop Ford from capitalizing immeasurably on his association with the 999 and Oldfield. Ford had actually given up on the 999 and the other Ford-Cooper before their racing debut; with the cars failing to show promise, he sold them to Cooper for "something like 600 or 800 dollars," according to Oldfield. Cooper, Oldfield, and an unsung hero mechanic named Spider Huff put the engines into racing shape. That he had disowned the cars weeks earlier did not stop Ford from materializing on the track after the October 25 race to be photographed with the winning car and driver. (Barney Oldfield, as reported to William Sturm, "Wide Open All the Way, Part One," *Saturday Evening Post,* September 19, 1925, pp. 52–54.) Ford used the race to secure the cash to start the Ford Motor Company and the early reputation that kept his product in high demand.

accident unless I got hurt going through or hurt someone on the other side."

Oldfield was far from the only driver having trouble keeping his rig within the confines of the old horse-racing tracks. Frank Day had replaced Oldfield on the 999 only to kill himself on it just a few months later. In 1905 Oldfield was racing his rival, Earl Kiser—once an internationally feared bicycle racer known as the "Match Race King"—when Kiser went through a fence and smashed his huge legs "to a pulp." Tom Cooper, Oldfield's old friend and partner, one of the greatest bicycle racers of his day, was killed while street racing in New York City in 1906.[24]

The auto-racing circuit turned out to be pure carnage, but, through it all, Oldfield continued to race. "Drivers don't want to stop or don't seem able to stop," he said, summing up much of present-day American culture in eleven words.[25]

Moreover, unlike his friends, Barney Oldfield never died. Well, almost never. Despite all expectations to the contrary, he lived to the relatively ripe old age of sixty-eight and died of a heart attack. (Folks say the cigar was still in his teeth when they put him in the ground.)* In the decades before his death, after a seventeen-year career as one of America's most visible daredevils, he traveled the country preaching an unlikely gospel: *safe driving.* (Cough.)

Before Barney Oldfield, automobile racing emulated horse racing as a kingly sport; the team crews were expected to be in spotless white uniforms, and car owners were given more credit than the drivers. The cars raced around the old horse tracks in a proper, orderly fashion—very civilized. Before Oldfield, the auto was exclusively a "gentleman's" toy (gentleman being, of course, an old-fashioned code word meaning someone who has so much money he doesn't know what to do with himself). Autos were such conspicuous signs of opulence that Woodrow Wilson voiced his concern that their very presence on the continent, as rare as they were, would tip the multitudes toward communism.[26]

Oldfield buried all that under a tremendous rooster tail of dirt. He was a foul-mouthed, working-class bad-ass in ratty clothes—no bleached whites for Barney. He and his mud- and blood-splattered compatriots made the aristocratic automobile attractive to tough guys, roughnecks, lowlifes, and farmboys. They made it seem *cool.*

It took a bunch of bike racers to do that. If your mama told you America wasn't a strange place, she lied.

---

* Not really, but Johnny Cash could have written a song like that.

A Dark Wave
Cometh

. . . the bicycle was a recreation and a fad. The automobile, while it is a recreation, is in no way a fad.[27]

—HENRY FORD, 1906

Unfortunately for us—the few, the proud, the cyclists—there turned out to be some truth in the first part of Ford's pronouncement, where he smugly waves bye-bye to the bicycle. And the second part was right on— the automobile was no fad. In the early twentieth century, ordinary Americans, when given half a chance, fell head over heels for the automobile and decided it was about as indispensable as the legs they were born with. Americans who had once laughed, cursed, and thrown rocks at the new machines, perceived to be obnoxious and unnecessary rich men's toys just a few years before, soon forgot how they ever got along without one.[28]

In 1908 Ford introduced his no-frills Model T. Ford's master plan was not original to him. There were 253 automobile companies in America at the time, and many of them had the same goal: to produce, as Ford put it, "a car for the great multitude." This industrial atmosphere in America was very different from the trend in Europe, where car makers were still handcrafting boutique, overtly pretty vehicles for an exclusive clientele. By 1914 the Euros were left completely in the dust. The United States cranked out almost 500,000 automobiles that year, out of a total of just more than 600,000 that were produced in the entire world. Clunky, black, reliable Model T's accounted for about half of new car sales as the United States entered World War I.[29]

At his new Highland Park factory, Ford demonstrated the winning formula for an industrial miracle. The famous moving assembly line allowed him to drastically reduce the price of the Model T, from $850 in 1908 to an incredible $290 in 1927. Simultaneously doubling salaries at his factory (to $5.00 per day) gave his workers the purchasing power to buy the cars they made. Ford has been criticized for all kinds of things,* but he was no dummy.

By 1927 Americans owned 80 percent of the world's automobiles. The industrial miracle, however, had sown the seeds of its own demise: "every American who could afford a car already owned one."[30] But the factory machinery ran amok and kept popping them out. Even during the Depression, Americans who owned automobiles were already so "dependent" on them that giving them up was unthinkable, destitute or not.[31]

The 1920s represented an early high point in the American love affair with the car that was diminished somewhat by the Depression, first of all, and then by the oil shortages and sacrifices of World War II, during which citizens were forced to temporarily rediscover the trains and streetcars. After the war, however, the auto reclaimed the high ground in American culture. Auto registrations doubled between 1950 and 1970.[32] In 1929 the average ratio of cars to people was 1:4.3 (California had already taken a substantial lead, with one car per 2.3 adults); by 1980 the nationwide ratio was very close to one car–one person.[33] And today in America, according to the Department of Transportation, there are more passenger cars than available drivers, because a lot of folks out there own more than one vehicle. And the average number of adult bicycles per household has fallen below one.[34]

During the oil shocks of the 1970s, Americans rejected the giant boats (or tanks, if you prefer) that were being produced by domestic companies at the time, in favor of more efficient foreign-made models. The little Volkswagen Beetle became the best-selling car of all time, passing Ford's Model T, in 1972. Toyota and Nissan soon surpassed VW to become the leading exporters to the American market,[35] and worldwide, Japanese companies became the leading suppliers of motor vehicles by 1980.[36] This time it was the American manufacturers who were left in the dust, and it seems doubtful they will ever recover from the drubbing applied by the Japanese. The

---

* Most of Ford's critics focus on his far-right political tendencies. He was one of America's most outspoken anti-Semites. He also sent goons from his "Sociological Department" on regular forays into his workers' homes to make sure they were "living properly" and weren't tempted to join any unions. The strings attached to the five-dollar day—the announcement of which caused unemployed mobs to riot outside the factory gates—proved to be too much for many of Ford's workers. (Robert Lacey, *Ford: The Men and the Machine* [Boston: Little, Brown and Company, 1986], p. 121; see also Flink, *The Automobile Age*, pp. 113, 121–22.)

Frankenstein's Monster

consumers have spoken. The 250-plus independent American car companies of 1908 diminished to the Big Three, and now, since Chrysler was acquired by the German Daimler-Benz in 1998, just *two*. The remaining two are hurting, despite the nation's monstrous appetite for trucks and SUVs.

Fake
Gas Tanks

While bicycle track racing remained popular in America through the 1930s, cycling by ordinary adults—nonracers—evaporated into memory as the country embraced the automobile. When the auto fever was in full burn, during the 1920s, bicycles resurfaced as toys for children, styled to resemble motorcycles and airplanes. From the 1930s through the 1950s, almost every bicycle produced in America had balloon tires and a fake gas tank attached to the top tube. *A fake gas tank on every bike!* Doesn't that say it all?

American grown-ups shunned bicycles until the 1960s, when the European passion for cycling filtered back to the States as a trendy novelty for the style-conscious. Since hardly any Americans were into it at the time, riding a bike became a badge of individuality, a quirky college professor thing to do.

America's Vietnam—era bicycle envy grew into a fad of respectable proportions. In 1973 American retailers enjoyed what is still called the "bike boom," selling more than fifteen million adult bikes. This number stands as the all-time yearly record.[37]

The 1970s also ushered in BMX dirt-track racing, which was quite significant, as it gave bicycles undeniable cool status with American kids. Many of the most obsessed cyclists of today are graying adults who grew up jumping BMX bikes or BMX knockoffs on homemade plywood ramps. Their love for cycling was thus ingrained at an early age, along with a fair amount of skill. Today's little thrill seekers, on the other hand, are just as likely to choose a skateboard, in-line skates, or one of those godawful "razor scooters" for their wheeled transport. (Poor little bastards.)

The birth of the mountain bike, which was mass-produced and mass-purchased beginning in the early 1980s, brought cycling back into the mainstream of American culture after a short lull. Since the beginning of this movement, the majority of bikes sold have been all-terrain bikes or cheaper knockoffs of all-terrain bikes.[38] These dirt-inspired machines are worthy vehicles for transport, and indeed, that is how most of them are used. Which is to say, most of them are used hardly at all.

The bike boom of the 1970s, and the second, mountain bike–inspired boom of the 1980s and 1990s show that America has a long smoldering lust for bicycles that is prone to flaring up from time to time. The 120-year-old flame shrinks and flickers, but will not be snuffed out completely. That speaks well for America, but the lust for bicycles tends to be based almost entirely on fun, thrill, and fitness. Bicycles are considered sporting equipment, rather than serious tools for efficient transportation. Average Americans do not fully appreciate the utilitarian value of the machine. Even during the fuel crisis of the early 1970s, bicycling could not transcend its primary designation as "a recreation and a fad," as Ford predicted. When the mountain bikes were flying out of the shops in the 1990s, the buyers often had grandiose intentions of riding their new bikes to work and to the store, but it usually didn't turn out that way. They didn't ride bikes instead of driving, but *in addition* to driving, generally on the weekends.

Transportation and the
Shape of Cities

Before the advent of steam railroads in the early to mid-1800s, American cities were packed together and centralized to facilitate foot travel. Only the very rich enjoyed the use of horse-drawn carriages, so, naturally, people wanted to live within a few miles of where the action was so they wouldn't have to trek all day to get there. When the steam railroads came to town, these dense cities sprouted fingers of development along the rail corridors, and many urban areas assumed pointy, starlike layouts as a result.

The first, primitive urban "mass transit" systems emerged soon after the intercity lines. Widespread use of the horse-drawn omnibus, essentially a big stagecoach for about a dozen passengers, encouraged city dwellers to move another mile or so farther away from the city centers. Almost 600 omnibuses were rolling around New York City by 1885, on twenty-seven different routes.[39] The omnibuses caused the star-shaped cities to fill in between their points.

This filling-in process was amplified by the first *intra-urban* rail systems. The primal rail transit systems used horses to pull the cars—"horsecars"— then, in the 1870s, evolved into cable-car systems that used ungainly networks of continuously moving steel cables to move the coaches. Electric trolleys, drawing power from overhead wires, became standard and ubiquitous soon after Starley invented the safety bicycle.

The electric streetcar became the preferred method of urban travel for the vast majority of Americans, perhaps putting the bicycle on the back burner of utilitarian transport long before autos became popular. By the turn of the century, there were more than 10,000 miles of electric streetcar lines in America, and the mileage proliferated rapidly thereafter.[40]

The streetcars had a profound effect on the physical form of American cities, causing the dense centers to bloom outward, and even stitching outlying satellite towns together with the primary areas into unbroken conurbations. On your next ride, you can check out the result of the streetcar effect in your hometown. The streetcar suburbs of the late nineteenth century now form the heart of the city—rows of stately, antique houses that once gave their owners the warm illusion of country living, but have since been encased in layer after layer of development.

Automobile
Suburbs

Contemporary Americans tend to use their cars for almost every trip, no matter how short or insignificant. What we see around us today, stretching from horizon to horizon, are cities shaped by this devotion to the internal combustion engine—*unshaped* by it, really—a process that began in earnest in the 1920s.

Travel by rail modestly expanded the cities' residential districts, but it also had a strong centralizing effect on the nation's downtowns, by virtue of the fixed nature of the rails, most of which led right into the central districts of the cities. By contrast, the almost universal use of the car by individual Americans was—and still is—incongruous with the concept of a central business district. Widespread use of cars and trucks made necessary the decentralization of American cities, while simultaneously making such decentralization possible. It was inevitable that American cities would sprout multiple centers in the Petroleum Age, and sprout they did.

The time just before World War I brought an unprecedented degree of congestion and chaos to American city centers. Automobiles and trucks joined a thick stew of horse-drawn wagons, streetcars, pedestrians, and bicycles, all competing for space on the streets. There were no parking lots, no highways, no traffic signals, and few paved roads. The cars just forced their way in there somehow, and the infrastructure, the laws, the whole cities started to morph to accommodate them—slowly at first, then massively.

Downtown was clearly the first major obstacle standing before America's automotive future. Therefore, developers started to build commercial areas out in the boonies, away from the congested traffic and scarce parking of the downtowns. The first strip malls began to pop up around the nation, with Southern California, of course, leading the way. The primary characteristic of this type of outlying commercial development was, and remains, the vast parking lot that surrounds it. An uncompromising new calculus flattened the city and its outskirts; for every square foot provided for the human occupants within a building, one and a half square feet had to be provided outside for parking their cars.[41]

The 1920s also saw the spread of the first automobile suburbs—suburbs built around the idea that cars would provide the primary mode of transportation to the occupants therein. These suburbs assumed a much different form than the earlier streetcar suburbs. While the streetcar suburbs were laid out in a predictable, orthogonal* fashion, many of the suburbs of the 1920s used curvilinear street layouts to emphasize the suburb's separateness from the city. The automobile allowed for a general increase in the faux pastoralism that had been a feature of suburbs from the

---

* orthogonal: characterized by right angles; streets in an orthogonal layout are parallel, perpendicular, straight, regular. This "authoritarian and legalistic" type of city design dates from ancient times. (Hugo-Brunt, *The History of City Planning*, p. 63.)

beginning. The houses were of a new type as well. They had driveways and attached garages. That the car got its own bedroom in the family home was a striking indication that something pretty bizarre was going on.

Spurred on by government home-loan guarantees and new highways, American suburbanization went nuts after World War II, and has continued to the present. A majority of Americans now live in Suburbia. These suburbs are maturing just as the old city centers did. With maturity comes a surprising degree of diversity—diversity of race and class, variety of commercial offerings, jobs, living situations. The suburbs have really become the new American cities, performing all the functions of the old.[42] Diverse or not, all American suburbs have one factor in common: They were all shaped by the near-universal use of the automobile.

The automobile suburbs mean different things to different people. One man sees freedom, opportunity; another sees a prison.

The Great
Streetcar Massacre

Once upon a time, every decent-size city in America, including Los Angeles, was thoroughly tracked with its own electric rail network. In a few large cities with dense and bustling centers, the old rail transit systems have been preserved, at least in part. Almost everywhere else, the systems were completely dismantled before 1960.

Where have all the streetcars and urban rail systems gone? If you smell a corporate conspiracy, join the club.

Liberal critics of urban development in America love to tell the story of the Los Angeles rail network. It goes like this: General Motors Corporation purchased the old rail company in Los Angeles with the intention of running the system into the ground, or, depending on who is telling the story, replacing the electric trolleys with buses; GM's devious plan, ultimately successful, was to make sure that gas-powered buses and cars would be the only remaining transportation options available to the city's commuters. That's the lore.

In fact, the conspiracy was much more widespread than that. Columbia University professor Kenneth Jackson, in his study of American suburbanization, *Crabgrass Frontier,* points out that General Motors had tried to work this same scheme in Manhattan as early as 1926. Jackson writes: ". . . by 1950, General Motors had been involved in the replacement of more than one hundred streetcar operations—including those of Los Angeles, St. Louis, Philadelphia, Baltimore, and Salt Lake City—with GM-manufactured buses. A federal grand jury ultimately found the giant corporation guilty of criminal conspiracy for this effort [under the Sherman Antitrust Act], but the total fine—$5,000—was less than the profit returned from the conversion of a single streetcar." The conspiracy extended well beyond Los Angeles, and many more companies besides GM were involved, including Standard Oil, Phillips Petroleum, the Firestone Tire and Rubber Company, and Mack Truck.[43]

The motorized interests, led by GM, assassinated the streetcars. No doubt about it. But, it's important to remember that this deathblow was delivered to an industry already on its last legs. America's streetcar operations were down and out before the auto interests piled on, leaving nothing to chance.

Folks became sentimental about the urban rail systems *after* they were torn out, but they held no shortage of contempt and criticism for them while they were in place. For decades, citizens loathed the overcrowded trolley cars and cursed every rate hike demanded by companies widely perceived to offer less than the minimum of service for the maximum price. And many of the traction companies were thoroughly shady and muckrakable entities, associated with greed, corruption, and the general stench of political impropriety. Before the triumph of the auto industry, streetcar companies were some of the progressives' favorite targets. The early popularity of the automobile among city dwellers was fueled largely by a grumbling dissatisfaction with the rail systems.[44]

Some of the chronic failure of urban rail, and the sweeping success of the automobile, can be explained in terms of public and private investment. When the streetcar companies struggled, private investors withheld their capital, resulting in a vicious cycle. Many of these companies went bankrupt in the 1920s and 1930s. It's possible that the streetcar operations could have been made viable with an infusion of public funding, but none was forthcoming. The streetcars, run by private companies from the beginning, were always expected to pay their own way. In sharp contrast, the auto infrastructure enjoyed a *built-in* source of funding—the gas tax*—and received a massive helping of regular government tax revenues as well.[45]

Just a few decades after the tracks were torn out, American cities were pining for their old rail systems. Predictable, eh? A 1973 federal provision allowed for a portion of the sacred federal highway funds to be diverted to mass transit, and, across the nation, politicians and municipal transit authorities proposed the building of urban rail systems as if this were a shiny new idea. Today these second-generation rail systems have been *re*-installed, at great cost, in many American cities.

Congestion

Amid the prosperity of the early decades of the twentieth century, there was a sense that American downtowns, built for a different era and choked with pedestrians, streetcars, and an increasing number of cars and trucks, were standing in the way of progress. A bright future was envisioned by those who were lucky enough to own an automobile. What this bright future primarily looked like was a wide, clean highway, with a sprinkling of cars, each traveling zippily along at a previously unheard of speed.

Images of the *limited-access freeway* occupied the happy daydreams of many city planners of the era, most notably of Le Corbusier,** the Swiss-born architect and artist who became the most influential city planner of the twentieth century. Corbu (as Le Corbusier was known to friends and innumerable disciples) created fanciful designs for entire cities based on the idea that vertical density (i.e., apartment towers) should be combined with wide, green spaces on the ground. His critics called this vision "sky-scrapers in a park," but the attempt at derision paints a somewhat less than horrifying picture.

---

* Oregon was the first state to implement a gas tax, in 1919. By 1929 every state had established these "user fees," which provide the majority of highway dollars. Gas taxes are probably the most popular taxes of all time. (Rae, *The Road and the Car in American Life,* pp. 62–63.)

** The name applied by Le Corbusier's parents was Charles Edouard Jeanneret.

More important than his argument for vertical density, Le Corbusier urged a wholesale transformation of old-style cities to maximize the auto's potential. In 1929 he declared, "wide avenues must be driven through the centers of our towns . . ." The visual is one of a stake driven into the heart of the nineteenth-century grid city. Conventional street layouts were conspicuously absent from his plans. Corbu wanted to *kill the street* and create a world consisting only of grass, buildings, highways, and walkways. Oh, and parking lots. "We must create vast and sheltered public parking places . . .,"[46] he wrote. Corbu, although a thinker of large thoughts, was not a keen cyclist.

Looking around us now, in a spaghetti bowl of on-ramps and flyovers, it is tempting to pin the whole ordeal on Le Corbusier and his brethren in black spectacles, the modernist planners of the early twentieth century. Really, these hopeful individuals are down a bit on the list of influences on American urban development. It is always more practical to follow the money, rather than the utopians, if you want to get to the bottom of things. In this case, follow the taxes on gasoline and tires that were placed in a national Highway Trust Fund. This grew into a massive pile that was doled out by the federal government in a streak of monumental appropriations, most notably the Interstate Highway Act of 1956, which allocated $31.5 billion over thirteen years to stitch together what was formally called the National System of Interstate and Defense Highways.* The Federal Aid Highway Act of 1973 and the Intermodal Surface Transportation Efficiency Act of 1991 are best known for their encouragement and funding of alternative transportation, but generous funding for new urban highways was also included in these packages, $18 billion and $120 billion, respectively. A 1998 law provided another $175 billion just for highways. In 2005 Congress approved another massive transportation bill that was primarily about highway construction and maintenance. Even as we acknowledge these extraordinary financial incentives, let's not be too quick to blame (or credit) the mysterious powers that be in government or their shadowy lobbyists and pressure groups. Popular choice is a critical factor determining the actions of our (somewhat) representative government and the look of our new cities. Urban highway projects are popular

---

* As is evident in the name, partial support for this massive undertaking came from the belief, rational or otherwise, that a system of wide highways would be necessary in the event of a nuclear war and mass evacuation. It was, after all, the duck and cover era. As the specter of civil defense creeps back into the national consciousness in the post-9/11 world, we now know that the National Defense Highway System is a woefully inadequate facilitator of mass exodus.

expenditures in spite of themselves. The 2005 tranportation bill was vigorously skewered for its undeniably porked-up nature, but few batted half an eyelash at $200 billion worth of highway spending.

People have plenty of love for their highways. And if they aren't loved, they are tolerated.

Ultimately, the shape of the American city is the product of a complex blend of ingredients. The most important single factor, by far, has been the citizenry's inclination to motor around everywhere in private automobiles. But this reality, in turn, has been influenced in unknowable proportions by multiple inputs, mainly consumer choice, government edict, and capitalist persuasion, with a sprinkling of failed utopian fantasy thrown in.

Through a spectacular confluence of interests, the urban highways have been built—lots and lots of them. The street survives, but the highway is triumphant. Every major city in the country is crisscrossed with elevated highways and ringed with beltways. In some cases, small neighborhoods in forgotten parts of town were bulldozed to make way for the Paved New World, just as the early auto boosters dreamed. As legions of well-read critics are quick to point out, urban highways often cut cities into disjointed sectors and create hundred-yard-wide swaths of dead space right through the guts of the urban village. On the other hand, the defenders will remind us that the highways allowed Americans to relocate to suburbs, escape their dirty downtown digs, and elevate their standard of living.

Strictly in terms of transportation efficiency, we can say now with some confidence that the highways' beneficial effects have not been exactly as hoped or, at least, as advertised. The cars on these urban freeways, they aren't exactly zipping along much of the time. What's this? *Congestion.* The very same problem the freeways were supposed to solve. Here are the proud freeways, overwhelmed from the first day they are put into service and nearly every day thereafter. One can set a watch by the rush hour floods of motorized commuters that turn the urban highways into parking lots. Facilitating the breezy travel of the huge numbers of cars seen in the typical American rush hour would require the building of highways that would be, for once, unacceptable in their colossal girth.

There is another built-in difficulty that continuously frustrates those who hope a new highway, or a wider one, will make their congestion problems disappear. Just as nature abhors a vacuum, a crowded city abhors an empty highway. You can add all the lanes you want—the new, wider highway will fill up and become just as busy as the old skinny one. Even better, you can build a highway out where there is nothing, and the highway will create its own demand, sprouting developments along its length. This effect, of course, could be exactly what the developers want. The citizens who pay for the new, wider highway, however, are usually sold the project on the basis that it will alleviate congestion for the current population, and the fact it will enable more population growth and congestion is left out of the sales pitch. Even with examples of the failure of the highway ideal all around them, decades of examples, citizens tolerate still more and wider highways through and around their cities, in the vain hope that these projects will alleviate traffic congestion.

Urban planner Rem Koolhaas explains how the hopeful dreams of a fast-moving automotive future got shucked aside by the automobiles themselves: "This century has been a losing battle with the issue of quantity."[47] Who could have predicted the sweeping popularity of the automobile among a spiking population? The battle has been lost to sheer numbers of people and vehicles, but more importantly the battle has been lost to square footage. Cars are peculiar in that they take up a great deal of space. *One* car takes up a lot of space—something like 150 square feet— which means one person takes up a large amount of space (some might say an inordinate, unrealistic, and unsustainable amount of space) when they drive back and forth from work in their personal SUV. In the one-person-one-car society, it only takes a handful of people to create a bottleneck.

Especially to developers and their allies in cities with lots of room to expand, it's been easy to rationalize traffic congestion away as a nonprob-lem. Congestion is, after all, a symptom that a city is doing a lot of busi-ness. Congestion means big numbers, and big numbers are good. In this view, congestion is an unavoidable product of success, so there is little, if any, criticism of citizens' transportation choices. However, a much more cynical, critical view is competing for supremacy among those with the power to do something about it. This view holds that traffic congestion is, essentially, waste. Lost time, productivity, and profits. Those in this camp point the finger of blame at the automobile, its large footprint, and its unnecessarily singular occupant. This is the attitude that has led to various forms of car-curbing legislation in the world's most congested cities, from Manhattan to London. While this sentiment is starkly opposed to that which led to the frenzy of highway building in decades past, there is noth-ing new about it—Julius Caesar was moved to ban wheeled traffic from

Rome's center during peak hours. The same simple reason was given then as now: too many space-hogging vehicles and not enough space.[48]

The future of American highways could be interesting. There is much talk of automated highways, on which cars would move on autopilot at high speeds while the drivers attend to their morning rituals. But we should be on guard against claims that such systems will alleviate congestion rather than enable it. As always, traffic congestion is part of the reality of the city, which only has so much area to devote to its pampered commuters. People still need to get out to places in the Internet age, and they still overwhelmingly choose a few hundred square feet of private automobile to get them there. Meanwhile, the population isn't getting any smaller. These numbers don't add up. You don't need a slide rule to predict a congested future.

It seems likely that American drivers, as consumers of transportation facilities, will quietly absorb even more obnoxious doses of traffic congestion than they currently endure. Commuters in the Washington, D.C., area spent about seventy-six hours sitting in traffic jams in 1997[49]—is there any indication that this is anywhere near the limit of human traffic jam endurance? Congestion is like an old friend to American drivers. You got your coffee, your mean-spirited morning DJs . . . it just wouldn't be the same without the traffic congestion. Without it, commuters would arrive at work too quickly.

Cyclists needn't worry too much about the problems of congestion as the world grinds to a halt around them. The more congested the city gets, the more efficient the bicycle becomes in relation to motorized forms of transport, and the happier cyclists are in relation to drivers.

Enclosure

There is one important thing automobiles provide that bicycles do not: *enclosure*.

Since the 1920s, cars have been built with closed, lockable, watertight passenger compartments. In addition to the practical benefits, like keeping occupants out of the weather, protecting them from crashes, and holding their valuables for safekeeping, this enclosure has also helped the automobile ascend to a place of surprising importance and esteem in society. Cars have become extensions of the home—living rooms, or (ahem) bedrooms, on wheels.

But the enclosure of the automobile also holds some far-reaching negative implications for the general character of American cities.

In 1961 Jane Jacobs wrote *The Death and Life of Great American Cities,* which is considered by many to be the most important critique of urban development ever written. Perhaps the most valuable point in Jacobs's work is the idea that vital, flourishing, and safe city neighborhoods owe their success to what she calls "an intensity of users."[50] Such areas within cities have people from all walks of life coming and going, on foot, at nearly all hours, for a variety of reasons. This coming and going leads to face-to-face contact among strangers and neighbors. According to Jacobs, these seemingly insignificant social contacts are the basic building blocks of safe, vibrant cities.

In his book *Emergence,* Steven Johnson celebrates Jacobs's version of the city as an "emerging system," and compares it to the common anthill, in which individual ants at the bottom of the ant hierarchy exchange basic information in random nose-to-nose contacts, and, unbeknownst to these individuals, form a sophisticated community that can "engage in nuanced and improvisational problem-solving."[51] The same is true of the cells in the human body, and the people on the street in the city. They all contribute intelligence, from the bottom up, to create successful self-organizing systems.

However, when everybody climbs into a car for every conceivable trip, no matter how short or insignificant, the face-to-face contact among strangers is drastically diminished. When city dwellers stay enclosed even when they leave the apartment, going from garage, to drive-thru, and back to garage in their private metal pods with blackened windows, this behavior casts a chill over neighborhoods and cities. Instead of faces, all we see is metal and glass. If Jacobs is right, then, American car culture starves the cities of their self-organizing fuel. If a city cannot organize successfully into its proper form, presumably it will organize into something different, something a bit nastier.

Rage

We just might feel the harmful sociological effects of automobile enclosure every time we go for a ride, or drive. One noticeable effect is increased road rage, and the general ramping up of bitchiness among encased drivers, who, free from the encumbrance of face-to-face contact, decide to just speed past flipping the bird or yelling a few choice words at whoever fills them with hate at the moment, then bolt away. They figure they're never going to see that person again. Traffic is a bit like the Internet in that regard. Out on the sidewalk, where getting walloped violently is a more pressing possibility, suddenly all the road ragers are quite polite to each other.

Cyclists tend to take these hit-and-run road-rage encounters rather personally, which is unfortunate. Usually such an encounter is a simple example of traffic being traffic. Enclosure creates anonymity, which breeds tantrums. If we're going to be out in it, we should not get all bent out of shape about the unshakable realities of traffic any more than we should get down on the street and bang our heads against the pavement. Doing the latter might be a little more satisfying, actually.

Cycling the
New American City

Americans are broad-minded people. They'll accept the fact that a person can be an alcoholic, a dope fiend, a wife beater, and even a newspaperman, but if a man doesn't drive there's something wrong with him.[52]

—ART BUCHWALD, 1968

We could argue for years about whether the postmodern, motorized metropolis is good or bad for our souls. Hundreds of books have been written about this already. Better we should tackle a question that we can really sink our teeth into: how is it for cycling? The question is complex, and the answer, it turns out, has much to do with attitude.

Is your water bottle half empty or half full?

We cyclists hear, and do, a lot of complaining about the car-based development of American cities and the car-dependent lifestyles of Americans. Indeed, there is much to complain about. There are many dangers and special frustrations waiting for us on American streets. And current trends are not necessarily encouraging.

In a car-dominated society, of course cyclists are marginalized, physically and socially. It sometimes feels as if the cyclist is The Other, to be reviled. While riding a bike for transportation is a tribute to many of the basic ideas upon which this country was founded—common sense, self-reliance, and closeness with the land, to name a few—it is also, in many ways, a slap in the face to contemporary American culture.

Now wait a second. It sounds like a never-ending conflict. It sounds like war on the streets. How bad is it really?

A masterful cyclist, marginalized though she or he may be, travels with ease through the modern motorized city. *With ease*. No doubt there are many streets to avoid out there, many hazards, many drivers with bad attitudes. But there are usually enough friendly routes available for the urban cyclist to move along on with incredible efficiency and reasonable safety. The best riders don't depend on drivers for much, but when they do, most drivers are still courteous and reasonably aware of their surroundings. The new city can be had.

When bad-mouthing contemporary cities, a reality check is in order. We romanticize the preautomobile cities, forgetting that they were so overcrowded and drenched in green horse crap that the inhabitants were scrambling to evacuate. We lament the dreary sameness of the new cities, grumble about the invisible mechanism that stamps out the fast-food strips of Laramie or Cincinnati or New Haven and makes them almost indistinguishable—sometimes the only way to tell what part of the country you're in is to check the accent coming out of the speaker at the Taco Bell. But the nineteenth-century cities were all pretty much the same, too (although they confined their sameness to a less ridiculous amount of surface area). No doubt our current cities will be missed and romanticized in the same way, after they are consumed by yet another form of city, based on some revolu-

tionary form of transport that has so far escaped imagining by humankind—
not likely any time soon.*

---

* As we go to press with a new edition of this book, there is much to suggest that the world is on the verge of a watershed event: *the global peak in oil production.* Reaching the peak does not mean that the oil is running out. Rather, it means that the oil is about to start running out. After that point, global production will decline every year, and supply will most likely never be able to keep pace with demand. As we sit here today, it's hard to tell if such an event is actually upon us, but it sure seems like something profound is rumbling up from the depths—the price of oil shot up 40 percent in 2005 and continues to reach record levels in 2006, excess capacity is nonexistent, and demand from China and India promises to propel global demand ever higher for the foreseeable future.

The only way we will be sure the peak has occurred is by seeing it in the rearview mirror, after it's all said and done. After United States' oil production peaked in 1970, it has declined every year since. Still, the powers that be refused to believe that the peak had been achieved until probably fifteen years after the fact. The geologist who developed a formula for predicting the oil production peak for any given region, King Hubbert, successfully predicted the 1970 U.S. peak within one year, and also predicted the global peak would occur some time in the early 21st century. Some experts believe the global peak could be postponed for another few decades, but few continue to resist the assertion that a peak is imminent.

The immediate implications of a global peak are clear—the price of oil goes through the roof, and never comes back. How we are likely to cope with this situation is a matter that is being debated even as I write this. Some insist that market forces will take care of everything—as consumers change their behavior in response to rising prices, curtailing demand, and new but expensive ways of producing petroleum and so-called "unconventional oil" become economically viable, increasing supply. Some think we will simply burn a hell of a lot of coal to make up for it. Some have faith that a hydrogen infrastructure will be created to replace the petroleum infrastructure, or that some combination of renewable energy sources will save the day. But there are several analysts who harbor much darker predictions about the peak and its implications. They argue, essentially, that it is too late to salvage our consumer lifestyle with new energy sources. We would have had to start that project long ago, when oil was cheap. Darkly, some predict that the earth will no longer be able to support six billion inhabitants. Petroleum-based agribusiness will be finished. Wal-Mart will be finished—no more cheap goods shipped in from distant sweatshops. Some posit that the suburbs will be virtually uninhabitable due to the cost of heating expansive homes with natural gas. They predict a cascade of loan defaults and bank failures, and the collapse of the world financial system. And of course, China and the United States are slated to duke it out in the desert for the last remaining significant puddles of oil. At the outset of 2006 we are forgiven for suspecting that these possibilities might be played out sooner rather than later. Even if we locate some gigantic new fields, could it be too little too late? The global fan seems as if it may be getting hit as we speak.

It is interesting to imagine a world where Americans are forced to choose between paying, say, $500 a month on gas, or getting around under their own power. If the fuel shocks of the 1970s are any indication, Americans will turn to pedal power in droves as fuel prices skyrocket. And this time it will be a permanent rather than a temporary shortage. It seems quite possible that the global peak could finally usher in the elusive Renaissance of utility cycling that many of us have longed for, although only due to incredible pressure and dire circumstances.

For a persuasive, fact-based look at the peak oil debate, see Colin Campbell and John Laherrere, "The End of Cheap Oil?" *Scientific American,* March, 1998. In this article the authors predicted that the global oil production peak, and the point where demand outpaces supply and never looks back, would occur by 2008. For a more optimistic outlook that places the likely peak a few decades later, see Jack Edwards, "Energy in the 21st Century," *Denver Post,* December 4, 2005. For a somewhat overly serious and, in my view, overzealously dark picture of the post-petroleum phase of human existence, see James Howard Kunstler, *The Long Emergency* (New York: Atlantic Monthly Press, 2005). Kunstler has a great sense of humor, but he is scared straight by the prospects of the global peak.

Frankenstein's Monster

Sure you can imagine a better way to live. But we get what we get in this world. We change what we can, and make the best of everything else. As cyclists, we are in prime position to make the best of what we cannot change.

Invocation

The dedicated cyclist is a new kind of pioneer. Pioneers have an obligation to those who would follow in their tracks, to show them the way. Instead of highlighting the difficulties and frustrations, instead of obsessing about conflict, get out there and show the nation how *easy* it already is to cycle in the city. Wear "normal" clothes for short rides. Put the superiority of the bicycle on display. Be responsible, unflappable, and polite. Ride with style, grace, and intelligence. Ride with fear and joy.

the city surface

Pavement:
Get Over It

Much hated, ever implicated, thought by many to be the perfect symbol for everything that is wrong in the world, it is pavement that allows us to fly home from work on a flashy road bike, or embark on six-hour rides directly from midcity apartments. Let's give pavement some credit. Pavement lets us go far and fast.

Anyway, it is a useless waste of emotion to hate pavement. Best to get over it, literally, and ride the wave.

Even before bicycle riders, makers, and mechanics helped start the auto craze, they were agitating successfully for smooth, paved roads on which to ride their beautiful machines. Your ancestral cyclists, in many ways, gave birth to the paved environment. Now go out there and claim it!

There could very well be some pavement near you right now. Crouch down low to get a good look. With a few exceptions, pavement comes in two general types. These we refer to as *asphalt* (black) or *Portland cement* (white). Civil engineers and contractors call these *flexible* and *rigid,* respectively, the latter being more expensive and durable. Rigid pavement, made from chalk and clay, is the material of choice for sidewalks and bike paths (although asphalt paths are still common), airport runways, and the most heavily traveled streets, highways, and intersections. It is more likely that you are looking at a flexible asphalt surface—actually a combination of black asphalt and a special gravel (aggregate), a combo known technically as *asphalt cement concrete*.

Black asphaltic structures are the workhorses of earthbound transportation. They form the skeleton of America. Reach down and give it a pat. Made of rocks, it is. Little rocks of varying sizes, chosen for their angularity,* bound together with black tar. How does it feel? Depending on the budget and strategy of the road builders, the surface layer might be composed of relatively large aggregate, in which case it will be quite rough. The nicest asphalt surfaces are on freshly resurfaced streets topped with a dark, slick layer of tar and very small aggregate. These smooth surfaces are better to ride on, and better to land on.

Asphalt, the black "glue" of asphaltic concrete, is strange stuff, yet another petroleum-based substance ripped from the bowels of the earth. These days we brew our own asphalt by refining certain types of crude oil. In the very early days of asphalt paving, it was necessary to extract asphalt from natural deposits, the most significant of which was on the island of Trinidad. We didn't know exactly what it was, but we knew it made a nice road (while it lasted).[1]

Responsibility and
Surface Hazards

Unlike motorists, who can just putter along worrying only about traffic signals and other vehicles, the urban cyclist must always keep an eye out for hazards fixed on the city surface as well as hazards moving across it.

First of all, American cyclists need to accept the fact that their streets

---

* Angular, jagged aggregate, as opposed to smooth, rounded aggregate, "locks" together and helps to keep the asphalt structure from sliding apart under stress.

will be shot with holes, cracks, grates, waves, trenches, and craters. (And that's not to mention railroad tracks, "Bott's Dots," rumble strips, and roadkill.) We must realize that some degree of road damage is considered inevitable, and even acceptable, to the planners, engineers, and bureaucrats who are responsible for the condition of street surfaces. If they see it that way, so should we. The fact that streets will degrade precipitously is built into the equation. Cost, of course, is the major factor that determines the frequency and intensity of street maintenance, and the quality of the street in the first place. Street surfaces are not designed to be perfect, by any means. They are designed to hold up, just barely, and facilitate motor traffic over a certain finite life span.

Cyclists, and drivers as well, who are not clued in to the rapid aging process of pavement often experience a reflexive twinge of anger when they slam into unnoticed potholes. This is the same kind of anger felt by someone who, while stumbling through a darkened room, stubs a toe on the coffee-table leg, then must resist the urge to attack an inanimate article of furniture. Damn coffee table! You have harmed me! Of course the coffee table shouldn't be blamed for the stubbing any more than it should be praised every time someone walks past without smashing into it.

On American city streets and country roads, potholes happen. Cracks and waves are reality. Damage is the norm. Any cyclist who overlooks a surface hazard and suffers the consequences—ranging from shocked surprise, to bent rims, to full-on yard-sale wipeouts and broken bones—has only him- or herself to blame. Accepting this responsibility at the outset will go a long way toward preventing such occurrences in the future. Of course, there is a fair bit of luck involved in the cyclist's struggle against road damage. But if we focus on luck, and accept its power over our fate on the roads, we do ourselves a grave disservice. The safest cyclists do their best to eliminate luck as a factor in their daily travels. They tame what seems uncontrollable to lesser riders.

The Great
American Pothole

During fiscal year 2003, the [New York City] D.O.T. has filled 131,691 potholes.[2]
— NEW YORK CITY DEPARTMENT OF TRANSPORTATION PRESS RELEASE

Streets are generally torn up and resurfaced after about ten years of use. In the later years of this cycle, it is expected that the streets will be buckled, cracked, and cratered. This worn-out street, in its rickety old age, may be horrible for cycling, but it will still be minimally usable by motor traffic, and that is what really matters to the powers that be when it comes to streets. The design, engineering, and construction of street surfaces is a showcase for cost-benefit analysis, and also Murphy's Law.

Pavement structures are composed of multiple layers, each with a specific function. Unfortunately, the structure is only as strong as its weakest layer. If the base layer is thin or weak, or the ground on which it is laid is rutted or uneven, the top layer will never sit quite right no matter how durable it is.[3] There are many ways for pavement layers to go wrong. Maybe the construction company was trying to skim some money and used a substandard aggregate. Maybe the crew laid down a wavy subgrade or just didn't feel motivated enough to compact the layer properly.

Even the most carefully constructed streets fight a losing battle against American traffic. From the moment it is put into service, a street is under attack from the drivers it serves, and also from the environment. Temperature changes cause the structure to expand and contract, and thus to crack and break apart. The freeze-thaw cycle is the most brutal destroyer of asphalt structures, so potholes and other forms of road damage are a more serious problem in cities that go through wet, icy winters. Freeze-thaw potholes often form first around seams in the pavement, around manholes for instance, or where the asphalt meets a concrete gutter, because moisture infiltrates the structure through the seam. Any crack is a candidate to become a monster pothole if it allows water to seep in, which is why road crews stripe cracks with tar.[4]

Hydrology has further implications. Once a little chuckhole opens in

The City Surface

the pavement, it can fill with water. Then, every time a car tire slams into it, the water is forced toward the bottom of the hole, carving it deeper and wider. With all these destructive mechanisms working at the same time, the wet and cold spring months are the worst for road damage.

As the New York City Department of Transportation can attest, the repairing of potholes is a job that is never finished. The typical NYC pothole repair crew uses five tons of hot asphalt mix per day.[5] As soon as one pothole is filled and steamrolled, another opens up somewhere else. This is the Law of Conservation of American Potholes.

To cyclists, potholes are both an annoyance and a real danger. A really bad pothole strike can pinch a tube and put a flat spot on the rim. More seriously, potholes can finish off critical components that are on the verge of failure—faulty forks, cracked steer tubes, stem bolts. A surprise pothole might cause the rider to stack painfully against the stem, fumble the bars, and just plain wipe out hard. So the specter of potholes must be taken somewhat seriously even if hitting them usually amounts to little more than a wake-up call.

Avoiding potholes is a basic test of awareness and vision. The number one way to solve the pothole problem is to keep the eyes forward, where they can scan the road surface as well as the traffic. Potholes may not be too scary by themselves, but they become so when the element of surprise is added.

Avoiding potholes is also a memory game. While it sometimes seems like a pothole has popped up overnight, it nonetheless forms in one place and stays there, growing until enough citizen complaints are lodged and the street crew comes along to fill it up. Many cyclists manage to miss the significance of this simple fact, which is the observant cyclist's ace in the hole. Consciously note, and try to remember, the location of any potholes you come across—unfortunately, actually hitting the hole is the best way to memorize its location. You might hit that sucker once, but hopefully never again. The pothole won't sneak across the street to get you on the return trip. It will be waiting in the exact same place tomorrow, a rather pathetic ambush. Memorizing pothole locations is a crucial aspect of knowing the route.

Potholes are an insidious danger while riding at night. Riding without a bright illuminating headlight in dark areas is kind of like trolling for potholes. On very dark, unknown streets the rider needs to decrease speed and assume a sort of pothole-smashing "ready position," with the weight back, the arms and legs bent. You don't have to see the pothole to be ready for it.

Cracks and
Seams

Asphalt structures crack easily and often. Cement surfaces crack as well, perhaps not so easily or so often. That's just how it goes.

Heavily stressed asphalt street sections tend to sprout a labyrinth of cracks like the bed of a dried-up river. This is called "map cracking" or "alligator crazing." Map cracking on asphalt is a warning sign for potholes. Typically, streets that have degraded in this fashion are the same streets that sport massive potholes. Often these holes are born right in the midst of a heavily cracked area, as the cracks form little islands of pavement that are knocked out one by one.

The beauty of the typical crack in pavement is its chaotic form. The crack, in other words, is crooked and irregular. By themselves, before they have a chance to evolve into potholes, crooked cracks are benign cracks. We ride across them with scarcely more than a *bu-bump*. Straight cracks are of much more concern to the urban cyclist.

Certain high-traffic streets are constructed of white concrete, called Portland cement concrete (PCC). Cyclists should notice when they roll onto a Portland cement surface and should be very aware of an insidious type of surface feature that is found there: the *longitudinal crack*, running parallel to the path of the cyclist.

Concrete pavement structures are often built in sections with relatively large open seams between them. These seams are left open to give the slabs room to expand, contract, and move without cracking apart. Other PCC structures are laid down in one large, continuous slab, but, in the absence of openings between sections, *control joints* are sawed in at regular intervals to dictate where the structure will crack. This is the road builder's version of fighting fire with fire. When it's all said and done, PCC pavement has no shortage of straight longitudinal seams running along it.

Expansion-contraction joints are usually no more than about ½-inch wide, but this can be enough space to catch a typical road tire and throw down the rider. When the front wheel starts riding in the crack, the walls of the crack determine the path of the front wheel. This is seriously *no bueno*, as the cyclist needs freedom to adjust the front end in order to stay upright. The rider leans slightly to the side, pulling on the wheel, which goes nowhere as it is stuck in the crack, and something very bad happens, preceded by a moment of panic. In these types of wrecks, the bike seems to be removed by a mysterious force, leaving nothing but air between the rider and the concrete. Expansion joints are implicated in some of the most violent and dangerous of the solo, non-motor-vehicle-related wrecks.

The same nasty effect results from riding up against a small ledge in the concrete, where one slab is taller than the one next to it. A ledge just an inch or so tall has the power to inflict the same punishment as a full-fledged curb.

Longitudinal cracks and ledges become much more dangerous when moisture is added to the equation. In the snow a miniscule control joint on a sidewalk can wash out the front wheel. This danger is compounded greatly by the way snow hides the cracks from view. Look for subtle indentations in the snow that correspond to indentations in the pavement below.

The dreaded parallel cracks and seams show up on asphalt surfaces as well, but not as often. Many asphalt-paved streets have parallel cracks, ruts, and lips where the pavement meets the gutter, and around some manhole covers. Asphalt streets also are known to degrade in such a way that a long straight strip—not so much a crack as a groove—is worn into the top layer of aggregate, and these grooves have been known to throw down a cyclist or two.

Road-bike riders, with their skinny tires, have more to fear from straight cracks than the mountain-bike crowd, although the fat tires are not immune.

Waves

The elastic nature of asphalt structures becomes obvious when the pavement forms waves. Known as "hummocks" to transportation engineers, waves in the pavement are actual, rolling waves. They're just moving very slowly. Sometimes they rise so acutely that the pavement breaks, like a wave in the ocean. Sometimes the waves are perfectly smooth and elegant formations. They can be minor ridges, or they can be about 2 feet tall. Waves occur primarily around intersections, where cars apply a greater amount and variety of force to the surface through continual stops, starts, and turns.

More so than potholes, hummocks represent a small failure of the system. Somewhere along the line, somebody messed up. These street surfaces are not really doing their job to the acceptable standards. Heavily waved sections cannot be easily repaired in a piecemeal fashion like potholes and are a good argument for the superiority of Portland cement structures. Wave-prone asphalt streets become candidates for premature resurfacing, and thus they are inefficient and cost money.

Waves are particularly dangerous for a cyclist looking down, back, or anywhere other than forward. When encountered unexpectedly, waves are extremely efficient at tearing the handlebars from one's hands. If we see it coming, it is a small matter to negotiate the obstacle. Pick a good line, mindful of nearby motor traffic. Relax the arms and legs to absorb the bump, like a rider on a jumping horse, and just ride over it.

Lane Markers

It is not unusual for a lane line to be a good quarter-inch tall, piled with multiple layers of special reflective latex paint. This is a problem for cyclists. Especially when moisture is added, this little lip can cause a displacement wreck similar to those caused by longitudinal cracks.

Even a very thin coat of lane line paint can be extremely slippery in rain or snow. Don't carve a turn on a wet line, or stand up and lean the bike from side to side while the front tire is on the line. Don't you watch the Tour day France? Every few years, some sucker eats it on a wet line and takes out like ten guys.

Performing the same function as the lane line—marking lanes and wrecking unsuspecting cyclists—is the Bott's Dot. Bott's Dots are the little bumps with reflectors on them, stuck into the pavement and glued with epoxy. Although they may look cute and unassuming, if a rider hits a Bott's Dot while looking away, it could be very messy. The Bott's Dot and its cousin, the *rumble strip,* have been at the center of a fair bit of cycling-related controversy lately. Some cyclists claim that Bott's Dots and rumble strips installed on center lines keep motorists from leaving a safe amount of space when passing cyclists on the right side of the road, because motorists are unwilling to bump across the markers. Truly, the center-line rumble strip could also add to the cyclist's safety in certain situations.

Wet Metal

When coated with a thin layer of H_2O, metal strips, manhole covers, and grates of various kinds are probably the most treacherous—slippery—of all city surfaces. Wet metal is a real shocker to green cyclists. Ride over it, yes, but don't make any false moves while your wheels are on it—especially metal-grated bridges that will tear up a falling cyclist like a cheese shredder on a block of cheddar.

Drainage

Street drainage has been a constant struggle for American cities. The use of smooth pavements meant that sizable sections of the modern city became impermeable to water—the streets were inadvertent aqueducts. An underground world of pipes, tubes, and tunnels had to be constructed to tame the runoff. To this day the makers of cities and builders of streets still fail to exhibit a solid command of the drainage problems they created. Each pool of standing water is a shimmering monument to failure.

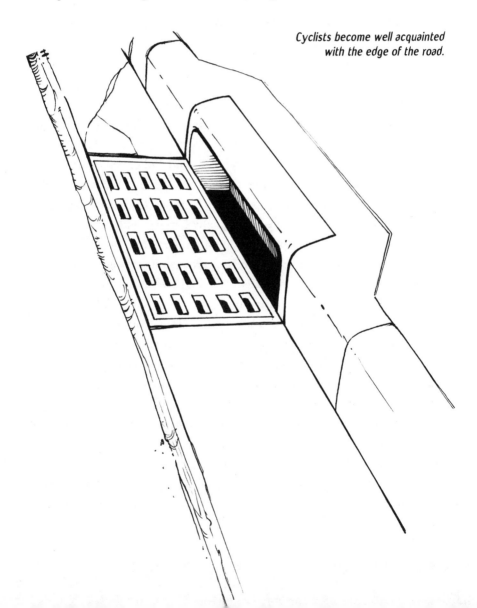

*Cyclists become well acquainted
with the edge of the road.*

In the interest of drainage, the modern street is "crowned," meaning it slopes downward slightly from the center to the sides. Riding on crowned streets has the effect of wearing out the tires slightly more on the left side.

More important for cyclists, the need for drainage implies the presence of various types of sewer grates imbedded in the street surface. Such a grate is often recessed a good 6 inches below street level, so the cyclist who succumbs to it actually falls off the edge of the world for a moment before striking metal. It may not seem like it, but most of the grates you see out there today have actually been designed with a hint of concern for the humble cyclist. Most of the grates with long, treacherous openings have been replaced with grates that have cross-members across the openings, so a bike's front wheel is less likely to be stopped cold or just eaten whole. Other grates have openings that are oriented diagonally to the direction of travel, also a nod to cyclists.

Grates are much feared—and understandably so, as grate-inspired accidents can be serious and bloody—but they are no longer the reapers they are rumored to be. When ranking the most injurious surface hazards in terms of overall danger, grates are no more damaging than longitudinal cracks, ice and other slippery stuff, potholes, sand and gravel, or railroad tracks.[6] Grates are truly nasty when they are undetected. Cyclists should expect a wheel-catching grate or pothole to be concealed beneath any substantial puddle on a street they are not totally familiar with.

Grates should only be a problem on unfamiliar routes. If the cyclist has ridden a street once or twice, any dangerous grates along the way should be detected, quickly inspected, and filed away for future reference. The next time the cyclist is cruising that street, he or she recalls the position of the grate and starts to take action to avoid it about a half block ahead of time. The same goes for potholes and as many other fixed surface hazards as can possibly be catalogued. They say we use only a small percentage of our available brain capacity. Well, here's your chance to use some more of it.

If you find yourself crashing through a catch basin on the edge of control, it's a sign you have been riding poorly up to that point, with a dangerously inadequate level of awareness. But these things happen. If you see a heinous recessed grate in your path, and can't safely get around it, one possible coping strategy is to slow way down, or even stop if possible, rather than just rolling into it. If the grate is unavoidable, size it up and actually pick a line across the metal slats. Keep the weight back somewhat—you may as well be traversing a little rock garden on a trail—relax, and visualize a successful crossing. Just don't grip the front brake and crouch stiffly over the front of the bike, or you might get bucked off. Another possible plan of attack involves speed. A skilled rider at speed should be able to lift the bike over the grate entirely for a soft landing on the other side. Riders who have mastered this "bunny hop" technique find occasion to use it several times per week. At slower speeds, a rider can perform a sort of stunted wheelie into the hole. If you can throw the front wheel all the way over the chasm, the rear wheel will usually just clunk through without major consequence. This clumsy technique may very well damage the rim or cause a pinch flat, but it's infinitely better than pitching over the bars. Whenever encountering a major hole like this, do yourself and your bike a favor by keeping the arms and legs bent, and stay light on the bike.

Railroad
Tracks

Ask around among any group of experienced cyclists, and you will find that more than a few have been felled by a railroad track. The most dangerous tracks are of two basic types: wet tracks (see Wet Metal, on page 50), and diagonal tracks. Railroad tracks that are both wet and diagonal to the cyclist's direction of travel are probably the most unforgiving of all possible forms of surface obstacles. Riders who wreck on such tracks report being slapped to the ground in a split second. There is nothing out there that is quite as efficient at ripping a rolling bike's front wheel to the side.

Railroad tracks cause quite an ugly brand of fall. The rider doesn't have time to get the arms out or prepare in any way. Serious injuries are common: smashed kneecaps, broken hips, broken wrists, broken collarbones, and broken skulls. Like the classic "dooring," the railroad-track wreck is almost like a rite of passage among cyclists, probably because, to inexperienced riders, it just doesn't seem like crossing a railroad track could be that serious of a proposition. But one encounter with a diagonal rail is enough to remove the rider from his or her suspended state of innocence.

"I woke up in ER, on the way to my CAT scan," writes one young woman of her recent railroad-track experience in Portland, Oregon. "They say that I constantly denied even owning a bike, so how could I have had an accident? Even though I blacked out and don't remember the accident, I don't ride bikes anymore."[7] That's how diagonal railroad tracks can cause a tragedy on top of a tragedy.

Negotiate railroad tracks by "squaring up." Cross the track at a square, 90-degree angle. If this is not possible, cross a diagonal track by lifting the front wheel over it. This lifting of the front wheel is an important technique for smoothing over all manner of road obstacles, and it should be second nature to any cyclist. Don't turn or lean the bike over when crossing tracks. They'll be time enough for turning when the crossing's done.

Toppings

So you've chosen a flavor: asphalt (chocolate) or Portland cement (vanilla). Would you like any *toppings* on that?

Your choices include: sand and gravel crumbles, oil sludge, water, wet leaves. Snow, ice, and even deicer. Also, upon special request, bum vomit.

Toppings make life so much more flavorful. All the toppings available here, even the deicer, ironically, serve to make streets more slippery, more difficult to ride, than they would be otherwise. Any mundane section of the city surface can be made terminally sketchy with the addition of the right topping(s). For instance, almost every experienced cyclist has slipped and crashed on a patch of sand at some point. Many have also learned the hard way that wet cement is twice as slippery as the dry stuff.[8]

Most street toppings can be dealt with fairly easily with a modicum of caution. Simply relax and ride across these problem sections without turning or using the brakes. A topping of ice, the Big Daddy of slippery street

A street that is empty of all other traffic could still be a problem for cyclists.

toppings, can pull the coefficient of friction down below an acceptable level even for straight rolling—the rider is just coasting along and the bottom falls out. And ice topped with water? Forget about it.

Riding in icy conditions is one of the most serious challenges a cyclist will face. It requires a very conservative, slow, upright style, and is not recommended for beginners. It is, however, quite possible to ride year-round even in the Great White North. Experienced winter riders adapt through the use of certain bits of winter-friendly equipment, including fixed gears, knobby tires, disc brakes, and internally geared hubs. Studded tires can also be purchased, or rigged at home. It should be noted that winter is known to destroy bicycles as well as streets, but that winter riding is good for the soul.

Plazas

Open plaza areas are standard equipment around buildings in American city centers. For this we can thank Charles Edouard Jeanneret, aka Le Corbusier, aka Corbu, and Ludwig Mies van der Rohe, aka Mies van der Rohe, aka Mies, and the legions of wannabes who followed along, pirating their ideas. Along with Frank Lloyd Wright, Mies and Corbu were the most-copied architects of the past century.

In a sharp departure from previous incarnations of the skyscraper, which were made of stone and so were necessarily wider at the bottom than at the top, use of reinforced concrete and steel construction allowed Le Corbusier and others to design tall buildings that appeared to be supported on *pilotis* (stilts). This style introduced a novel look and idea—that the land under and around the building could be left open as a park for the building's residents.

Mies van der Rohe used a version of Corbu's "skyscrapers in a park" vision, complete with *pilotis,* for his famous glass-skinned, steel-framed Seagram Building at 375 Park Avenue in Manhattan (designed with Phillip Johnson and completed in 1958).[9] The Seagram Building in itself was interesting, but the *negative space* of the design was the real novelty. The building was set back 90 feet from the street, and it consumed only 40 percent of the lot. With its expansive and elegant plaza, the Seagram complex became the model for corporate towers in every city center in America. The plaza was king.

The current version of the urban plaza is generally a second-rate copy of the Seagram plaza of 1958. It is a privately owned space administered by humorless guardsmen in blue blazers, who are directed via radio by monitor watchers in a remote nerve center. All the plazas are on camera. The primary task of the management company's rapid reaction force is to shoo panhandlers and skateboarding teens off the grounds. Secondarily, the guards are charged with keeping cyclists from locking their bikes to any railings. The railings are shiny and they'd like to keep them that way. Third, one hopes, they might want to set aside a moment or two after lunch to thwart any terrorists who might be planning to explode their buildings.

For cycling purposes, plazas should be treated like giant sidewalks. Pretend they belong to the pedestrians, even if they don't. Ride them only with great care and a sense of guilt, using the zero-impact style (see Sidewalks and the Law, on page 143).

Here's the deal with plazas, for those who wish to ride them. Plazas are often surfaced with granite or brick paving stones, which are then coated with slick, urethane-like substances. They're slippery as heck. A small grounds crew armed with pressure washers and power blowers is charged with keeping the plaza free of snow, ice, trash, leaves, and general munge. Truthfully, they could spare themselves the work of removing the ice. When wet, plazas are often just as slick as ice, and regularly claim uninitiated cyclists, and even a few pedestrians in their flat-soled shoes.

Curbs

Some cyclists claim that they never, ever have to hop a curb. Nor do they want to. These nonhoppers are devoted to the "vehicular" style of street riding, and vehicles, they say, should confine themselves to the roadways. When these riders decide to cross a curb, theoretically, they dismount and carry their bikes across the threshold.

As usual, the vehicularists have a point. If a rider is hopping on and off curbs all the time, it is an indicator of careless, dangerous riding. Riders who pop into the roadway in the middle of the block are often the ones who inflate the accident statistics. But—there is always a "but"—in the chaos of city traffic, curb-hopping skills are undeniably useful. For example, you might accidentally turn the wrong way onto a one-way, or make some other bonehead mistake that leaves you looking to get off a street as quickly as possible. In such a situation, you would not want to be limited by an inability to deal with a common obstacle, 6 inches high.

Realistically, cyclists will be faced with the prospect of negotiating the occasional curb or curblike feature, and should know enough to do it right. Curb hopping is undeniably part of the language of city cycling. Techniques range from smooth to crude and reveal a great deal about a rider's skill level.

The most common way to ride a bike up a curb is to pop the front wheel up with a little wheelie, then to simply let momentum take care of the rear wheel. In other words, the rear wheel impacts the curb solidly, which is a less than satisfactory situation, and awakens the dragons that live in the sewer. Those who employ this method should graduate to a more advanced style.

Somewhat more advanced is a quick one-two combination that is potentially quite smooth. As soon as the front wheel is on the curb, shift body weight forward, unweight the rear wheel, and lift it gently onto the ledge—no impact.

Even smoother is the fluid bunny hop: The rider lifts the front wheel just before lifting the rear, sails briefly through the air, and places both tires gently on the ledge. When performed by a master, this move is completely soft and silent. This application of the bunny hop is much easier with clipless pedals, although relying on clipless pedals to hop is frowned upon by purists and is truly the junior-varsity way of doing things. Bunny hops, after all, were perfected long ago by BMXers using platform pedals. Not very many riders can pull this off one way or the other, so most of us fall back on less-elegant techniques.

Curb climbing can be made easier by adding angle to the approach; in fact, climbing the curb dead-on at a 90-degree angle will be the method least likely to cause falls among beginners. Some riders who are really good can hop onto a curb as they ride parallel to it, but some of these same riders will tell you they have wrecked trying this move.

If the angle of approach is too small, or if the ledge is too high, or the timing is just plain off, use the one foot method. Unclip the inside foot, roll to the curb and turn almost parallel to it so your unclipped foot is close to the curb. Place your foot firmly on the step and finesse the bike up the curb using the hands as well as the outside foot, which is still clipped in.

When dropping off curbs into the street, the first and last concern should be avoiding motor traffic in the street. If the rider is speeding and launching from the street to the sidewalk, or vice versa, it's a bad sign. Cyclists need to exhibit more conservatism and patience in their curb-related freelancing. First and foremost, this means checking thoroughly with all the available senses for any traffic moving in the road. The rider should patiently check, re-check, and re-re-check for traffic before entering the roadway. No more speed and launch. Drop gently off the curb, using the arms to make the front tire's touch on the street as light as possible. This light drop is becoming a lost art in the age of suspension forks. Practice controlling the rear of the bike as well, holding it up in the air for a moment with the front brake, then setting it down with a little *tap* in the street. Your bicycle thanks you in advance.

Just because you have the skill to hop curbs doesn't mean you *should* hop curbs. The bicycle's versatility, it's potential to exploit both the vehicle and the pedestrian sectors of the city surface, and to move freely between them, becomes a liability in the wrong hands.

in traffic

Beyond
Vehicular Cycling

Responsibility, *n.* A detachable burden easily shifted to the shoulders of God, Fate, Fortune, Luck, or one's Neighbor. In the days of astrology it was customary to unload it upon a star.[1]

— AMBROSE BIERCE

The bicycle is the magic carpet of the urban traffic grid. It can squeeze between lanes of cars in a traffic jam; pop onto the sidewalk and snake around pedestrians, newspaper boxes, and hot-dog stands; or bust a tiny U-turn in the middle of the block. It can even go the wrong way up the middle of a one-way street, and not give a damn. This tremendous agility demands great care and discretion. In the wrong hands, it can be deadly. The bicycle's magic power is also its Monkey's Paw.

Crash statistics indicate that there are many, many cyclists out there who are abusing the bicycle's go-anywhere potential. Most of the nasty car-versus-bicycle collisions in cities occur when bicyclists succumb to temptation and fail to yield at stop signs, turn suddenly into the paths of motorists, or ride against traffic. Their riding style, if it can be called that, is characterized by chaos and unpredictability. These victims can't handle the freedom that the bicycle gives them. Freedom requires responsibility. Unfortunately, freedom comes easily to American cyclists, but responsibility does not.

In 1975 John Forester wrote the first edition of a book called *Effective Cycling*. Using these ugly accident stats as a guide, Forester implored cyclists to dispense with the anarchy and ride in a predictable, ordered fashion. The normal traffic laws governing motor-vehicle traffic, he declared, provide a ready-made framework that works just as well for bicycles as it does for motor vehicles. He boiled it down to a single statement: "cyclists fare best when they act and are treated as drivers of vehicles."[2] This he called the "vehicular-cycling principle." Forester's ideas won over the cycling community, if not the general motoring public. Today the vehicular-cycling principle is endorsed and taught by the League of American Bicyclists (formerly the League of American Wheelmen).*

Next to the absentminded anarchy practiced by many novices, the vehicular-cycling principle is a stellar guideline. Vehicular cycling is a great starting point for beginners. Just by obeying traditional traffic-law principles and riding predictably, a bicyclist will eliminate a large portion of the danger of cycling. However, the vehicular-cycling principle has a big hole in it: The strict vehicular cyclist who has eliminated many of his or her own mistakes by riding lawfully will still remain quite vulnerable to the mistakes of others. Because mistakes are common in the mix—indeed, mistakes are the rule—and because cyclists are especially vulnerable to the seemingly inconsequential "brain farts" of motorists, riders who have spent decades and hundreds of thousands of miles in city traffic naturally adopt a style that is quieter, more conservative, and somewhat less trustful of others than that of the vehicular cyclists. It's amazing how a few trips to the MRI room will color one's judgment of traffic laws and fellow road users.

---

* In recent years the League finds itself under attack from vehicular cyclists who once formed its core membership. The Foresterites charge that the LAB has lost its commitment to vehicular cycling education and principles, and have formed a feisty protest group known as LAB Reform.

One of the big problems with the vehicular-cycling principle, or any principle of cycling, for that matter, is that it fails to account adequately for the complexities, details, and chaos of the city streets. Evidence of this failure is provided in the fact that few experienced cyclists, even those who are vocal proponents of vehicular-cycling dogma, apply it consistently in their everyday travels. Instead, they use it whenever it suits their purpose and discard it when it doesn't. They're not above using an off-street bike path if it's headed in the right direction. They roll through stop signs, treat red lights like yield signs, and filter past lines of stopped cars in traffic jams and at intersections. Not very vehicular of them. That's the reality of cycling today. If cyclists were to suddenly start living by the vehicular principle in all situations, disregarding the special privileges and de facto rules they have built for themselves over the decades, the advantages of riding a bike in the city would be gutted.

It is apparent, also, that the vehicular principle lends itself to some very questionable interpretations. While Forester's advice is usually quite sound, a large number of cyclists have added a militant, confrontational tone to the framework of his message. They have taken the vehicular-cycling principle and bastardized it. Through their riding habits in traffic, which are often deliberately, theatrically antagonistic, they seek to make some kind of point to their special audience of other road users. One is never quite sure exactly what that point is—something about the rights of cyclists in traffic. Their riding often becomes little more than a passive-aggressive acting out of their disdain for drivers. What a waste of a good bike ride this is. The feisty neo-vehicularists claim they are standing up for their rights, asserting themselves, showing drivers that they will not be intimidated in the face of overwhelming pressure, and increasing their own safety in the process. Others claim these riders needlessly charge the air with conflict and do grave damage to all cyclists' ability to navigate safely and easily in traffic.

The vehicular-cycling principle may simply be outmatched and out-dated in the new millennium. Indeed, much has changed since the concept was formally introduced. The country's population has grown by about sixty-five million, and even more cars have been added than people. The national culture has become even more adoring of automobiles, and cities have sprawled out grotesquely to accommodate them. Americans are more devoted to and dependent on their internal combustion engines than ever before. As a result, traffic is much worse in just about every city in the nation. Drivers spend more time stewing in traffic jams and shaking fists at each other, and cyclists are even more unwelcome on busy streets. On the other hand, the bike lanes and paths, which drew such biting criticism from vehicular devotees for being unsafe and unfair to cyclists, have been greatly improved since the 1970s and 1980s, and look more attractive to cyclists than ever before. When it suits them, even seasoned veterans of city riding abandon the traffic-packed roads in droves for separate facilities. They feel no sense of loss when doing so. A prime example is Manhattan, where all the bridges onto the island are now accessible by bicycle due to new paths, and a continuous bikeway runs beside the Hudson River.

Decades ago, the vehicular-cycling ideologues had high hopes for their cause: They hoped that cyclists would be granted not only equal rights, but also equal respect, on America's roadways, that cyclists would be able to cruise *any* city thoroughfare alongside—or, to be more accurate, in front of—cars and trucks, and that the whole concept of separate facilities would wither and die from lack of usefulness. The dream has failed to materialize. America is further from a vehicular-cycling utopia than it was twenty-five years ago.

In this chapter, you will find a synthesis of sorts between old-fashioned vehicular cycling and the reality of modern street riding. We will pay homage to the masters who have taken the sacred vehicular-cycling principle and molded it to their needs, to create a more enlightened and nuanced style. Theirs is a safer style, and an easier style. Where the vehicular-cycling principle encourages cyclists to deny any off-street options and to boldly stake out a position among motor traffic, flexibility will be our guide. We will use the safest, easiest, and most stress-free option available at any given time. We will exercise all our rights to cruise the busiest city streets, but also our rights and abilities to use the quiet ones, and the off-street paths. We will have the best of all worlds.

While some cyclists preach assertiveness and militancy, we offer cooperation and facilitation. We will still get where we're going in a hurry, if we wish. We will recognize and respect the limitations of human nature as well as traffic law. We will recognize the basic human mistake as the salient feature of urban traffic, and we will seek to anticipate the mistakes of others. Where the vehicular-cycling principle leaves responsibility in the hands of motorists, and trusts that they will act properly, we will take back responsibility for our own safety whenever we can. We will not seek to dole out blame to anyone but ourselves. While Forester claimed that even children could ride safely on busy streets using the vehicular-cycling principle, our way is unquestionably for adults. Freedom will be our food and our poison. The streets demand from us an awareness and maturity that would be very rare in a child.

We will abandon the pretension of principles and rules and will adapt to the ever-changing chaos of city life. We will find the path of least resistance. Instead of attempting to dictate the flow of traffic, we will become the flow of traffic, and it will become us.

Above all, we will have fun and get home in one piece.

The style prescribed here is nothing new. It is put to work every day in just about every city in the world. The cyclists who use it have come by it organically as individuals. They did not get together at a conference to cook it up. They did not take a course or read about it in a book. It is a natural product of their long, sometimes painful experience. It works.

Quite unfortunately for authors of books about cycling, this enlightened style is difficult to describe with words. It is born of infinite details and will not be tamed by principles or paragraphs. This brand of cycling is an art form.

Blame Versus

Responsibility

The word "blame" came to the English language by way of the Latin word *blasphemare,* meaning "to blaspheme." The Old English version of the verb "to blame" had a very negative connotation. It implied dishonesty. Blame had roughly the same meaning as "malign" or "libel." Somewhere along the line, the definition of blame got all twisted up. Blame ceased to be a very bad thing and became quite respectable—not a proud or useful moment in human history.

Today's Americans spray blame around in great shotgun blasts to see what they can hit and where it might stick. They aim it everywhere except where it might actually do some good.

The proliferation of blame is rather useless for cycling. Blame is what happens when it's already too late. Obsession with blame is good for insurance purposes but not so good for safety purposes. The cyclist should cast the twin concepts of blame and legal liability onto the scrap heap and forget about them. Thinking in terms of blame while out on the road is a perfect example of self-fulfilling prophecy. Blame is dangerous.

The most effective way for a cyclist to stay out of trouble on city streets is to forget entirely about the possibility of blaming others, and to take on full responsibility for his or her own safety. This attitude will be fundamentally different from the prima donna mind-set displayed by many humans, drivers and cyclists among them, who put their safety in the hands of others, count on everything working out just right, and have a royal freak-out at the first sign of trouble. The successful cyclist counts on nothing but chaos and stupidity.

Blame! Who will you blame after that floral delivery van runs a red light and pulverizes your internal organs? As you wheeze your last wheeze, will you find the breath to bitch at the driver—"Nice driving, ***hole!"? Will you be planning your suit as you lurch around on the pavement like a trout?

From now on, if some bastard breaks every law in the book and runs you over in the process, it will be *your* fault and nobody else's. That is the meaning of true freedom. That is how we will keep such disasters from happening in the first place.

The delivery van example above is an overdramatization, of course. To illustrate this point more clearly, let us consider a more plausible example—an example, in fact, from real life, the life of someone who shall remain nameless. A cyclist is pedaling down a relatively pleasant street in an inner-city residential area. The street has a bike lane painted on it, and, because the bike lane is crowded with parked cars on the right, and this cyclist recognizes the general limitations of bike lanes, he is positioned very near the left marker of the 4½-foot-wide lane. He is moving along at a good clip. Suddenly (of course) a black Mercedes E320 comes ripping out of a hidden alleyway backwards and the cyclist bashes into it. The rider is injured but not seriously—a small matter involving chunks of pinky finger and road gravel in the forehead; the bike's frame, a sturdy old Columbus Battaglin, is broken. The butt end of the Mercedes is trashed. Battaglin 1–Mercedes 1.

In terms of fault, this is an open-and-shut case. The cop gives a ticket to the driver, despite her repeated unsubtle hints about being willing to "bargain." Failure to yield.

But whose fault was this wreck, really? A glance at the police report reveals that it has failed to pin down the true causes of the so-called accident. It says nothing of the cyclist becoming distracted by an attractive member of the opposite sex on a nearby porch before the collision. The rider wasn't even watching the road! It doesn't mention the cyclist's few miles per hour of excess speed, impatiently applied, that translated into a few tenths less available time before impact, or the sluggish action of the ill-maintained front brake, or the failure of the cyclist to respect and move away from a dangerous alley intersection hidden behind the plumber's van, even though he had ridden this same route literally thousands of times and had been nearly run down at this same spot dozens of times . . . a multitude of causes, coincidences, and consequences.

Any break in this long chain of the cyclist's failures would have neutralized the motorist's mistake and averted the final crunch. Car-versus-bike accidents require two parties: one to make a colossal mistake and another to be caught off-guard by it, one to screw up and another who fails to fully respect the potential of the other road user to screw up. Any way you slice it, it's two screwups, smashing together.

Smart cyclists, for whom the stakes are inordinately high due to their notable lack of protective sheet metal, have little use for the simplistic system of classifying accidents and assigning blame after the fact. The motorist's backing blindly and illegally into the roadway is just another something that happens in the city. Drivers back out of hidden alleys, parking spots, and driveways all the time. It must be expected. It must be prepared for. The law blames the motorist for such a collision—as it should—but the safe cyclist blames him- or herself for being distracted and unprepared. It's either that or get used to eating trunks and side-panels, which aren't very tasty and provide poor nutrition.

The cyclist's best chance is to gather all the responsibility that can be gathered. Hoard it from those around you. Have faith that you will do a

better job with it than they will, and make it so. Don't trust your fate to the police, the planners, the pedestrians, or the paramedics. Don't leave your fate to the stars, or to luck. Definitely don't leave your fate to the drivers.

Vigilance

Is cycling dangerous? Yes. Yes, it is. Deadly, no, but definitely dangerous.

This is actually a controversial thing to say. There are those who bristle at any suggestion that cycling is dangerous, because they fear it will scare noncyclists away from ever ditching their cars and trying a more healthy form of transport. This is a good point, but it doesn't change the fact that cycling is dangerous. This is not some urban legend that needs to be debunked. It is reality, and we need to embrace it. Of course, this argument is meaningless unless both sides have the same concept of what "dangerous" means, and they rarely do.

Now, is cycling any more dangerous than driving or walking in the city? Not really. Maybe a little bit more dangerous overall, depending on how vigorously you want to manipulate the statistics, but probably less likely to cause your death (see Chapter Four: Bicycle Accidents and Injuries). In general, people seem to be short on respect for the dangers involved in *any* of their chosen modes of personal city transportation, whether driving, or walking, or riding a bicycle. It's dangerous out there, period. The difference with bicycling is that it brings long-term health benefits and peace of mind that the other forms of transportation can't.

Realistically, it is not the prospect of dying in an accident, but that of being sent to the hospital with a serious injury, that hangs over the vulnerable heads of cyclists. The cyclist's primary goal should be, first and foremost, to avoid serious injury. This is the cyclist's bottom line. We must do whatever it takes to achieve this goal, short of staying at home. Our other major goals as cyclists—efficiency and enjoyment—are dependent on the goal of safety. Getting packed into the back of an ambulance halfway through our commute will obviously keep us from reaching our intended destination, and it probably won't be very much fun either.

Instead of just hopping on the bike and pedaling, we should take a moment before any ride to soberly consider the dangers we are about to face and how we will avoid them. We will need to carry this underlying seriousness into the ride and maintain it throughout, despite all the distractions of everyday life that compete for bandwidth in our skulls. It is absolutely true that accidents happen when they are least expected. The old warhorses of cycling—and there is not a single one of them who hasn't been hit at some point or another—will always say their worst wrecks came at a time when their minds were wandering. They had momentarily forgotten the danger. They let themselves slip, just a little. Just enough.

The good news is that the cyclist has the potential to control his or her own destiny to a great extent. The bad news is that as soon as the rider drifts off into a passive mode, goes on autopilot, unpleasant things seem to happen. The obvious remedy is to keep oneself from falling back into this passive mode. To always stay alert. To treat the potential dangers very seriously, all the time. This is a state of mind known as vigilance.

Vigilance goes hand in hand with accepting responsibility for oneself, and is the hallmark of the experienced city rider. Will it be possible, in a book, to teach beginning cyclists the value of vigilance, before the lesson is pounded into them by events? One can only hope.

In addition to constantly scanning the road surface for obstacles, the vigilant cyclist keeps tabs on other road users—motorists, pedestrians, and other cyclists—who have any potential to cause a collision. That's a lot of road users. The vigilant cyclist expects serious ineptitude from strangers in traffic, and therefore is not surprised or angry when it has to be endured. The vigilant cyclist keeps the head up and eyes forward unless it is absolutely necessary to look elsewhere, and the vigilant cyclist does not expect to be seen by others. The vigilant cyclist does not trust green lights or stop signs or bike lanes painted on the street or any of the other artificial trappings of traffic engineering. The vigilant cyclist is not a trusting cyclist, but makes up for this lack of trust with a load of patience.

Bicyclists may experience long intervals encountering nothing but rational and lawful citizens on the road, weeks or months with everything running smooth as silk. But the vigilant cyclist realizes this is only a setup. The vigilant cyclist will not be faked out or lulled into complacency by the semisadistic urban spirits and their tricks.

Luckily, maintaining a constant state of vigilance can be fun. A great trick is to meld the goal of safety with the goal of enjoying the ride. Turn your dangerous trip through the city into a kind of game. The concentration required of the cyclist in heavy traffic is not unlike the concentration demanded of the mountain-bike-trail rider on a descent. Constant scanning ahead, constant adjustments, unbroken focus on the task at hand. It pushes everything else out of your head when practiced correctly. It can be, paradoxically, totally relaxing and fun.

Cycling is no stroll in the park. As with many of the world's most enjoyable games, the penalty for a loss of focus while cycling can be serious injury or even death. This is not a game you want to lose.

Route
Choice

There are two competing philosophies about route choice in cycling. One says that cyclists should not be overly concerned with route choice at all, except to choose the fastest and most direct route to their destination. It is a corollary of this belief that all city streets and boulevards, with few exceptions, are suitable for cycling. It's simply up to the cyclist to stake a claim to the road. Cyclists are granted that right by law, so why not? If we don't exercise our right to use the public roadways, they'll take that right away. Cyclists who believe this often urge others to make heavy use of busy arterial boulevards. Whether or not they actually follow their own advice on this is questionable.

Another philosophy maintains that the cyclist is better off choosing a route with as few traffic hassles along the way as possible. Cyclists who believe this prefer to avoid busy and narrow streets, whenever practical, in favor of wide, quiet streets. They are not averse to using well-designed bike paths. They will sacrifice a bit of time in exchange for a reduction in overall stress. Although these riders may be quite well versed in the methods of riding busy streets, they feel no ideological need to do so when alternative routes are available.

The first of these views is perhaps a relic from a bygone era. The second is more realistic. In a perfect world, a skilled cyclist would be able to travel on any street in the city, with no problems. But this is not a perfect world. In our traffic-jammed twenty-first-century urban sprawl, cyclists subject themselves to needless hassle and stress by trying to ride streets that are bad for cycling. Many newbies, embarking on their first commutes, simply attempt to follow the same exact routes they've been driving in their cars every day. This is ill-advised. The best routes for cars very rarely correspond to the best bike routes. Riders who attempt this are often so frazzled by the experience that they never look at their bikes again. If that's what cycling is all about, then they want no part of it. But that is not what cycling is all about. It's simply the consequence of a classic beginner mistake—failure to recognize or appreciate the available route options.

Know that your cycling experience should not be marked by frequent conflict. Occasional conflict, sure. But the ride should actually be pleasant. No yelling. No fist shaking. No screaming in terror. Every commute should be a bit of a vacation. If it's not, perhaps a little creative route finding can solve the problem.

It is extremely difficult to generalize about the problems associated with different types of streets and paths. As with the other important aspects of cycling, the only principle that really works with route choice is one of total flexibility.

When choosing streets, the first priority should be to minimize the danger of the route, of course. But there should be an underlying recognition that all streets and bike paths will be somewhat dangerous. Danger can never be eliminated through route choice. Vigilance must be maintained, no matter what route is used. Don't be lulled to sleep by a quiet route.

Route choice has as much to do with minimizing hassle and stress as it has to do with safety. With this in mind, look to avoid lane conflicts and turning/crossing conflicts rather than simply being concerned with volume of traffic. Find streets with low *intensity of traffic*. Traffic intensity, an official-sounding term that the author has just now made up, is a function of volume, speed, frequency of turning/crossing vehicles, lane width, and a certain frantic disposition. Traffic intensity will vary on the same streets at different times of the day. Some very well-traveled boulevards may also have relatively low traffic intensity. Some near-deserted streets cross a heinous intersection every block, and are insidiously problematic.

Really, what you are looking for are wide curb lanes or wide shoulders, with a minimum of motor vehicles traveling across your line. The fewer intersections the better. The presence of an on-street bike lane is, at least, an indication of a wide curb lane. Avoid when possible hectic commercial streets bordered with many parking lots and parking-lot entrances. Riding these streets will mean dealing with an inordinate amount of left- and right-turning vehicles, and therefore lots of confused and angry drivers, lots of harrowing near-misses, or worse. Low speed limits—30 mph or lower—are nice. High speed limits are of no use to cyclists. Remember that a cyclist will travel basically at the same speed on a 30 mph street as a 75 mph freeway, all other factors being equal. One-way streets with moderately high speeds and lots of lanes, streets designed to move a huge amount of cars in one direction in a hurry, are probably poorly suited for safe cycling if the curb lane is skinny. Unfortunately, these tight one-ways are extremely common in urban centers. One is tempted to make the claim that streets with lots of on-street parking are always bad for cycling, due to the dangers that parked vehicles imply, but in fact some parking streets are quite nice if there is enough space. Streets where the cyclist must block the lane to stay out of the Door Zone are bad cycling streets (see The Door Zone, on page 116).

Traffic intensity and lane width are not the only factors to consider. Cyclists also put a premium on streets that are smooth, clean, fast, and direct. Mix and match depending on your priorities and preferences. These attributes can be competing, but not always.

Often the urban or suburban cyclist will find that the most direct route to a destination is a very narrow, high-speed roadway where the mere presence of a cyclist causes a major disruption to motor traffic. Faced with these situations, the cyclist is advised to chart a longer route, even a meandering route, on streets with less intensity of traffic, if any such route is available. It's not so much that the busy, narrow-laned, conflict-prone street is dangerous—all streets are dangerous. It's the continuous hassle with motorists that is the real deal breaker on such a street. It's just not worth it most of the time. Use these streets only as a last resort—when no other option is available, or in a serious time crunch. A cyclist may occasionally decide to subject him- or herself to a good deal of additional contention over lane space in order to take the fastest route. Already fifteen minutes late for work? You might need to jump on Suicide Parkway and fly. It happens.

Circumstantial evidence strongly suggests that cyclists in this late-to-work mode are more likely to be involved in collisions because of the increased intensity of traffic on their chosen routes, and because of their own impatience. There's hardly anything out there that could make you quite as late for work as a side trip to the hospital (although that does provide a good excuse). Perhaps the best safety tip is to leave early enough that you don't have to hurry and can afford to take a luxuriously mellow route.

◆ ◆ ◆

The first attempt at any new destination will consume excess time because it will naturally include some backtracking, inadvertent forays onto poor cycling roads, and other general floundering. A first attempt is always something of an adventure and is to be relished. Some riders like to just hop on the bike and go exploring, and others like to look at a detailed street map before embarking. Be careful with the special bike-route maps; these are good for locating the bike paths but often fail to show all the city's streets.

One of the first challenges with charting a route through the modern American city is finding a way across freeways. Freeways are like huge rivers. We can't ride on them, there are only a few places to cross, and many of the crossing points will be horribly inhospitable to cyclists. So the cyclist's options are already, shall we say, simplified dramatically for any cross-city ride. Urban freeways, rail corridors, rivers, and other colossal barriers always seem to cause the most route-oriented delays during any ride through unknown territory. Know the crossing points.

Contrary to the insistence of some misguided souls, American cyclists are lucky that continuous, fully separated bicycle/pedestrian mega-paths have been and continue to be constructed in many cities. These paths flow unbroken under (or over) freeways and major boulevards, and must be distinguished from the old-style asphalt bike paths and the "side paths" that are little more than glorified sidewalks. Rather than cutting down on cyclists' available options as some fear, fully separated paths make the bicycle an even more versatile and efficient tool for urban transportation. Ideally, the best route would consist entirely of a wide concrete bike path cutting diagonally across the city, directly to your destination, with not a single intersection or stop sign along its entire length. Of course, such a route is rarely so perfectly placed, but you might be able to pick up a segment of a good path and insert it into your route.

Experienced riders know that cruising these separate paths brings an increased total chance of minor collisions, something that seems counter-intuitive to many beginners. Make no mistake, bike paths are dangerous. Cyclists will have to deal with hazards on the path that they would never see on the roads. But the complete lack of traffic stops and car interactions on separate facilities is much appreciated and makes the new bike paths the most attractive of all possible cycling routes. If only they led everywhere we need to go.

Once a good route has been sniffed out, the cyclist will gain a significant amount of security by riding it consistently and repeatedly. The rider will learn every pothole, every intersection, every hidden garage exit, every thin section of road, and will grow to understand and predict the personality of the traffic at different times. Just in terms of learning the idiosyncrasies of the road surface, route repetition is extremely valuable.

Route repetition can also be boring. To add variety, scout a few alternates and learn those as well. These alternate routes will come in handy when the normal route is under construction or bombed by North Korea.

Road Position and
Location

Newbie riders are often puzzled by the question of where to ride in the street. "Where should I ride in the street?" they ask, puzzled.

There are no easy answers to this question. The intricate art of positioning is downloaded into cyclists' brains by experience. They don't analyze where they ride or why they ride there, they just do it. After having been passed hundreds of thousands of times by cars and trucks, after hundreds of near misses and more than a few collisions, highly experienced riders gain a *feel* for what is easiest and safest in different situations. They ride where they are most comfortable, and the details are based largely on personal preferences.

If we were to gloss over all sorts of variables and use gross generalizations, however, we could hang the positioning art on a framework of four not-so-simple guidelines:

1. The cyclist should ride in the same direction as motor traffic.
2. Cyclists should avoid riding within about 3½ feet from the sides of parked cars, unless speed is slow enough that collision with an immovable object called a car door would be relatively benign (see The Door Zone, on page 116).

3. When approaching intersections and when exiting them, the cyclist should be positioned in the appropriate sector of the appropriate lane, depending on whether he or she is going to turn right, turn left, or continue straight through—on the right side of the far-right lane, in the rightmost left-turn lane, or at the right of the rightmost through lane, respectively. Achieving proper position for a left turn can be extremely difficult, or even impossible, depending on traffic. For this reason, left turns are a special case (see Left Turns, on page 103).

The previous three guidelines are fairly straightforward. They are standard vehicular-cycling fare. This next one is far from straightforward. We could qualify it, question it, and pick it apart until the sun dies out.

4. Use the BUFFER ZONE. Choosing road position on busy streets in dense urban areas—as opposed to wide, quiet boulevards with few pedestrians and near-perfect visibility of any side streets and driveways—is a delicate art. When no cars are gaining from the rear, or approaching from the front, the cyclist should ride way out in the heart of such a street, not tucked over on the side. How far out? That's where the art comes in. Many savvy veterans enjoy riding near the center of the right lane, on the hump between the right lane's wheel depressions, or in the right wheel depression. Others like to ride farther out toward the left of the lane. Whatever your preference, consider a centralish position to be the *default position* of cycling.

There are a few very good reasons why the cyclist should take this position on streets with lots of side traffic. The rider will be more visible to motorists and pedestrians on the periphery and will be less likely to have these other road users move into his or her path. More importantly, the "buffer zone" created by this positioning gives the cyclist a better view of what may be coming from the wings, which translates into precious milliseconds when the inevitable intrusion occurs. If a car bolts out from a driveway, alley, or side street, or a jaywalker with a fresh set of running shoes pops out from between parked cars, the rider will want to be as far away from the hazard as possible while still accounting for the possibility of additional hazards. This buffer zone increases the cyclist's safety, of course, but also allows the cyclist to continue rolling at a consistent clip in an obstacle-prone world, without having to swerve harshly or slam on the brakes every ten seconds.

Increases in speed bring increases in the importance of space. The more speed carried by the artful cyclist, the closer he or she gets to the center of the street. At moderate, ho-hum cycling speeds, the rider will not have to be too concerned about maintaining a buffer zone unless the street is lined with parked cars. Streets with clear edges, few pedestrians, a view all the way to the curb, and good lines of sight to any driveways, alleys, or intersections can be ridden safely all the way to the right if one wishes. Lines of parked cars seriously compromise the cyclist's vision and visibility, in addition to the other dangers they pose, and change the equation drastically.

Quick speeds that are easily attained by the bulk of riders—around 20 or more mph—require the rider to maintain a serious buffer zone between the bike and any parked cars on the right side of the road. Ten feet or more. This means that, on a very narrow side street lined with parked cars, the fast-moving rider might take a position *right down the middle of the street.* When forced back to the right on such a street, the rider should respond with a decrease in speed. On wide roads with multiple lanes, the cyclist probably won't have to drift any farther left than the left side of the outside lane.

The rider should always ask him- or herself: "How much am I leaving to chance here? How dependent am I on other people?" And then the rider should adjust his or her location and speed in such a way that this dependence is minimized, while taking traffic law, the need for speed and efficiency, and courtesy for other road users into account. Clearly this endeavor is entirely dependent on the rider's awareness of the position, speed, and vector of every other vehicle in the vicinity.

Leaving the comfortable default position to move closer to the curb or parked cars is often necessary for sharing the road with vehicles on a parallel path, oncomers and overtakers. When faced with oncoming vehicles in the opposite lane, the cyclist might not want to continue riding near the middle of the street. (What if the driver doesn't notice the rider and decides to crank a sudden left?) Instead, the cyclist might drift to the right, relinquishing the default position, for the same reason he or she assumes the position in the first place: to create a buffer. Moving to the right for an overtaking vehicle—a vehicle traveling in the same direction as the cyclist—is more a matter of courtesy. How far over should we move for overtaking vehicles, if at all? More art.

Safety is the cyclist's primary motivation for shifting position left or right—to reduce the chances of getting hit or running into a pedestrian. Cooperation is another reason to change positions. Subtle shifts of road position can send signals of goodwill to drivers. When a cyclist who has established position near midlane looks back, then shifts toward the curb as a car approaches from behind, this one-two combination sends a signal to the driver that the cyclist is aware of the vehicle's presence and passing is welcome. This accommodating move is one of the fundamental building blocks of safe, swift, and hassle-free cycling, but many riders view it as a display of weakness.

The cyclist's approach to road positioning should be characterized by flexibility. Accept that the best possible line will be shifting on a near-constant basis. Don't cling grimly to a favored spot in the road while the disposition of traffic shifts wildly around you. City cyclists should switch their positions, toward the curb and back out, and adjust speed, quite often in dense traffic as conditions fluctuate. These movements should be smooth and subtle, not swerves or weaves or lurches, and should be based on 360-degree awareness of surrounding traffic.

At times the rider will have to accept that position on one street should be abandoned altogether for position on another street, or an off-street route.

The Invisible
Cyclist

Well out in the lane, the cyclist may be more visible to others, especially crossing drivers, pedestrians, and oncoming drivers setting up for a left turn. *May* is the operable word here.

The cyclists' struggle for visibility has been a noble and long-fought effort. Problem is, it hasn't worked. No matter how much tinsel and ornamentation we attach to ourselves, no matter how many flashing beacons we strap to our backsides, no matter what previously unseen degree of neon insanity we manage to surpass in our jersey selections, some drivers continue to look right through us, as if we were—that's right—invisible.

The dream of visibility is a sweet siren's song that will, eventually, lead us into the rocks. Not that visibility is a bad thing, mind you; we all love visibility. It's just that an attitude of faith in visibility puts the rider on a slippery slope on the way to complacency, which is a very dangerous place for a cyclist to hang out. Guard against the creeping assumption that taking a more conspicuous position will actually make you visible to all drivers. Go ahead and take measures to enhance your visibility—the orange vest, the flashers, et cetera—just don't fool yourself into believing these measures will always work. It's better to stubbornly assume that you are unseen until it is made absolutely obvious that you are seen.*

Cyclists are often overlooked, no matter how or where they ride. We should accept this as reality, and proceed from there. We should deal with reality as it is, not how we hope or wish it to be.

Space Versus
Visibility

Adjusting position on the road to maximize visibility is a fool's game. It should not be a guiding principle.

Much more important than adding to visibility, riding in a position away from the curb and parked cars, out in the street, gives the cyclist precious *space* should a sudden hazard emerge from the right side, and

---

*This stubbornness can be tempered a bit with respect to vehicles overtaking from behind. Motorists overtaking from behind are the most likely to see a cyclist, because they are generally looking forward in the cyclist's direction and have more time in which to notice him or her. For this reason, the rider can usually maintain a fair buffer zone on the right even as vehicles come up behind. Shifting position to the right in these passing situations is usually more a matter of courtesy and practicality than a safety issue. Drivers crossing the rider's path are much less likely to notice a cyclist. This pattern is reflected in the accident statistics. Pedestrians rely heavily on their hearing and therefore are prone to stepping into quiet streets, in front of cyclists, without looking at all. The phenomenon of nonlooking pedestrians is one of the best reasons to maintain a fat buffer zone.

maneuvering room should a hazard emerge from either side. Space becomes time, which transforms collisions into near misses.

It's interesting—riders who position like this to maximize space will often find themselves riding the same line as cyclists who position to maximize visibility. Both cyclists are pedaling along in the same road position, but for completely different reasons. One cyclist rides in the default position in the hope they will be seen by others, another cyclist rides there precisely because they assume they will *not* be seen. Both have maximized visibility as well as space, but the attitudes of the two are fundamentally different: One readily abdicates a bit of responsibility and places it in the hands (or eyes) of strangers; the other cyclist assumes all responsibility for his or her own safety. One is pedaling innocently toward disaster, the other expects it and will be ready for it.

The Myth of
Lane Ownership

The Master said, those whose measures are dictated by mere expediency will arouse continual discontent.[3]

—CONFUCIUS

It is a common belief among cyclists, and even among drivers, that cyclists have "the same rights and responsibilities as motorists." Many cyclists take this to mean they will be protected by the law when consuming an entire lane, even if this slows or blocks motor traffic.

While it is generally true that bicycles are classified as vehicles, and cyclists are governed by the same traffic laws as motorists, there are some crucial exceptions. In most municipal traffic codes, a cyclist is *not* allowed to occupy an entire lane whenever he or she wishes. In this respect, bicycles are not equal to cars in the eyes of the law. Cyclists are usually required to ride as far to the right-hand side of the roadway "as practicable."* This law

---

* Many cities, New York City and Seattle among them, allow cyclists to ride on the far-left side of one-way streets. Many cities specify that the cyclist is entitled to the 3- or 4-foot-wide strip to the left of the right-hand edge of the roadway. Albuquerque law requires that motorists allow at least 5 feet when passing cyclists.

is not in place to increase the safety of the cyclists, but simply to facilitate traffic flow—to get slower vehicles out of the way of faster vehicles. For this reason, the law is often attacked by vehicular-cycling activists.[4]

Only where the lane is too narrow for a car to pass a bicycle, where there are parked cars, grates, or piles of debris near the curb, where the bicycle is moving at the same speed or faster than motor traffic, or where the rider is maneuvering for a left turn, can the cyclist legally take charge of an entire lane. The exact conditions that would relieve the cyclist of the legal requirement to keep right are generally not specified. How narrow is too narrow? How much debris constitutes a hazard? In practice, these decisions are left up to the judgment of the rider. And then it's up to the whim of individual police and judges to sanction any cyclist who oversteps the subjective and imaginary bounds.

The ride-to-the-right rule is one of the major sources of confusion in the traffic codes. It baffles cyclists, motorists, and police alike. Faced with a rule that is arbitrarily formulated and arbitrarily applied, cyclists need to take responsibility for themselves and interpret the ride-to-the-right rule for the benefit of their personal safety first, and with consideration for other road users second. The trick is not to take this quest for personal safety so far that it does more harm than good.

There are certainly situations where the cyclist should stake out an entire lane in front of motor vehicles, no matter what the law states. For instance, any time the cyclist is moving at the same speed as motor traffic. There are many other scenarios when lane taking will be the best temporary option; these are determined by subtle variables—the speed and personality of traffic; the proximity of curbs and parked vehicles; and the presence of grates, potholes, and debris, to name a few. Recognition of these situations will come with experience, and will be difficult to learn from books and pamphlets.

Often, those who regularly practice deliberate lane blocking say they do it to prevent any motorists coming up behind from passing too close. On narrow streets, and in the well-used curb lanes of busy boulevards, they say, motorists will buzz right by the cyclist's elbow when given half a chance. These cyclists attempt to prevent these unwelcome and dangerous intrusions into personal space by moving well into the middle of the lane. This forces motorists either to run the rider over or move completely into another lane to pass. These riders feel they can control motor traffic through lane taking, are prepared to absorb the ire of motorists, and are comfortable in the assumption that they will always be visible to those approaching from behind.

Sometimes, without a doubt, exaggerated lane taking like that described above is justified and proper. It is the opinion of this author, however, that total lane consumption in front of faster vehicles is necessary less often than one might think, and that the safety benefits it brings are usually marginal enough to be canceled out by the sheer hassle of the endeavor. Some cyclists resort to it far too quickly, and for too long. They block lanes on a regular basis, thinking somehow that they have found the best method. For these riders, more intensive route finding will be the best medicine. Some riders use lane taking as a crutch for shortcomings in cycling technique. When riding in a normal, wide curb lane they feel as if they are caught in the narrows of the Callejon.* These are often inexperienced riders who are completely twizzed out by vehicles passing closely, or they have little tolerance for the normal obstacles of city riding, like sand on the road. Even the most militant lane takers will have to deal with plenty of all of this, no matter how assertive they are in their positioning, and they will find out soon enough that riding the lane is no magic force field against dangerous passes. It is recommended that these riders face their demons and shake the habit. Lane taking is a poor substitute for finesse, skill, and experience.

It turns out that there are some high-maintenance cyclists out there who are regularly abusing their lane-blocking abilities, consciously or not. On the other side of that coin, many drivers are just as high maintenance. Even when the cyclist is clearly correct to take a lane, and causes no delay to the motorist by doing so, some drivers will boil over with anger at the very sight of a cyclist taking a lane. They gun it to get around even though there is a stop sign 30 yards ahead. Cyclists have every right to use the roadway and should not have to cater to the lowest common denominator of aggressive drivers. We shouldn't coddle them. But we shouldn't be surprised by the reaction or bent out of sorts by it, either. Greet these irrational drivers with a cool stoicism.

The bottom line is that lane conflicts are occasionally unavoidable, inevitable to a certain degree, but need not be a regular feature of the cycling experience. The artful cyclist rarely needs to commandeer an

---

* The *Callejon* is the last section on the route of Pamplona's *Encierro,* the Running of the Bulls. It funnels bulls and runners into a narrow tunnel that enters the bullring.

entire lane in front of faster traffic. The artful cyclist is comfortable riding in tight spaces and rarely feels threatened—physically or psychologically —by passing vehicles. Indeed, the artful cyclist rarely affects the flow of motor traffic in any significant way, is rarely put out by it, and moves with an effortlessness in heavy traffic that the habitual lane takers can only dream about.

Most often, if the rider has chosen a good route, plenty of room can be given to passing drivers without any real sacrifice on the part of the cyclist. If there's enough room, find the seam that will allow cars to pass while you continue swiftly and safely on your way. This is cooperation and compromise—the rider moves over a bit to the right, the driver moves over a bit to the left, and everyone coexists in harmony. If no such harmonic seam can be found on a street, and the cyclist is constantly fighting cars for one available line, that's as good a definition as any of a street that is bad for cycling. Find a different one. Save the evil street for special occasions. If it's a simple matter of feeling uncomfortable with cars passing close, practice riding relaxed and straight in tight spaces until it becomes second nature. The ability to share a narrow curb lane with motorists comes with experience and handling skills.

Share the lane, if possible, and make the world a better place.

Running
Green Lights

When an experienced adult gets smacked by a car, it is most likely that the cyclist was riding lawfully and predictably at the time. Now, consider, if you will, the common American bicycle messenger. The veterans of this species are likely to bust through several hundred thousand red lights over a career. If anyone is in a position to find out just how dangerous it is to break the law while riding bikes in the city, it's these guys; and yet, overwhelming circumstantial evidence suggests that experienced messengers almost never get hit while running red lights, and are actually much more likely to get hit under green lights than red ones. This isn't a suggestion that running red lights is a good idea. But, clearly, following the traffic rules alone isn't necessarily synonymous with safe riding. There must be something else, a more important ingredient that keeps riders out of trouble when they sneak through red lights, but somehow turns up missing when the light is green. That critical ingredient is the rider's own awareness.

The trick is to bring your red light awareness to the green light intersections.

Rather than simply cruising through a green light with your eyes glazed over and your head in the proverbial clouds, begin to check all the trouble spots vigilantly and anticipate conflicts before they arise. Anticipate the mistakes of those around you. There are five distinct sources of trouble:

1. Well before reaching the intersection, direct your awareness left and behind for cars that might be preparing to turn right across your path. Bicyclists on sidewalks or side paths are less likely to be seen and less likely to be respected if they are seen. Even if the little green man is showing on the walk signal, be prepared to stop completely before entering the intersection to stay out of the way of furious right-turners. *Right-of-way means nothing.* Don't roll into the intersection without first looking behind you.

2. Check quickly for red-light runners moving quickly from the right and left and

3. wayward pedestrians on the loose, stepping blindly into the street.

4. As early as possible, give the street ahead a thorough examination in search of left-turners. Is that oncoming vehicle going to turn left? There is no reliable way to tell if a vehicle is going to turn at you until it does or doesn't, so assume it will. Be ready for it. Left-turners are particularly dangerous because they often carry a great deal of speed, their turns are often not telegraphed, and in their haste they often fail to notice cyclists. To avoid one, you may be forced to veer right or left, speed forward, or stop quickly.

    Watching for left-turners is important even on little streets, where the only intersections are minor driveways. Whenever a car approaches, going the opposite direction on the same street, consider all the potential vectors the vehicle could reasonably take—driveways, alleys, parking spaces, streets, or straight ahead. A little alarm should go off when you are passing by some kind of parking-lot entrance or street on your right just before an oncoming vehicle goes by, because you are crossing through that vehicle's possible path. Avoid these little moments of potential disaster by watching well ahead and subtly adjusting speed and position. This probably sounds excessively cautious to those who don't have much experience riding in the city. But driver-turns-left-into-cyclist is an extremely common scenario, and an extremely bloody one as well. A little paranoia is warranted here. You'll notice nothing is said here about watching for turn signals, except this: turn signals—*ha!*

5. The cyclist will have a little more time to scan the right front for possible right-turners. Leave an adequate buffer zone between yourself and any vehicles as you exit the intersection on the far side. Try not to roll right across in front of any bumpers. If you are entering the intersection on a yellow light, be very aware of any overanxious light-timers rolling up in the right lane of the intersecting street.

So, let's see . . . that's two different types of right-turners, in addition to the left-turners, light-runners, and wayward pedestrians. Every busy intersection is a green garden of mistakes. Two forces need to be balanced when riding through all busy intersections: the instinct to leave space on the left, and the instinct to leave space on the right. Both instincts are correct.

Eye Contact, Stop Signs, and
Fake Right Turns

Some cyclists have so much faith in the concept of *eye contact* with motorists that they end up confused and bitter. It's sad to watch. They're out there, riding along, doing no harm to anyone, and duly making eye contact with all drivers who represent a direct threat to their well-being. And yet, some of these drivers still pull out right in front of them. These encounters start the gears turning in the poor confused cyclist's head. But I had *eye contact!* That guy must hate bicyclists! Just because he's got a big-ass Yukon he thinks he can do whatever he wants! Other victimized riders come to the less-emotional conclusion that the drivers have seen them but misjudged their speed.

These explanations usually represent a fair bit of overthinking. The most likely reason for a driver to pull out in front of a cyclist is far less complex. It's just the Invisible Cyclist thing again. Here is an important newsflash that any would-be rider needs to hear: Just because a driver's eyes are pointed directly at you does not mean the driver sees you. Direction does not imply detection.

It's no surprise that cyclists are baffled by this phenomenon. The driver's eyes are pointed right at you, a pleasant expression on her face, like "Ah, look at the nice bicycle rider," but really she's looking right through you somehow, trying to remember the lyrics to Neil Diamond's "Sweet Caroline." *Sweet Caroline . . . Bop buh bah . . .* It's a creepy feeling to be that invisible. Get used to it.

To be fair, most drivers are looking for cars when they look. Cyclists can blend into the background of parked cars, trees, pedestrians, even when riding out in the middle of the road. Motorcyclists get the same foul treatment quite often. Unfortunately for motorcyclists, they are more restricted in terms of where they can be on the road. Bicyclists have more capability and leeway to avoid the seemingly blind drivers, should they choose to utilize it.

Most of the phantom eye-contact incidents occur when the cyclist "has the right-of-way" *(ha!)* on a through street, with cars pulling up to stop signs on side streets. Drivers are known to space out stop signs completely, but the more common danger to cyclists comes from drivers' "failure to yield" upon restarting. "Failure to yield"—these are the words that appear on the driver's summons and complaint after such a mishap, but a more accurate description of the offense would be "failure to notice."

When the driver comes from a stop sign on the cyclist's left, the cyclist has more time and space to avoid disaster. This extra buffer is much appreciated, as drivers at stop signs on your left are less likely to notice you pedaling down the road, and are thus more likely to launch their vehicles in your general direction. Next time you're in the driver's seat of a car, look to your right, past your wildly gesturing passenger with his gigantic head and comically large sombrero, fight through the glare of the sun on the dirty windshield, you know, that little triangle of mud-splattered glass where the wiper doesn't reach, and imagine how hard it might be to see a fast-moving cyclist out there. And notice how the doorposts in new cars have grown plenty large enough to completely block the view of an approaching cyclist—total eclipse of the cyclist—potentially for several seconds at a time if the driver is inching the car forward. A driver on the right has a much easier time seeing an approaching rider, but an intrusion from the right is more urgent due to the proximity of the vehicle.

By the time the rider is actually passing in front of the stopped vehicle, if he or she has been able to leave a decent amount of space and is holding good speed, the danger has pretty much passed. But if the vehicle arrives at the stop just before the cyclist gets there, the cyclist becomes at least partially dependent on the driver's vision and awareness. Experienced cyclists feel it in their bones when they pass through these "sweet spots of danger"—*if that guy goes right now I'm toast*. This is when most of the desperate attempts to establish eye contact are made. At such a late stage, looking for eye contact to save you is not a good sign, to put it mildly.

It is not practical to forever avoid passing through these zones of vulnerability. In our quest to hoard responsibility, we cannot gather it all in. Some responsibility will always escape our grasp. But we still can, and must, cut down on the danger by recognizing it, by leaving healthy buffer zones, and by remaining physically prepared to execute evasive maneuvers when some driver launches 4,000 pounds of weaponized steel in our direction. These drivers usually don't have murderous intentions toward cyclists, they're just bad drivers.

Next time someone pulls out in front you after seeming to look right at you, watch their face while you execute a smooth turning-braking evasive move. Notice at which point, if any, they become aware of your presence. Watch their mouth form a wide "O" of surprise. When you see this, it can actually be quite reassuring. The successful cyclist sees the driver make this face from the comfort of the bicycle, not while doing a fly-by past the windshield.

One of the most useful moves that the cyclist can perfect is the tiny curlicue turn-and-stop that is made in perfect anticipation of a driver pulling out into the rider's would-be path. Upon the first sign of premature movement in the vehicle, the rider brakes smoothly while turning sharply, usually to the right. This sharp turn keeps the cyclist from ever crossing in front of the vehicle. Although this is a reactive move, it is not a panic stop, because there is no panic. The rider expects the pullout all the way and is ready for it.

The Fake Right Turn is an example of a *proactive* technique. The controversial Fake Right Turn is an advanced—plain stupid, in the opinion of some—method of dealing with jumpy cars at stop signs on the cyclist's right. It is favored by heavily scarred, very untrusting riders, and can be executed only when there are no vehicles present other than the one in question. Here's how it works: Instead of simply continuing straight in front of the car, the cyclist who wishes to leave as little as possible to chance slows down and pretends to make a right turn onto the street with the stop sign. Usually, as soon as the rider starts the fake turn, the driver hits the accelerator and blasts across the intersection. The cyclist then veers into the space vacated by the car and continues on his or her way with a minimum of disruption. By "springing" the driver, the cyclist has made the driver's questionable grip on reality a nonissue. If there are any other vehicles or pedestrians around—or any other cyclists—such a deceptive move would be more dangerous than crossing normally. Otherwise, it can be beautifully smooth: It cancels danger in a way that the fattest buffer zone could not, and allows the rider to keep moving. Many riders use the Fake Right Turn as a more courteous way to avoid stopping at four-ways, passing behind vehicles rather than stealing the right-of-way by crossing in front.

In general, riding in an unpredictable fashion is a stupid way to move through city traffic. The carefully applied Fake Right Turn, however, is one example of how a little bit of deception can benefit a cyclist.

The

Gap Effect

Mind the gap. The gap is brutal.

Consider the condition of some of the drivers locked in the typical traffic grid. They're trying to make a left turn, but all they see is an unbroken line of fast-moving vehicles coming at them, with no end in sight. They're late. They're hopped up on four cups of coffee. They're about to

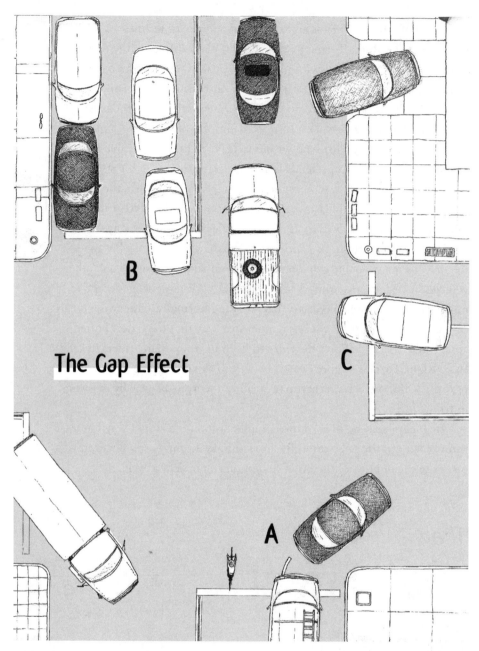

The Gap Effect

While riding in a proper position in the street, to the left of the right-turners (**A**), this cyclist is nonetheless entering the intersection at a dangerous time. The light has just turned yellow, and an illusory gap has appeared in the traffic. As she rolls through, the rider will be at the mercy of two impatient drivers: the left-turner (**B**), and the right-turner (**C**), both looking to shoot the gap.

pee their pants. They've been waiting to make that left turn since the Mesozoic Era. Actually they've been waiting about thirty seconds or so, but to them it seems like a very long time. Like the dinosaurs of the Mesozoic Era, their eyes are bigger than their brains. Suddenly, a small *gap* opens in oncoming traffic. They're going to hit that gap if it's the last thing they do, which it may very well be. They stomp on the gas and crank the wheel. This is the Gap Effect in action.

One big problem, though—there's a cyclist in the gap, puttering along. The motorist doesn't see the cyclist or else misjudges the cyclist's speed, or, so in love with the idea of the gap, simply denies the existence of anything that could possibly spoil this golden opportunity. In any case, the cyclist is going to get hit, badly, unless he/she can flash some serious evasive maneuvers. In this way, the dreaded gap is often a factor in the kinds of statistically overabundant car-versus-bike incidents that claim very experienced, streetwise cyclists—the wrecks where the motorist turns left into or pulls out in front of the cyclist.

As a bike rider in the city, it will be nearly impossible to avoid riding in dangerous gaps around intersections. Too many gaps, too many intersections. The best way to avoid gap disasters is through recognition and anticipation. The Gap Effect is one of the best reasons to remain on high alert in traffic. Don't just mosey along out there. Recognize that a gap exists, your position in relation to it, and the presence of vehicles that might want to blast through it, from the left and right. If your view of any potential gap shooters is blocked, their view of you is also blocked. Assume they are there with their clodhoppers poised over the gas pedal.

Old hands who have had bad experiences in the gap develop an instinct for gaps and some very cautious techniques to solve them. Rather than occupying a gap through an intersection, the rider might jump forward to hug the space of the car in front a bit and hang about 6 or 8 feet off its right rear, to use the car as a sort of shield against crossing traffic. If the cyclist can't get into that position in time, it will hopefully be good enough to stay loose, maximize space, and keep the fingers poised on the brake levers.

Four-way
Stops

Picture this: You're riding along and you arrive at a four-way stop five seconds *after* a big Buick arrives at the stop sign to your right. Being a proud semilawful road user, you come to a complete stop and put your foot down, waiting for the Buick to make its move. But the Buick doesn't even flinch. Several seconds go by as you stare at the driver and he stares at you. Then you notice a flurry of activity inside the car—the driver is flapping his wrist at you in a distinctly impatient fashion. This is the international symbol for "get the hell across the intersection, you *@#$* cyclist! What are you waiting for?"

The driver of the Buick, naturally, expected you to roll right through the stop. After decades of cyclists rolling through four-way stops, this behavior is now considered normal, and the general motoring public has been trained to expect it. When confronted with lawful behavior (i.e., actual stopping) from cyclists at four-way stops, drivers tend to freeze. They become indecisive and confused, and the whole system breaks down, if only for a brief moment.

Some of the drivers you encounter at four-ways will be seething with anticyclist resentment (like the driver of the Buick perhaps), while some have a soft spot for cyclists and appreciate the importance of momentum in bicycling. Both types get impatient when the cyclist doesn't fulfill expectations. Both types may recognize that the unwritten law—that which gives cyclists special leeway to roll through—actually benefits the driver, too, because it means the intersection will clear sooner. Either way, the written laws have not kept up with reality on the street. The cyclists, with the drivers as accomplices, are molding their own special laws.

Minor misunderstandings at four-way stops are a common component of the cycling experience, and there is no easy cure for them. Luckily, such annoyances are more a matter of convenience than safety. They may sap the efficiency of your commute, stop sign by stop sign, but they are unlikely to lead directly to a crash. Cyclists can minimize the hassle for all road users, while still holding onto responsibility for their own safety, by taking a realistic approach to four-way stops.

As with any stop sign or traffic light, cyclists need to treat four-ways with great care. Slow to a walking pace as you near a four-way stop. Assume that a huge LaFrance fire truck is going to speed through the intersection right on top of you until you can actually see down all the intersecting streets and can verify such a thing is not going to happen. If the intersection is completely, verifiably clear, exercise your special power to roll through. Slowly, though. Now, if you arrive at the four-way several seconds before a vehicle coming from another direction, first make sure that the vehicle is really going to stop; then roll through slowly, but give the driver a little wave, a goodwill gesture to display your awareness that the move is technically illegal, although convenient for both of you. That's about as lawless as we should get at four-way stops. Not exactly a capital offense.

If other vehicles have beaten you to the intersection, or arrive at the same time, or there are pedestrians present, go by the letter of the law. Which is to say, stop completely. Put your foot down to minimize confusion. Take your turn like everyone else—first-come, first-served, or, in the case of simultaneous arrival with another bike or car, yield to the vehicle on the right. When the confounded drivers, bless their hearts, wave you impatiently into the intersection, you can flap your wrist back at them and get into a little wave-through war, which is always fun. Or you can accept the invitation and roll through out of turn. Be careful not to ride out in front of a driver who has given up on you. In all your dealings with stop signs, be realistic, but stay conservative.

Every now and again, the rider who rolls through a four-way stop will be greeted by disapproving catcalls from drivers who observe the move from a distance—*Hey, that's a stop sign!* The hecklers are most often older males, which is not surprising, as the idea that cyclists should come to a complete stop at four-ways is an old-fashioned one. It's nearly extinct. Like the elephants, the idea is being systematically eliminated by poachers.

Momentum

Pedal cyclists, engineless by definition, have more use for momentum than drivers of motor vehicles. The quest to preserve momentum in traffic is one of the main reasons cyclists roll through stop signs and red lights, generally make a nuisance of themselves on the roadways, and get themselves hauled off to the emergency trauma centers of this fine nation. They're impressed with the thought of not having to crank back up to speed. Your grandfather might have called it laziness.

Whether you call it laziness, sneakiness, or pure stupidity, cyclists should be much more subtle and conservative about their efforts to preserve momentum than they historically have been. Cyclists should give up entirely on the unrealistic goal of holding onto high speeds through urban areas with lots of intersections. After this leap of faith is made, there will still be a few opportunities for a mature and careful rider to maintain low-speed momentum. Even at low speeds, it's an art to preserve momentum while still moving in a fashion that is reasonably safe, predictable, and ethical.

The most persistent momentum sapper out there is the stop sign. An intelligent rider can deal with many stop-sign situations in a way that involves, how should we say this, a *liberal* treatment of traffic laws, but also respects the rights-of-way of other road users. The first step is to approach stop-signed intersections with patience as the primary emotion, at subdued speeds. Even the momentum lover needs to think safety first. Once you get a good handle on what's coming and what's not, try to time your movement through the intersection for maximum smoothness, not speed. It does no good to speed toward a stop sign, slam on the brakes, and then have to wait for some minivan to clear the intersection. Instead, slow down well in advance, triple-check the intersection for other obstacles, and roll across behind the minivan. Smooth. Even the incurable stop-sign busters should get used to the idea that walking pace is about the maximum speed a rider should ever go rolling through a stop sign, and, not only that, they will have to accept the fact that they will actually need to stop and put a foot on the tarmac more often than not.

At a stop sign, a rider who would otherwise have to stop in the literal sense *might* be able to make a very small, very low-speed turn within the lane to allow a driver with the right-of-way time to cross. If executed slowly and smoothly enough, this Figurative Stop seems proper to others but also allows the rider to stay in motion—if the rider can maintain even a very slight movement, this will be greatly significant for preserving momentum. When practiced sloppily, such methods can confuse drivers and pedestrians, or even put the rider in the paths of vehicles. A small hook in either direction, for instance, applied at the wrong moment, could leave the rider staring down the business end of a right-turning vehicle. Like some other momentum-conserving techniques, the Figurative Stop is an advanced move that demands careful treatment. It should be left to experienced riders.

Not all lost momentum is lost at stop signs and intersections. There are plenty of little opportunities to lose or save momentum all along the route. A rider can preserve momentum simply by looking far up the road and anticipating the normal proliferation of road damage and the ill-advised movements of motorists.

A rider who looks ahead and thinks ahead can flow much more smoothly through traffic, and thus preserves energy and momentum, in addition to riding safer. But cyclists should avoid some momentum-related temptations that dangle before us like fruit ripe for the picking: Don't move at speed through traffic jams, for instance. Always slow to walking speed when passing close to any large stationary vehicle, which creates a blind corner as efficiently as any brick wall. Buses are the worst. Don't succumb to the most egregious form of pathological momentum poaching: blatant running of stop signs and lights at high speed. And resist the temptation to latch onto the perfect handhold formed by the swing arm of the spare tires of Nissan Pathfinders and certain other SUVs, or the tail-gates of pickups or the wheel wells of taxis.

Overall, preservation of some momentum is a nice bonus, especially when navigating residential streets with lots of stop signs. But momentum remains a secondary consideration, often at odds with safety concerns. As with any other hard drug, the addiction to momentum can be fatal.

Notes on
Traffic Lights

Long before the dawn of the automotive age, vehicular chaos at big city intersections led to the employment of various forms of lights, signs, and traffic cops. With the growing popularity of the automobile in America, the need for such measures became obvious, and urgent. Hundreds of different variations on the traffic signal were patented in the first decades of the twentieth century. Before too long, folks were thinking about how to link multiple signals into a coherent system. William Potts adapted railroad signals for a string of automated traffic lights in Detroit in 1920. A few years later, New York City flipped the switch on its first automated traffic control system.

From the beginning, the trend has been toward greater automation and control over traffic. The dark cloud of control rolled into every American city, until, one day in Los Angeles, 1925, motorists in the Shangri-La of automotive freedom began to take orders from a mechanical device for the first time.[5] With understandable reluctance, the people began to obey. Red. Green. Stop. Go. A little of the dream died that day, and it's been downhill ever since.

The early, automated systems didn't help much but they were nonetheless the primitive ancestors of the very impressive adaptive systems that are being used in American cities today. The modern traffic control system gathers information from hundreds of intersections, through video cameras and buried sensors, and sends that information almost instantaneously via fiber optic cables to a mainframe computer, and to engineers in a central control room who watch the dance unfold in real time. With the aid of sophisticated hardware and algorithms, the engineers tweak the system as they see fit, and, theoretically, keep traffic flowing. Sounds like fun, actually. Seen from that far up, American traffic probably looks pretty orderly and reasonable.

Computerized traffic lights can cause problems, because some motorists hold an unrealistically high opinion of their own ability to time the cycles just right. A light-timer who is just a wee bit off in his calculations might roll into an intersection before the green light and smash into someone who is coming through the other way after the light turns red. Being slightly slower than motor vehicles, cyclists who are late through an intersection are extremely vulnerable to the light-timing crowd. To prevent this class of wreck, traffic engineers program a substantial delay after a light turns red before the other light goes green. This period of "all red" must be subtle, or else it would be noticed, and ignored.

Lights on side streets may be coordinated with the lights on the main streets, or may be activated by vehicles. Activated, or "actuated," lights depend on some sort of vehicle detection system to set them off. Video cameras and radar are increasingly used to detect vehicles at intersections, but this is still relatively rare. For about half a century, the typical detection system has consisted of an electrified wire loop buried in the pavement. When a lot of metal gets parked right over the coil, it changes the frequency of the current in the wire through induction. This change of frequency causes an electronic signal to be sent to the signal box, which changes the light. Induction loops are rigged to detect beastly large metal objects, and tend not to notice bicycles or even motorcycles.* The devices could be tweaked so that they always detect bicycles, but then they would be so sensitive that vehicles on other streets might also set them off. A cyclist may be able to get some action from one of these detection systems by positioning the bike directly over one part of the coil, some visible sign of which should be apparent at the road surface, but don't bet on it. And those with carbon bikes are probably out of luck here.

New technologies are taking over for the buried loops. One wonders how long it will be before every major light is controlled by a video camera that can detect traffic while performing other important tasks, like scanning license plates, notifying the black helicopters, and sending out summonses. The induction loop seems to be on the way out, but we are hesitant to declare it dead just yet.

Waiting at
Traffic Lights

When approaching a signaled intersection, the cyclist should be figuring out how to achieve proper *destination positioning*. This means getting to the rightmost left-turn lane, if possible, for a left turn (see Left Turns, on page 103); moving to the right lane for a right turn; and establishing position in the rightmost through lane to continue straight. Try not to hug the curb of a right-turn lane, as this invites right-turning drivers to pass and turn or just turn into you. If you are turning right, own the right-turn lane like a vehicle would, and if you are going straight, try to get to the

---

* There are many different loop configurations, and some are better than others at detecting bicycles. The failure of signal systems to detect motorcycles was the rationale behind new laws in Tennessee and Minnesota that allow motorcyclists to ride through red lights, after coming to a complete stop and when no other vehicles are present. Such laws are no doubt being proposed in other states.

In Traffic

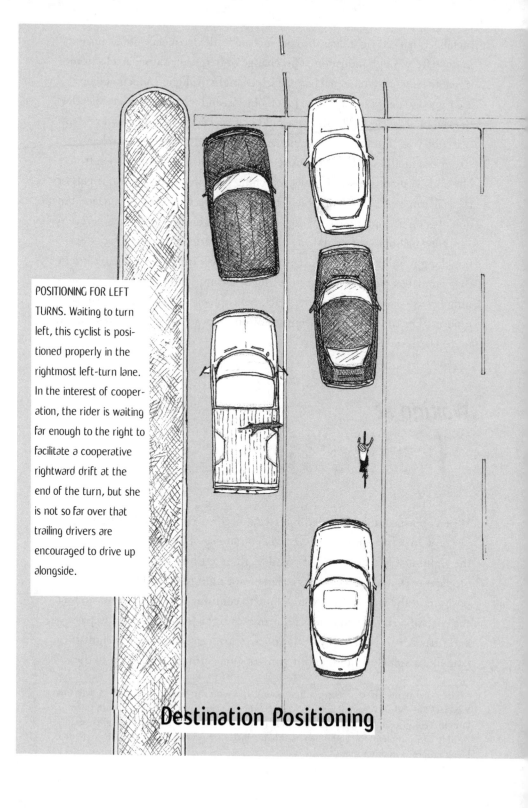

POSITIONING FOR LEFT TURNS. Waiting to turn left, this cyclist is positioned properly in the rightmost left-turn lane. In the interest of cooperation, the rider is waiting far enough to the right to facilitate a cooperative rightward drift at the end of the turn, but she is not so far over that trailing drivers are encouraged to drive up alongside.

Destination Positioning

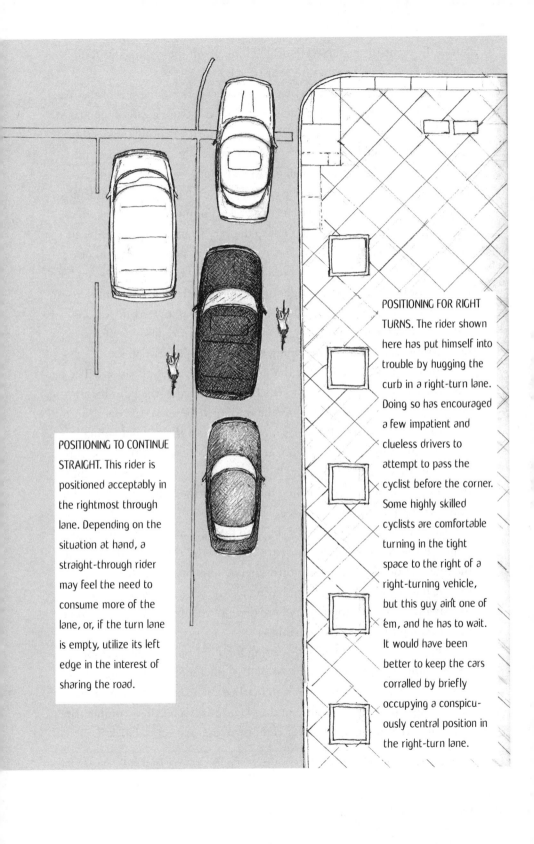

POSITIONING FOR RIGHT TURNS. The rider shown here has put himself into trouble by hugging the curb in a right-turn lane. Doing so has encouraged a few impatient and clueless drivers to attempt to pass the cyclist before the corner. Some highly skilled cyclists are comfortable turning in the tight space to the right of a right-turning vehicle, but this guy ain't one of 'em, and he has to wait. It would have been better to keep the cars corralled by briefly occupying a conspicuously central position in the right-turn lane.

POSITIONING TO CONTINUE STRAIGHT. This rider is positioned acceptably in the rightmost through lane. Depending on the situation at hand, a straight-through rider may feel the need to consume more of the lane, or, if the turn lane is empty, utilize its left edge in the interest of sharing the road.

left of the right-turners. No big deal. Think about these things well in advance and it will greatly ease your travels.

Generally, even though cyclists can usually sneak up the side of the road to the front of a line of vehicles at a red light, cyclists are legally supposed to wait out the light *behind* any vehicles that are already waiting (unless there is a segregated bike lane or a curb lane of vast acreage). Regardless of the laws in your community, you will occasionally find yourself sneaking up front—the incurable nature of the cyclist, taking advantage of an undeniably skinny machine. In the parlance of cycle-commuters, this is known as "filtering."* Some riders like to filter to the very front of the line and wait about 4 feet to the right front of the lead vehicle, if there is enough room, where the cyclist's presence will presumably be obvious. Other riders prefer to lurk just behind and to the right of the lead vehicle. The key consideration when positioning beside a line of cars at a light is to be aware of, and out of the potential paths of, any cars that might turn right—to enhance one's visibility but to avoid becoming completely dependent on it.

Filtering to the front of the line comes with certain obligations. The ethics of sneaking up front, past vehicles that arrived at the light before you, suggest that you should allow the trailing vehicles to pass once the light turns green and traffic starts moving again. If there is not enough room for them to pass here, then you should have stayed at the back of the line in the first place. There is really no way to justify filtering up to the front of the line and then blocking the lane after the light turns green, but some cyclists pull this one on a regular basis.

Even if you have beaten everybody to the light and are rightfully first in line, it may be a good idea to drift slightly to the right, into the void of the intersection, when the light turns green. This shows the following drivers that a pass is welcome and available. It will make your life easier to coax them into passing here, where there is usually ample space, rather than keeping them bottled up behind.

Often you will find yourself waiting for a light to change, positioned on the right of the vehicles going straight, with a motorist inching up behind you. Even though there is no marked turn lane, the driver hopes to make a right on red. But you're in the way. This is a needless conflict. Be mindful of the space available for right turns and try not to block it.

---

filtering: The term is also used to describe the act of riding between lanes in jammed traffic.

There is an easy way to solve the problem if you find yourself blocking an ersatz turn lane. With one foot in the pedal, and the other resting on the street, squeeze and lock the front brake, then lean forward on the locked front wheel so that the rear wheel floats in the air. Swing the backside of your bike to the left and set it down, then pick up the front end and move it over. Repeat as necessary to make enough room for the right-turner to squeeze by. This courteous maneuver will be much appreciated and will foster goodwill.

Depending on the available space and other characteristics of the intersection, you may be more comfortable waiting on the sidewalk and crossing as a pedestrian.

Running Red Lights

Cyclists are legally required to obey all traffic lights, just like motor vehicles. We're supposed to go when it's green and stop when it's red. You knew that, right? This comes as a surprise to nobody, and yet few of us consistently obey the law when it comes to traffic lights.

As with stop-sign running and other questionable activities, red-light running by cyclists is basically expected by some motorists. But it is certainly not accepted. Red-light running engenders more bitterness in motorists than stop-sign running, maybe because the driver must stay waiting for the light to change, watching the little cyclist, often clad in tight black shorts, pedal off into the distance.

Now, y'all gather 'round. What you are about to hear is a realistic yet constructive method of dealing with traffic lights, given that many of the lights are not triggered by bicycles and will not turn green until a car comes along. It is not exactly a lawful method, although it's very close. It is far more conservative and careful than the method practiced by the majority of cyclists today. Still, some folks out there will get all agitated at its mere suggestion.

In Traffic

First of all, always come to a complete stop at a red light. Position yourself well and wait for the light to change.

But what if the intersection is completely deserted, and the light is clearly not being triggered by your bicycle? A rider might need to treat such a light like a stop sign in order to get anywhere in a reasonable time. If busting the light would mean crossing in front of cars on the intersecting street, don't do it, even if there is plenty of space. If there are any cars behind or across from you waiting at the same light, resist the temptation to go through. This is just good form. It sends a message of solidarity: If you gotta wait, buddy, I'll wait too.

Treating the occasional red light like a stop sign is a practice for mature, adult riders only. The traffic lights are in place to keep people from thinking for themselves. When bicyclists think for themselves, they often make horrible, costly mistakes. You think you can do a better job of thinking than a traffic light? Don't be so sure.

In downtown areas, the cycles of traffic lights are very often set up to give pedestrians their own special time during which motor traffic is stopped in all directions. Many cyclists cannot resist the lure of the pedestrian phase of the cycle. They come up between two lanes of stationary traffic stopped at a light, or between the right traffic lane and a line of parked cars. Moving quickly, they see that walk signal or the flashing hand and realize the intersection is in full-on pedestrian mode. So they accelerate toward the intersection. If it is done absent-mindedly, this is one of the biggest mistakes in cycling. This cyclist is begging for a ped-bike collision, as a walker pops out from behind a van or sprints out at the exact wrong time, trying to get across before the light changes. A poetic bike-bike collision with some other carelessly opportunistic joker is another strong possibility. Cyclists hoping to exploit the pedestrian phase of the signal cycle often get served with Instant Karma.

Left
Turns

Because of the cyclist's usual position in the rightmost lane, making a left turn in traffic is one of the trickiest maneuvers in cycling. Theoretically, the cyclist should execute the left turn just as a car would, by changing lanes all the way over to the turn lane, well in advance of reaching the intersection. When circumstances are right this is the method of choice. Unfortunately, in today's world circumstances often conspire against the cyclist hoping to make a left turn. On busy streets with fast-movers it can be extremely tricky to get across to the turn lane. Some cyclists are used to forcing their way across on streets like this. They throw hand signals, look back, look back some more, and pull out in front of cars that are moving much quicker than themselves. The rider is pedaling as fast as he can and feels that should be fast enough. Meanwhile, the drivers behind step on the brakes or stare into their rear-views looking for an opportunity to change lanes. The drivers behind them hit the brakes, then the drivers behind them, and so on down the line. The rider gets to the turn lane, but at some cost to overall traffic safety and flow.

The smooth cyclist, by definition, does not have to force anything. There comes a point when the vehicular left turn is more trouble than it's worth, when it becomes impossible to accomplish smoothly. Even experienced riders make frequent use of a more submissive way of turning left: stay right and carefully take a place on the far sidewalk to cross as a pedestrian. If the road is really busy, this method will probably not cost the rider much time at all. The cyclist who chooses this approach on a street with oppressive traffic displays a healthy acceptance of reality.

Lots of riders who use this method make a habit of freelancing their way into a position in the street rather than rolling all the way to the sidewalk, where they never wanted to go in the first place. Like many of the freelancing moves of cycling, this can be effective and smooth, or it can lead directly to a collision. Left turns are tough on busy streets. The rider is damned if he does and damned if he doesn't.

There aren't too many other decent options available to the left-turning cyclist. Whatever you do, don't turn left from the right side of the street.

In Traffic

Corner Cutters

You pull up to a stop sign on what seems to be a quiet, residential street. You put your foot down and wait patiently for a break in the heavy, fast traffic on the intersecting boulevard. With not a care in the world, you have placed yourself far enough forward that your front wheel is almost even with the near curb of the busy boulevard. Tucked away within 3 feet from the curb, you feel quite secure.

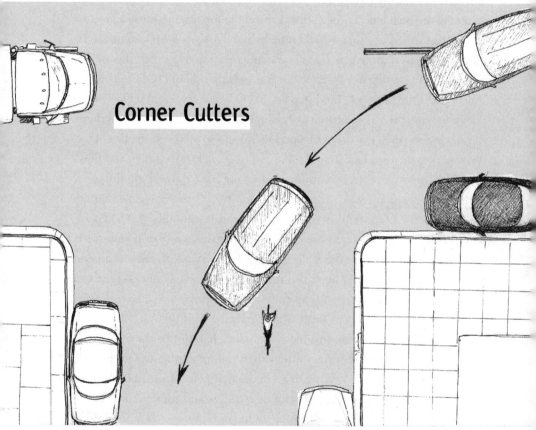

Corner Cutters

This diagram shows how common, modest corner cutting and common, reasonable cycling might lead to a disaster for the cyclist. Cyclists should be mindful of this phenomenon at every intersection.

Suddenly—a screech of tires from your right side. A car turning left from the far side of the boulevard carves directly at you. This guy's spotted a minuscule gap in the oncoming traffic, and, rather than wait ten seconds, has chosen to risk the health of several motorists, including himself, to shoot the gap. His line is taking him directly toward the apex of the corner, across the wrong side of the street, directly at your front wheel. Unfortunately, he hasn't seen you at all, he's so focused on oncoming traffic.

Be especially wary of corner cutters upon approach to the intersection, because the offending drivers haven't even had a chance to see you yet. They may be in the process of cutting that corner just as you arrive. The corner-cutting phenomenon is a good reason to roll slowly toward intersections, to be patient, and to stay 5 feet or more back from the corner, just out of the cutter's favored path. That way the cyclist's well-being is not dependent on drivers who don't think twice about who or what might be waiting for them around the corner.

Looking
Back

Cycling demands frequent look-backs. Whenever preparing for any significant lateral movement—to avoid jaywalkers, piles of glass, potholes, parked cars, or to change lanes in preparation for a turn, to name a few examples—the rider usually needs to check behind first. And there are a multitude of scenarios where the cyclist might be maintaining a steady line but would still benefit from taking a little peek to see what's back there. Riding away from the curb, in a comfortable *default position* or toward it, is dependent on a 360-degree awareness of traffic.

What we have here, then, is a real dilemma, because cycling also demands that the eyes point forward as much as possible. Every microsecond spent looking anywhere other than ahead is borrowed time. Eventually, the look-behind will get you. A common scenario is to hit a road crater just as the head swivels back. This type of encounter could easily lead to a crash if the rider is really overdoing the look-back—for example, sitting up and holding onto the bars with the fingertips of one hand. Another scenario involves coming in contact with the butt end of a car after looking back just in time to miss the car's brake lights coming on. Look-backs rob you of precious moments. If a look-back or look-away begins a short chain of events that leads to your next accident, it wouldn't surprise anybody who has had any experience on the streets. We've all been there.

When checking behind, make it quick, but not so quick that the move is wasted. You only get so many chances to look back, so use these chances wisely. In tight traffic, where milliseconds matter, and the dangers of the road surface are compounded by the dangers of motor vehicles, avoid looking back unless absolutely necessary, and then allow yourself just a lightning strike of a glance.

Here is the secret of looking back while cycling: The first step in a safe look-back is the look-*forward*. Before diverting the eyes, scan the road surface well ahead for potholes, grates, manholes, and waves. Note any vehicles, currently moving or stationary, that might move into your path. Notice all driveways and other intersections from which vehicles may emerge, and scan lines of parked cars for heads, brake lights, and other signs of life (see Reading Parked Vehicles, on page 118). Notice pedestrians who may step out in front of you. Calculate the time and space at your disposal assuming a worst-case scenario involving all potential hazards. Veteran riders accomplish this forward scan almost unconsciously in about one second, cataloguing anything that could get them when they turn their heads.

In busy areas, it is normal for sizable helpings of time to pass while the rider is unable to steal a single safe look-back. The artful rider recognizes these spells and respects them. If the road ahead becomes clear enough that its potential hazards are outweighed by the need to look behind, swivel the head smoothly to the left. If you just need a little semi-look to check on a passing car, a quarter turn of the head should be enough to pick up the car's general location and attitude in the peripheral vision. It's usually not necessary to turn the head all the way around. Keep both hands steady on the bars, just in case you missed a pothole or other trap with your initial forward scan. A half-second glance should be enough to determine whether vehicles or other cyclists are approaching, their position in the lane, and even their speed. The ability to make these determinations quickly will come only with experience. Sometimes a more thorough and time-consuming look-back is needed.

The physical act of looking back while riding a bike is not as simple as it sounds. It requires some skill to keep the bike tracking straight while moving the head around. Practice in a safe location, such as an empty parking lot, glancing back quickly and smoothly without swerving even a little. Beginners should refrain from serious city riding until they can manage this skill.

The look-back, when practiced correctly, is actually quite a production. In tight traffic, cyclists must check behind often enough that the process of scanning forward in order to scan backward consumes a great deal of attention and concentration. This information-gathering process becomes meditative as it cleanses the mind of nonessential thoughts. It is not a passive activity.

Seeing without
Looking

Given that diverting one's eyes from the road ahead is asking-for-it dangerous, cyclists help themselves a great deal by developing a sense for what is coming up behind without relying on frequent look-backs.

The most solid, nonvisual clues about the netherworld behind the cyclist's back are gathered through the ears. Let your scraggly, rather-bizarre-looking human ears become your rearview mirrors.

The first audible indication of approaching vehicles is usually not engine noise, but the sound of tires on pavement. Most modern passenger cars are extremely quiet. Some are near-silent at low rpms. They can sidle right up on you at low speeds, completely undetected. At normal city speeds, however, their tires give them away. Tire noise can be a hiss or a sort of ripping sound. The sound will vary with different vehicles, tires, street surfaces, and speeds. Tires that are rolling quickly make noise at a higher pitch than tires that are rotating slowly. The noise from an accelerating vehicle rises in pitch. With practice, a cyclist should be able to hear what type of car or truck is coming, how fast it is moving, whether it is speeding up or slowing down, and how far to the right it is.

Cars that are turning, stopping, and accelerating make noises that reveal a great deal about the habits of whoever is behind the wheel. The chirp of a tire accelerating hard out of a turn, for instance. Riders should listen for the rip of tires that are struggling to hold the road, versus the dull nonnoise of a normal Sunday turn. Engine rpms can also be very informative. Anger, impatience, conservatism, timidity—the attitude of the driver is revealed before the vehicle can be seen.

In recognition of the basic importance of ears for cycling safety, some cities—Philadelphia, for one—have banned the use of headphones by cyclists. They don't want folks out there weaving around, rocking out to *Doug E. Fresh* while unable to hear vehicles, horns, sirens, and screaming pedestrians. Coming from noncyclists, these laws are somewhat paternalistic and hypocritical. After all, the passenger compartments of modern cars are designed to keep out as much street noise as possible. Half the drivers seem to have the stereo cranked, and the rest are talking on the phone. They can't hear jack.

Like the typical passive motorist, the headphone-wearing cyclist willfully disregards a symphony of useful information. Rearview mirrors do much of the same work as ears, and therefore are absolutely recommended for riders who crank music through headphones or are hard of hearing.

A mirror won't provide a complete enough picture to eliminate the need to turn the head, but the helpful snapshots it provides will allow the rider to cut out a substantial percentage of necessary look-backs. Experienced riders seem to prefer the eyeglass- or helmet-mounted style of mirror.* Riding behind a friend who is using a good eyeglass mirror, and examining their little migrations on the road, will give an appreciation for the device. The mirrored rider, without turning the head, sees potential trouble early and starts dealing with it well before the nonmirrored rider becomes aware of it. Mirrors are very helpful on narrow, busy roads and in bustling downtown areas that have high levels of background noise.

---

* The long-stemmed handlebar-mounted mirrors are doomed to be broken in any kind of sustained city cycling.

Precisely because it negates some of the need to look back, however, reliance on a mirror can cause problems. The cyclist who looks back in traffic is actually sending helpful signals to drivers. Because riders with mirrors don't have to look back as often, they end up alienating themselves, in a sense, from other road users, often to the point that they are viewed as unpredictable and dangerous. On the other hand, a rider who swivels the head around to look back is clearly aware of the following traffic, a revelation that clarifies the cyclist's movements and gives confidence to drivers. A cyclist who looks back seems to be up to something. Even the most dense of motorists will usually figure out that the rider who checks behind in a certain way is preparing for some kind of turn or move. Turning back can have almost the same effect as a turn signal.

In addition to ears and mirrors, riders can employ plain old common sense to visualize the situation behind them. The cyclist who passes the exit of a busy grocery store parking lot, for instance, knows there is a good chance that a bogie will appear on the street before too long. Artful cyclists subconsciously calculate the possibilities and odds of what might be happening behind them, even if they can't see or hear it. It helps that they usually have a long history of navigating that street or, somewhere, a street very similar to it.

The look-back will never be made obsolete by these other techniques. Never. No matter how uncannily aware you fancy yourself to be, with your well-honed sense of hearing, your nifty little mirror, and your eerie supernatural powers, try not to make any significant lateral move on the road without first turning the head and getting visual confirmation of a clear path.

Instinct
Unveiled

An expert tracker might look at an elk track and know immediately how large the animal was, how fast it was moving, and, with startling accuracy, when the track was made. He notices a few blades of grass out of place in a field and can tell what moved through there and when. Some trackers have honed their craft to such a degree that they have actually learned to track ants over rock. To the general public, these skills can only be explained by a crazy sort of magic called *instinct*. The tracker must be "tuned in" to the rhythms of the forest in some preternatural way. But this talk of instinct cheats the tracker out of the credit he deserves. One does not enter the world with a mysterious talent for tracking already built in. One learns the craft, by spending every waking hour in the forest, face in the dirt, watching. Trackers spend weeks at a time observing what fresh tracks of all kinds look like and how they degrade over time. It's not magic that gives them such a masterful knowledge of their surroundings, but hard work and intelligence.

Cyclists should take a page out of the tracker's book. Ride constantly, and consciously try to learn from the thousands of little interactions you will have on each ride. Try to crack the code. The city moves according to laws that are more powerful and more interesting than the traffic ordinances. These laws are mysterious, but not unfathomable. The cyclist can crank up the powers of observation and collect knowledge on a level so advanced that most folks won't be able to understand how it might have been obtained. They will call it instinct, but it's just active learning.

Some riders apparently feel that the tumult of heavy traffic constitutes an incomprehensible chaos, an overload on the senses that could not possibly be sorted out. But in fact we are faced with a finite and manageable amount of useful information at any given time. There is only so much that can happen out there. There are only so many vehicles and pedestrians to be concerned with, and these are ultimately limited in their potential movements by the physical laws of the universe, if by nothing else.

Separate the known from the unknown, and respect the unknown. Blind corners and alley entrances, the penumbra of hulking buses and trucks—what's back there? The world of traffic is teeming with hidden life. It's replete with things that are moving and happening just out of view, things that could well be on a collision course with your personal well-being even if you can't yet see them. What exists in the shadow of knowledge? And even if we are able to track a vehicle with our eyes, in full view, that does not mean we will be able to predict its movements. The known, and the unknown. So much of what is called instinct could simply be a recognition of what is not seen and what is not known, and expecting the worst from it.

So open your eyes, that is the first step. Take it all in. See the whole playing field. Process the vectors, the sounds, and the possibilities. Sort out the known from the unknown. Learn from your mistakes and the mistakes of others. Constantly adjust position and disposition as you examine the environment, then, seamlessly, undetectably, become part of it. In the end you are some pedal strokes ahead and laughing all the way when traffic reaches out to bludgeon you with one of its tentacles of disorder. "Tentacles of disorder"—yeah I said it. It's not instinct that makes this possible, but ordinary human faculties put to good use.

When tuning in Zen-like to one's environment, route repetition is massively helpful. Find a number of good routes and ride them consistently to become intimately acquainted with all of their idiosyncrasies. Like a tracker who has been watching the same track for a week, when some detail is out of place on your route, you will know how and why.

Turn
Signals

They leave the signal on for no reason, use the left signal when they want to turn right, or just forget their minivan was ever equipped with this startling new technology. Drivers are so unreliable about signaling their turns that bicyclists should approach the whole enterprise with an underlying skepticism. In fact, it may be better if cyclists completely forget about trying to look for turn signals on cars and trucks in traffic. The act of looking for a turn signal reveals some degree of faith that drivers will actually use their turn signals properly, and no such faith should be forthcoming. Such faith is actually dangerous.

Now, if you should happen to notice, through no fault of your own, a blinker flashing on a nearby vehicle, by all means take it into account. But don't go searching for turn signals to answer any questions you might have about a particular driver's intentions. Instead, simply assume poor performance from all other road users and note any potential paths their vehicles might take. This is the cyclist's version of keeping an open mind.

A cyclist who is perturbed by a driver's failure to use a turn signal reveals a still-lingering reliance on the proper habits of others that holds disturbing implications for the rider's future. Expect nothing, and you will never be disappointed. Demand nothing, except from yourself. The proper response to a driver's failure to signal is calm indifference. Perhaps the cyclist's head is filled with things of real consequence and the turn signal is not even noticed, one way or the other. Turn signals matter little to the experienced rider.

Hand Signals

Many states and cities require cyclists to signal every turn. The big problem with this law is that removing hands from the bars while riding is generally bad policy, especially in traffic. The cyclist needs both hands on the bars, to hold the rig steady over potholes and to keep in close contact with the brake levers. Signaling is a bit like looking behind. The road ahead must be verified as smooth and clear before the hands come off the bars. For this reason alone, it is not recommended that cyclists signal each and every turn. Hand signals should be used only when they will really do some good.

Problems aside, there will be situations when the hand signal is very useful. At relatively high speeds, with a vehicle coming up behind, the rider does well to pop a quick hand signal before slowing down for a turn. Moving from lane to lane might require looks back as well as hand signals. Group cycling is much safer when riders signal their turns and stops to surrounding riders.

The best way to signal a turn is simply to stick the arm out briefly in the direction you plan to turn or move—right arm for a right turn, left arm for a left. The ol' left-arm-bent-up-at-a-90-degree-angle-to-signal-a-right-turn method is quickly going out of style—if it isn't there already—and will be unrecognizable to many new drivers. Some riders put an arm straight down, palm open, to signal an impending stop. This last one is more useful as a signal to other cyclists in your group that you're slowing down for a stop, so they don't come up on you quickly and can also prepare to stop themselves.

In Defense of
Gutters

It is often declared, for many reasons, that cyclists should *never* ride in the gutter. Never is a scary word. It applies to many aspects of riding but not to gutters.

Rarely is riding a gutter the best option, but we shouldn't be dogmatically opposed to it. Gutters can't be lumped together into a single category, any more than streets can. There is tremendous variety in gutters. Some gutters are quite wonderful places to ride, spotless runways of fresh white concrete. Some gutters provide a more hospitable riding surface than the road itself. But some are horribly dangerous debris-filled little canyons that fall away into gator-mouth drainage portals every 10 meters. Most are somewhere in the middle.

Gutter riding is occasionally useful on busy, multilane roads with narrow curb lanes and no on-street parking; streets where the right lane is as well-used as the left, and cars are moving fast. In these situations, traveling in a smooth gutter for a short while may be safer and stir up less general hassle than riding in the lane.

Yes, there are good reasons to consider gutter cruising that have little to do with safety. Some folks get vigorously agitated when they hear any hint of a suggestion that cyclists might want to move over for the sole purpose of facilitating motor traffic. But the fact remains that riding the gutter can occasionally help keep traffic flowing and stress levels subdued, and this is a good thing.

The most-often-cited safety problem associated with riding in the gutter, which is that it presents a near-open lane to drivers and causes them to pass dangerously close to the rider on very narrow roads, is certainly a consideration, but not a deal breaker. It is really no less likely that a driver will make a close pass on a cyclist who is out in the lane. In fact, some drivers will recognize and appreciate a cyclist's attempt to share the lane by moving to the gutter, and they will often leave more space when passing, not less.

The most important traffic-related danger of gutter riding has to do with turning and crossing vehicles rather than passing vehicles. The natural inclination of motor-vehicle drivers, as a species, is to creep through stop signs, especially when turning right. This is something that drivers and cyclists have in common. The drivers hope to creep through, look left, and make the turn all in one furious motion. Actually stopping at the stop sign or red light? So old-fashioned. Gutter riders, tucked away in the peripheral vision, will often evade detection by drivers looking left into the traffic lane. The gutter rider will also be less visible to oncoming drivers (potential left-turners). For reasons of compromised visibility, the gutter option is best when it is easy to reclaim your rightful place to the left of the gutter well in advance of crossing any intersections. Gutter riding and intersections don't mix well. Consider the gutter for a temporary option, but don't spend too much time there. Move there from a normal, established default position in special situations, and then move back into the street once conditions allow.

Safely leaving the gutter to climb onto a raised layer of asphalt may require lifting the front wheel, or both wheels, or subtle steering tricks to add angle to the exit. When exiting a gutter, don't veer weakly into a lip of asphalt, and don't start the turn before checking thoroughly for traffic.

There are other inherent physical difficulties in riding gutters, the most obvious of which involve proximity to the curb (although the presence of a gutter does not automatically imply the existence of a curb). It's possible to catch a pedal on the curb, for instance. Curbs also cause steering troubles. Due to the physics of countersteer, it can be very difficult to steer away from the curb, because pointing the handlebars to the left begins to turn the bike to the right (see Turning and Cornering, on page 128). With the bike very close to a curb, steering in either direction is a challenge because you can't move the wheel. Curbs tend to have a troubling sort of gravitational pull. Just how much the gutter limits your physical options depends on handling skills.

So, to review, the biggest problems associated with riding the gutters have to do with visibility, the expectations of other road users, and the physical limitations of riding there. These practical contraindications not withstanding, one could be forgiven for thinking that the zealous rejection of gutters so common in the cycling community might have more to do with psychology than safety. There is something about gutter riding that really touches a nerve in some folks, and they are religiously opposed to it.

Many cyclists believe quite passionately that riding in the gutter is necessarily demeaning, and that it sets a bad precedent that erodes the ability of all cyclists to navigate the streets in a properly "vehicular" fashion. People who buy into the emotionalist rejection of gutters cheat themselves by dangerously narrowing their range of acceptable options. A cyclist should be prepared to use every inch of available space on the road, including the gutters. Rather than banishing gutters to purgatory, cyclists should understand their inherent dangers and learn how to solve them. The gutters are calling, *"Help me help you."*

You will need the gutters some day, so don't let them freak you out. The best way to learn the gutters is to ride them. Try it first at subdued speeds on streets with sparse traffic. Notice what kind of debris and obstacles are there and build a tolerance for these—a tolerance through mastery rather than passivity. Especially on skinny tires, there will be some types of street drainage grates that you shouldn't go anywhere near unless you're looking to enter the sewer in several pieces. Learn the grates. Get the feel of hugging the curb and moving between the gutter and the street (looking back prior to each move). Note how the curb is better approached with the right pedal positioned high. Observe the alarming tendency of pedestrians to step off the sidewalk into the street without looking—a great reason to ride in the middle of the lane when possible. Pedestrians won't expect you to be in the gutter, and neither will motorists.

The best way to avoid having to choose between the gutter and some other bad option is clever route finding. Route choice, people, route choice.

The
Door Zone

Some of the worst streets for cycling are narrow, busy streets (narrow, busy—you should see a pattern developing here) lined with parked cars, where the cyclist is faced with the choice of getting out in front of much faster motor traffic, or riding in the Door Zone (DZ). The Door Zone is the area within about 3½ to 4 feet of the parked cars, where doors pop open seemingly at random into or in front of cyclists, with disastrous results. On bad cycling routes with oppressive traffic and lots of on-street parking, taking the lane can be a nasty prospect, but is usually more palatable than venturing into the DZ.

The Door Zone is a brutal, sadistic taskmaster. The Door Zone is a total beeyotch.

Getting "doored," as it is universally known in the language of cycling, is a violent, completely unpleasant experience. Unfortunately, it's also a rite of passage for urban cyclists, who remain difficult to convince about the treacherous nature of the DZ until they experience it for themselves. Then they never want to go near a door again.

Smacking a door almost always results in the cyclist being launched head first. With luck the rider might hit the door square and fly cleanly over it to roll in the street beyond. That's a best-case scenario. More often, a door disaster will result in violent secondary collisions with various things, like the bicycle, the door, the window, and the pavement.

Passenger-side doors also pop open, which means there are DZs on both sides of a car. This is of crucial importance for riders who like to "filter" between lanes when traffic is jammed.

Cyclists should realize the futility of trying to scan the passenger compartments of parked vehicles for potential door openers. We can never spot them all. Since there are no consistently reliable ways to tell if a door will open until it opens, cyclists should adopt a strict zero-tolerance policy about riding fast in the Door Zone. There are times when a little foray into the DZ can be helpful, but the DZ-cruising cyclist needs to slow

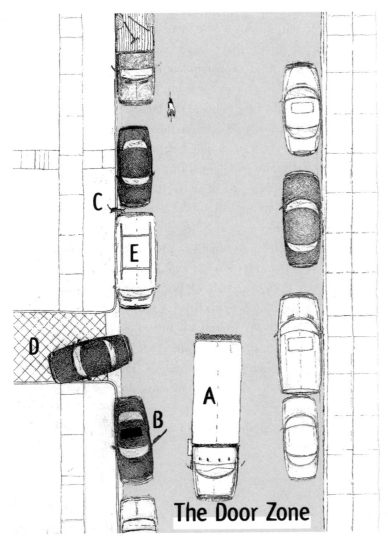

The Door Zone

Even though this is a narrow street, the rider does not need to ride in the DZ to allow the dock truck **(A)** to make an easy pass. If this street were much busier, however, with traffic in both directions, it would be more than a little frightening to ride. This relatively quiet inner-city street holds plenty of danger as is, compounded by the lines of parked cars. The rider has spotted the open door ahead **(B)** and will be positioned nicely to avoid it—if he makes it that far. He will narrowly miss hitting the dog **(C)** that is running out into the street, and will probably smash into the car **(D)** that is in the process of rocketing backward out of the driveway. The rider's view of the moving car will be blocked by the plumber's van **(E)** at a crucial moment. The driver will get the ticket, but the rider will get the injuries. To avoid such typical right-side hazards, this cyclist should check behind and move several more feet toward the center of the street after the dock truck has passed safely.

enough that a collision with a door would be noncatastrophic. Luckily, most streets are sufficiently wide that a cyclist can ride *between* the DZ and the path of passing traffic at a constant, comfortable pace. It is only on the really bad streets that the cyclist is confronted with the necessity of commandeering a busy traffic lane to avoid the Door Zone, and these uncomfortable streets can usually be deselected from the route.

Traditional placement of on-street bike lanes on many streets— sandwiched between traffic and parallel parking spaces—endangers inexperienced cyclists by encouraging them to cruise the Door Zone. Add this to the other criticisms applied to bike lanes (see Bicycle Lanes and Paths: Good or Evil? on page 134). Since almost all painted bike lanes are 4 feet wide or more, cyclists can usually cruise on the far left of the bike lane to stay comfortably out of reach of any evil doors. New bike lanes in Denver and Seattle have been placed out of the DZ in their entirety.

Doors are far from the only hazards lurking in the DZ, unfortunately. A mob of potential dangers floats around any line of parked cars, like fish around a coral reef. There are strange creatures that live behind parked vehicles and then pop out at inopportune moments. These include adult jaywalkers, toddler ball chasers, drunken transients, dogs and assorted other locomoting balls of fur, et cetera. As if that weren't enough, parked vehicles outdo themselves by pulling out into traffic at exactly the wrong time and place.

Reading
Parked Vehicles

Several years ago a bike messenger named Ray was riding through the downtown of a midsized American city during the afternoon rush. Traffic was very heavy, four lanes, solid. There was a little silver Subaru parked against the curb in front of him, nothing out of the ordinary. Ray starts to move around the Subaru. Suddenly, a guy comes crashing out of the bank on the right and jumps into the Subaru's passenger seat head first. Bank robbery! Just as the guy throws himself and a gym bag full of loot and exploding-dye-packs halfway into the car, the getaway driver guns the engine, pops the clutch, and fishtails into Ray's lane, missing him by just a few feet. The guy didn't look once before he stomped the pedal, and Ray was almost toast.

The driver then put on a display of getaway bravado that was absolutely jaw-dropping and uncharacteristic of drivers in beat-up Subarus: careening all over the road on the edge of control, jamming the car into tiny gaps in the choked rush-hour traffic, missing dozens of other cars by inches, and finally disappearing out of sight. It was like all the *Rockford Files* episodes condensed into twenty seconds. Ray tried to chase after, just to watch the driving, but the Subaru bandits escaped. His amazement turned to anger as reality seeped in: *Those bastards almost took me out!*

Ray then did something that was totally out of character. He went back to the bank where the cops were starting to gather and gave them a description of the vehicle.

◆ ◆ ◆

Ray's near miss with the getaway Subaru is an extreme example of a common problem: parked vehicles pulling out suddenly in front of, or in to, passing cyclists. In this case, Ray should have been able to see trouble coming. When a passenger runs and jumps in a waiting parked car—especially when the passenger is carrying out of the bank a bag of neatly stacked twenties—that car is probably about to burn rubber away from the curb.

There are other meaningful signs besides bags of loot, but cyclists shouldn't be overly obsessed with scanning lines of parked cars for clues. Attention, as always, should remain primarily forward. Instead of trying to pick up warnings of impending pull-outs and door openings, just leave a minimum 3½-foot buffer between yourself and any parked cars, much more space if practical, and keep tabs on the little buggers out of the corner of your eye. But if the parked cars are talking, you might as well listen. Predict the future by taking note of the following details in parked vehicles.

HEADS? Actively scanning car interiors for heads, again, is probably more trouble than it's worth for cyclists who need to keep focus forward. If you happen to notice movement through the car's windows, or in the side mirrors, however, don't blow it off. The appearance of a driver is usually the first and most obvious clue that a parked vehicle could become a problem. Over time, an observant commuter may begin to notice subtle patterns in the behavior of drivers and passengers. The slight shoulder hunch of someone in the first stages of opening a door, for instance. Where is the driver looking? A driver who is looking back over his shoulder or intently into the rear-view may as well be holding up a warning sign that he is about to thrust his car into the next gap in traffic—are you in the gap? Beware the gap (see The Gap Effect, on page 89). As always, be prepared for the worst, whether or not you see a driver. Darkly tinted windows, oversized headrests, tiny, shrunken heads, and other problems keep the head-watching method from being consistently reliable.

Is the ENGINE running? You may or may not be able to tell. Obviously, a vehicle with a running engine is a vehicle that could move at any moment. During daylight hours, in the noise of the city, it can be nearly impossible to tell which engines are running and which aren't. The only policy is to assume they all are. When the city tosses you a solid clue, such as TAIL LIGHTS or visible EXHAUST, which is a common sight in cold weather, be thankful and put the sudden windfall of information to use as best you can. Always remain vigilant, even in the absence of such signs. NOISE from the vehicle is generally not a useful indicator when passing parked vehicles. By the time you can hear the modern engine idling, or distinguish it from others, it's too late. Sometimes there will be an audible clue or two—the clunk of a transmission, the change in rpms as a clutch releases—that can serve as a helpful warning for cyclists in close quarters.

The TIRES tell a story too. Tires that are in the process of turning one way or the other are a definite symptom of vehicle movement. Either the driver is parking, or getting ready to bolt. A sharp eye for the disposition of nonmoving tires is also helpful: Which way are the front tires pointed? Give special attention to cars parked against the curb on your right with wheels cranked to the left. Such a car could launch directly into the street, without the typical reverse adjustment needed to exit a curbside space. Urban cyclists are vulnerable to being smacked by harmless-looking parked cars that suddenly jump into the road with one vicious stomp on the gas pedal, not unlike the getaway car that nearly got Ray. At five o'clock they *all* become getaway drivers. On tires that are pointed into the curb, there can be no instant getaway.

In a line of parallel-parked vehicles, REVERSE LIGHTS are a beautiful sight. Shining reverse lights represent at least two or three seconds of advance warning before a pullout, because drivers simply don't leave parallel parking spaces by backing out. Doesn't happen. As long as those soothing beacons shine from its butt end, a vehicle remains a known quantity, accounted for and predictable. Contrast this to streets with diagonally parked vehicles, and parking lots, where reverse lights are the opposite of soothing.

Another comforting sight, among the innumerable frightening omens that the cyclist must recognize in traffic, is that of a DRIVER'S ARM poking out of an open window. Arms that are resting like that don't open car doors.

Close Combat:
Positioning in Heavy Traffic

In many ways, very congested streets are easier to navigate than less-congested streets, because traffic tends to move at a reasonable cycling speed or lower when the streets are clogged. This speed matching allows the cyclist to claim an entire lane without difficulty, change lanes, and generally flow with ease. Proximity to vehicles is also a by-product of congestion, but proximity to vehicles that are moving in the same direction, at close to the same speed, is not necessarily dangerous and should not, by itself, cause a cyclist to freak out. Proximity combined with speed discrepancies, proximity to turning and crossing vehicles—these are more legit reasons to freak out.

When patiently cruising behind a car—a common situation in congested traffic—try not to stare grimly at the car's rear end. Instead, from a safe distance off the bumper, try to look through or around the vehicle to see what's going on ahead. The best riders will notice red lights or obstacles ahead before the driver does, and will have already decided how they will deal with the driver's likely reaction to them. Keep the fingers poised on the brake levers. As long as the rider has awareness of a vehicle and accounts for all its potential movements, it doesn't matter much if its driver sees the cyclist. This point is hard to get across to bicyclists who figure that being seen is the most important thing.

One of the key points for riding in heavy traffic is to avoid passing or just squeezing into the space on the right of slower vehicles in the same lane. Those who succumb to this temptation put themselves in a position to be cut off or run over by a vehicle from the line on their left. Expect the vehicle to turn onto any side street, alley, or driveway, or pull into any open parking space, even without a turn signal—*especially* without a turn signal, some veteran riders might say. Rather than passing on the right, stay behind slowish vehicles and observe. If you feel the need, pass these vehicles by switching lanes to the left, vehicular style. This lane switching will open the cyclist to a new set of dangers, however—like frantic drivers who have the same idea—and should (also) be treated with much caution.

Bicyclists in congested traffic could easily find themselves in a position to pass slower vehicles, especially as the right lane begins to back up. At these times, the line of stop-and-go traffic in the right lane is possessed of a troubling sort of potential energy. It's likely that there will be some drivers stuck in that line who don't want to be there. Consider that these drivers are even less likely than others to see you because they must use their mirrors or crane their necks around to do so. An insidious version of the Gap Effect (see The Gap Effect, on page 89) is in full effect in these situations. To counter it, give all the potential gap-shooters—the overeager, the unaware, the nonnoticers, or just plain nonlookers—a healthy buffer while passing, and maintain your awareness of a potential intrusion. Expect it and stay one step ahead.

The rider who exhibits much patience in regards to vehicles in front may remain vulnerable to vehicles behind. Any assumption that the drivers around are aware of anything beyond their own eyelids should be avoided. Cluelessness is a constant threat that causes, among other things, the common rear-end collision, *collisionus americanus*. As drivers and passengers in motor vehicles, most of us have at some point experienced a rear-end collision caused by drivers who momentarily fail to notice what is going on in front of them. They reach down to fiddle with the radio, or brush some McMuffin chunks off their Dockers, and *wham!* Rear-end collision. These wrecks are typically inconsequential for motorists, a matter for the insurance companies to sort out, but for cyclists the prospect of the rear-end collision is much more frightening. Can you imagine being smashed between two cars? Thanks for comin' out!

Cyclists should maintain rearward awareness of approaching vehicles when slowing for a stop. Use the ears for this purpose. A slowing vehicle makes a distinctive sound as the engine and the tire noise both decrease in pitch. The rider who follows a car relatively closely should not execute a full look-back, but can turn the head about 45 degrees to the left. This allows the cyclist to keep tabs on the lead vehicle as well as the trailing one. Some of the more jaded urban riders prefer to slide to the right, out of the way of potential rear-enders, as traffic slows.

Cars and trucks are kind of like bulls at a rodeo. As long as we can avoid the business ends of the beasts, we can contend with them quite easily. We can mess with them and use them as our toys. But if we get careless—horn up the yang.

Riding
a Straight Line

Riding straight is a crucial skill for navigating many types of situations. If gutter riding feels sketchy, or you squirrel out in tight traffic, get busy with some straight-line exercises before you go too much further. Don't try to jam your poorly skilled self into situations that demand good skills. Cycling in traffic without being able to ride a straight line is like trying to climb a frozen waterfall in bare feet. It's going to end badly.

Urban riders have at their disposal an easy and effective teacher of straight-line skills, built right into the transportation infrastructure. The traditional way for a cyclist to practice riding straight is by attempting to ride on top of one of the many solid white lines painted on the street. Use one of the standard 4-inch-wide lines, not one of the honkin' 8-inchers that are so popular these days. Look ahead instead of down, and let your eyes pull you along. The eyes are powerful. Relaxation is key. The bike is steered, veered, and jerked around with the legs as well as the hands and arms—relax them all. Do this straight-line exercise while pedaling. The pedaling motion should not cause the bike to weave.

When it becomes easy to roll right on top of the line for long stretches, get used to glancing back quickly while holding the line. Resist the natural inclination to veer left when swinging your head back to the left. Turning the neck can start a chain reaction that causes the bike to go haywire. Break the chain by turning only the neck and keeping the shoulders relaxed and square. Don't lean the bike over and don't turn the bars. Whatever it takes to hold the straight line. It is not recommended that city cyclists succumb to their temptation to look back by pulling one hand off the bars and sitting up (see Looking Back, on page 105).

After the cyclist learns to ride easily on a 4-inch line and learns how to hold a straight line while looking back, the next step is to learn how to ride a straight line at very slow speeds. Using the same 4-inch line, slow to a walking pace, and then slow down even more, and see what happens. Ideally, the cyclist should be able to hold the line at any speed, all the way down to 0 mph, while swiveling the head all over the place. This drill will expose any basic shortcomings in balance and control. The ability to balance and control the bicycle at low speed is another very important skill that should be viewed as part of the minimum requirement for safe cycling.

The rider's straight-line skills will be tested at some point on every ride in the city—suddenly narrowed gaps between side mirrors, grates to be traversed, long cracks and lips in the pavement to be avoided, not to mention most lane-sharing situations. When faced with such challenges, concentrate on the line you want to ride, and not on the obstacles you need to avoid. Any skier or mountain biker knows that if you fixate on a tree or rock you'll run right into it. Instead of looking at where you don't want to go, look where you want to go and go there. Relaxation, confidence, and visualization are the key building blocks of bike-handling skill.

The ability to ride straight will generally decrease the space required by you to operate your bicycle and will thus open up much more of the road surface for your use. This can only be a good thing. It will instill confidence not only within the rider, but also in other road users who observe and appreciate the rider's command of the machine. This keeps everything moving smoothly. Erratic weaving and flounderage, of course, has the opposite effect—it causes following drivers to get frisky with the brake pedal and ruins the traffic flow.

This is not to say you need to ride straight all the time, but it is guaranteed that you will need this skill. Riding straight also saves energy and lets you go faster.

Track Stands

One of the most exciting and strategically interesting events in all of bicycle racing is the one-on-one track contest called the match sprint. Although the match sprint is only three laps around the velodrome, the racers usually hold off until the final lap to unleash their full fury. The first two laps are usually spent playing mind games, jockeying for position, and keeping an eagle eye on the opponent.

During the first lap, one of the racers is designated to lead at a walking pace or better. After the first lap, the walking-pace requirement is scrapped, and the lead rider often slows to a complete stop, balancing on the bike in an attempt to force the other rider into the lead. Thus the term "track stand." Track stands are an important part of sprint strategy because, for most track sprinters, the trailing position is the coveted position. From the back, a racer can launch a surprise attack or take advantage of the draft when the other racer attacks in full view. When both riders have it in their heads that they will steadfastly refuse to lead the final lap, a track-standing duel results—a race to see who can go nowhere the longest.

Track stand-offs in match sprints rarely last longer than a few minutes, and rarely test the human limits of track standability. Track-standing contests at messenger competitions are usually won by a rider who is able to balance in one spot for forty-five minutes or longer. These riders are such masters of low-speed and no-speed balance that maintaining balance is no longer an issue. Instead, the track-standing contest becomes a bizarre test of physical endurance, as the muscles start to shake and seize, usually after about fifteen or twenty minutes. Today's messengers are such accomplished tricksters that to keep things interesting, their contests usually require riders to keep both hands off the bars, and then balance with one foot on the pedal and the other hanging in the air.

Probably the most useful application for the track stand, outside the velodrome, is that learning the technique helps riders achieve the low-speed balance that is very helpful and important for city cycling. If you can ride 0 mph, you can also ride relaxed and under control at 2 mph.

Solid points in favor of track standing at intersections are few, frankly. A true artist can employ track stands to smooth out and quicken a ride, just a little. Because the track-standing rider is able to keep both feet in/on the pedals throughout a stay at a stop sign or traffic light, starting from the intersection is slightly easier and the rider gets up to speed faster. But is it worth it?

Unless the rider is quite skilled, the attempt at a static balance will consume much more energy than it saves as the rider flounders around, strains, and struggles to hold position. A good track stand is silent and near motionless. Before the rider is even able to fake one of these graceful moves, he or she will have to suffer through dozens of sorry, energy-sapping performances. Even if the track stand is perfected, after years of practice, it is hard to imagine how the rider would actually conserve much energy by using it.

Also, the track-stander's effect on nearby motorists and random passersby should be considered. This conspicuous activity has two effects on citizens of the outside world: (1) it confuses them and (2) annoys them. Imagine the nifty track-stander at a four-way stop. The cyclist has come to a complete stop and is waiting lawfully. But the driver with the right-of-way has been hypnotized into submission by the track-stander, who appears on the verge of powering into the intersection. The rider finally puts a foot down, everybody breathes a sigh of relief, and the normal sequence resumes. In areas with lots of pedestrian traffic, sloppy, substandard track standing often results in the rider's migrating up into the crosswalk and blocking it.

It is also worth considering, at least for a moment, how a noncycling citizen who has no appreciation for the limited practical benefits of a track stand might experience it entirely as an alienating force. To the untrained eye, a track stand looks to be little more than showing off, a cry for attention. And those in the metal boxes are left to wonder, even if they are not directly affected by the track stand, what kind of world is this where grown men and women have learned to stand still on their bicycles? Could this be one of the seven signs of the Apocalypse? These are fair questions.

That many drivers will feel an urge to exit their vehicles and knock track-standers over is undeniable and unfortunate. How much we should care about this, if at all, is unclear. The bottom line with track standing is that it's fun. Even if it won't save energy or put the rider on the short list for a Nobel Peace Prize, balancing and rocking back and forth on a stationary bicycle (the real meaning of the term "stationary bicycle") can add a little challenge and spice to a mundane commute or ride to the store. And if some drivers are annoyed by it, to what extent is that my problem, and to what extent is it just something that these people will have to deal with on their own? Anyway, some riders really like annoying others, deep down. That's the only possible explanation for those dinosaur jerseys.

Whatever the initial motivation, it is a natural progression for city riders to try to learn a passable track stand, just like basketball players eventually learn to spin the ball on their fingers. Start by looking at the street. Notice how it slopes downward to the curb. Some streets might have pronounced bumps at intersections around the recessed wheel tracks. This is all the incline you need to get a good track stand started. Because streets generally slope down from left to right where cyclists ride, most track standing is accomplished with the front wheel pointed to the left, up the incline. Don't use the brakes, just let gravity stop the bike, then hold it with a slight pressure on the crank. The back end of the bike can be pointed down the slope or up, as long as the front wheel is pointed up. Most riders find it easier to stand on the pedals, with the cranks near level, or with the forward pedal slightly above level. Track stands can be performed with either foot forward, but most riders find it easier to put the left foot forward when the wheel is pointed to the left. If nothing else, this position keeps the shoe from hitting the tire. Really smooth riders can balance with the feet in any position, and in any gear.

Micro-adjust the track stand using the cranks, the handlebars, and body position. It's easy, but you might want to go through the initial stages of learning in a semiprivate place. The track-stand learning process is not pretty, especially if the rider has not yet mastered a set of clipless pedals. Nothing looks uglier than a wobbling, meandering track stand followed by the toppling over of the rider, who then thrashes helplessly like an overturned turtle.

Master a regular track stand, then move on to sitting down, one hand, no hands, one foot. The ultimate is to learn to ride the bike backward while facing forward. That's when you know you're really going slow. You'll never lead out a sprint again.

Turning and
Cornering

It sometimes becomes necessary for cyclists to remind themselves of the freakish steering behavior of their bicycles. To do this, perform a little demonstration. Ride down the street with a very light touch on the bars, so light that you may as well be riding with no hands. Let the bike steer itself. Then, very gingerly, pull the right side of the handlebar toward you slightly, forcing the front wheel to point to the right. As most will probably expect, the bike begins to track to the right. But, almost immediately, the bike tips over to the left and the right turn becomes a solid left turn. This is a demonstration of *countersteer* in action: Turning the handlebars to the right turns the bicycle to the left, and vice versa. It sounds crazy, and it is.

Bicycle steering is a bizarre phenomenon that eludes complete understanding. Even highly skilled veteran cyclists may be quite surprised to learn of the fundamental madness ingrained in their bicycles. All this time they thought they were using their handlebars to steer their bikes. Turns out they've been using a mysterious combination of body English and handlebar adjustments to get the job done. Turning is achieved by leaning the bicycle, and the lean is controlled by adjusting the handlebars. Widespread ignorance of this strange phenomenon of countersteer isn't too surprising. When we're out riding, we don't analyze how we steer the bike, we just do it. Our bodies have known how since we were kids, but our brains never bothered to figure it out.

The cyclist in a turn should not be thinking in terms of countersteer, or hitting the apex, maintaining speed, or anything sexy like that. The cyclist should really only be worried about tracking a safe line through any debris or road damage, and what large game—cars, pedestrians, other cyclists—they may encounter in the turn or when coming out of it. Save the fast cornering for races on closed courses. Overzealous cornering causes trouble in two important ways: (1) it increases the likelihood that the rider will wipe out, usually with sand or gravel on the road as a contributing factor, and (2) it often causes the rider to veer wide into oncoming traffic lanes upon exiting the turn.

The more the bike is leaned over, the more likely it will be to slide out while turning. Straighten the bike up to vertical as you ride over sand, ice, wet metal, or wet brick pavers. This straightening of the bike will make the turning radius wider, so the cornering speed needs to come down in order to keep the bike in the proper lane. Scan for road damage and micro-adjust your line accordingly. Notice the variable slope of the street when cornering. A few degrees on the surface might make the difference between cruisin' and bruisin'.

One of the best cornering tips is to stay loose on the bike and to unweight the saddle and handlebars enough that the arms and legs can act as the perfect shock absorbers they are. Don't push the bike away stiffly in the turn. Instead, let it come to you. Use the eyes to pull you through the turn. Don't look down, but instead look where you want to go. The bicycle has a tendency to track right to where the eyes are looking.

Panic
Stops

The formula for calculating g-force in braking looks something like this: $g = (velocity)^2 \times .0333 / stopping\ distance,$ where velocity is mph and stopping distance is measured in feet. Notice that there is no mention of weight or mass in this formula. G-force is a simple matter of speed and distance. A 3,000-pound car executing a .6-g stop will have the same stopping distance as 200 pounds' worth of cyclist and bicycle executing a .6-g stop, assuming identical reaction times and initial velocities for both. The car's brakes will have to do a great deal of work transferring kinetic energy into heat energy to achieve such a stop, but, with power-assisted brakes on all four wheels and a low center of gravity, the typical car is actually able to stop in a shorter distance than the typical cyclist traveling the same speed.

For a very long time now, cyclists who think of themselves as quite knowledgeable have repeated amongst themselves the statement that the maximum g-force a cyclist can generate while braking is about .6 g. Conventional wisdom held that anything much more than .6 g would flip the bicycle and send the rider over the front wheel. This calculation was based primarily on the relatively high center of gravity of the cyclist, and the coefficient of friction between rubber and road.

Few of these cycling illuminati have ever bothered to check their formulae in an actual physical experiment with skilled riders. If they did, they would find that skill level has a huge effect on stopping distance. In fact, the really skilled cyclists among them, those having achieved a certain intimacy with their machines, would be surprised to learn they could generate close to .8 g or more under heavy braking and stay on their bikes. The rear wheel would stay on the ground the whole time. In real-world terms, this means that a very good cyclist traveling at 20 mph (about 30 feet per second of initial velocity) can achieve a complete stop in 16 or 17 feet. This is better than many cars.*

---

* The Lotus Esprit Turbo, with its air-cooled discs and computer-controlled antilock braking system, is limited to about .89 g in a stop, a typical number for high-performance automobiles. More down-to-earth vehicles are usually capable of .75-g stops.

How do great riders achieve such stops? First of all, they have practiced the maneuver repeatedly, often by necessity, and have developed a
remarkable feel for the brakes on their bikes. Rather than simply squeezing the brake levers as hard and quickly as possible, they are able to apply a
smooth gradient of force over a very short period of time. They understand
that the front brake will do almost all the work in an effective stop. Most
importantly, they have learned to use and control their own body weight
under forceful deceleration. They throw themselves back to cancel some of
the force sending them forward. Just enough of this forward momentum is
canceled that the bike stays on the ground and under control.

Hard braking on a bicycle has much more to do with the rider than
the bike. The rider who sits on the seat passively and jams on the front
brake is going over the bars. A successful and safe panic stop requires an
exaggerated, well-timed body movement. It is an athletic move, like sliding into second base or dunking a basketball. The butt is pushed well

behind the seat, and the arms are outstretched but slightly bent. If you don't look too closely, the proper body position for a maximum stop looks a bit like that of a sprinter at the finish line, throwing the bike forward.

Unlike cars, bicycles are somewhat maneuverable under heavy braking, which allows for even shorter stops. Even under substantial g-force deceleration, a cyclist can turn the bicycle sharply. Such a turn may not be an available option in a tight space in traffic, but the cyclist in crisis should think immediately of turning as well as braking to avoid trouble. It may also be possible to enhance a maximum stop by pushing the rear wheel to one side, a smaller, quicker version of the "power slide" most of us performed as preteens. The rider may as well utilize the inevitable rear-wheel skid that occurs under hard braking.*

Theoretically, the most effective stopping force that can be applied to a wheel comes at the moment just before the wheel locks up. This leads many to believe that the shortest stops will involve no skidding. On a bicycle, it doesn't work that way. Trying not to skid the rear wheel in most hard stops is like trying to keep the eyes open during a sneeze. The rear-wheel skid is almost automatic when the front brake is applied correctly. Maximum stops can only be achieved with a very forceful application of the front brake, and heavy application of the front brake tries to bring the rear of the bike off the ground. Even though a good cyclist can keep the rear tire on, or almost on, the pavement during all but the most intense stops, the rear end always lightens up enough that friction between the tire and the road is reduced, and a skid occurs. The front tire should not skid at all, but the rear pretty much has to, if it's not off the ground entirely.

Cyclists should definitely practice this sort of hard stop. The damage that will occur to the rear tire—from the inevitable skid—will be worth it. Strap on a helmet and find a fairly deserted strip of blacktop. Start with

---

* An example of all these tricks being put into action came in stage nine of the 2003 Tour de France, just after Joseba Beloki crashed heavily on a descent. Lance Armstrong, who was closely following Beloki at the time of the wreck, at about 70 kilometers-per-hour, slammed on his brakes and locked up his rear wheel. In a display of exquisite control, Armstrong twitched his bike left under heavy braking and was able to avoid the carnage narrowly. This is the move that took him overland across rough ground. Armstrong's "shortcut" across the switchback will be forever enshrined as one of the legendary moments in bike racing. His initial braking reaction will never get the attention it deserves.

slow speeds and work your way up, stopping as quickly as possible. Stay light on the bike and learn how to turn sharply to either side under heavy braking. Get a feel for what kind of force brings the rear wheel off the ground. Try some stops using only the front brake. This drill will quickly, perhaps ruthlessly, educate the rider about front-brake modulation and how the body must move under heavy braking.

The term "panic stop" is a bit of a misleading way to describe the braking maneuvers described above. There are still faster and more brutal ways for panic-stricken cyclists to stop, which involve increased levitation of the rear wheel. In the most extreme of these, the front brake is squeezed so hard that the front wheel sticks right where it is. This is occasionally necessary to avoid a collision, unfortunately. At decent speeds, no body movement could possibly counterbalance the forward momentum of the bike and rider involved in this last-ditch evasive maneuver. The bike flips over and the cyclist is forced to eject. This is the real panic stop. Stopping the bike this way does not have to end in ugliness as some may assume. The cyclist can still retain some control. Rather than surrendering completely to head-first momentum and dropping like a rag doll onto the street, a rider might be able to clip out and *hurdle* the handlebars when the bike goes vertical, landing on the feet or on all fours as the bike crashes behind.

Short reaction times are even more important to the safety of the cyclist than panic stops. Reaction time is the time between the point when the need to stop arises and the point when the rider actually starts the process of stopping. You could be the best panic stopper in the world, but if your reaction times stink, you're still going to find trouble and pain on the streets. Reaction time can be reduced by such physical preparations as keeping the head up, the eyes forward, and the fingers on the brake levers, but the best way to cut reaction time is through disciplined vigilance.

It is good to master all versions of the panic stop, but it is better to anticipate problems well ahead of time and to avoid situations where problems elude anticipation. Panic stops are a symptom of cyclists' mistakes. Riders who have mastered the art of anticipation rarely have to flash their most serious stopping skills. The riders who know best how to execute panic stops are the riders who least often need to.

Youth is wasted on the young, and experience is often wasted on the experienced.

Bicycle Lanes and Paths:
Good or Evil?

What's food to one may be fierce poison to others.

—LUCRETIUS

During the "Bike Boom" of the early 1970s, Americans started taking bicycles out onto the car-clogged roads in significant numbers, and the results weren't all that pretty. The cyclists didn't know how to ride in traffic, and the drivers didn't know how to deal with cyclists. Wouldn't it be great, folks started to wonder, if we could build separate facilities for all these bicycles, keep them off the roads and out of the way, and simultaneously make things safer and more pleasant for cyclists? Cyclists as well as drivers were asking this question. At about the same time, as the country experienced a fuel crisis and generally stank like a tailpipe, Congress allocated funds for alternative transportation projects, including bicycle facilities. Cities and states started to build bike paths and paint bike lanes on their streets. These were popular projects all around.

Before too long, problems became apparent with the new facilities. Bike lanes and bike paths were packaged and sold to the public as safer facilities for cyclists, when in fact the best available statistical evidence showed that use of these facilities was actually more dangerous than riding on the road. By one estimate, cyclists were 2.6 times more likely to experience an accident while riding on a bike path.[6] The bad news about the danger of bike paths did not fit well with the goal of urban transportation engineers—to get bikes out of the way of motor traffic—so they just ignored it and kept building.

Structurally, the early asphalt paths were crude. They were often as narrow as suburban sidewalks, about 6 feet across and didn't endure well. They cracked badly and gave cyclists a very rough ride. The typical off-street bike path was really just a glorified sidewalk known as a "side path." Side paths—which are still being built today—repeatedly send cyclists into intersections, which explains much of the elevated accident rate for separate facilities. Cyclists on side paths are less noticeable to motorists and tend to be seduced by a false sense of security. They carry this false sense of security into the intersections and get crunched. Invisible and blind—it's an unfortunate combination. The first generation of painted bike lanes also had some unsafe design features. At intersections, the lanes often guided riders into slots to the right of right-turning vehicles, leading to conflicts and collisions.

This illustration depicts three cyclists trying to negotiate a tricky intersection at the entrance to a popular mall. As shown, the cyclists all own the right-of-way through the intersection. Each is in a position to find out exactly how little that means.

Cyclist One is riding against traffic on the side path and must contend first with right-turning motorists in the near lane (A). These motorists look almost exclusively to the left and are patently unaware of any cyclists approaching from their right. For this reason, the rider is smart to pass behind this vehicle. Next, Cyclist One will have perfect vision of those turning right into the mall (B, F), which is good, but will also have the critical task of keeping tabs on frantic left-turners (C) over the right shoulder. If Cyclist One makes it across, hazards on the other side include the awkwardly placed signal box (D), on a raised concrete pedestal, and the ever-popular man being dragged by dog on long leash (E).

Cyclist Two enters the intersection from the other side, lulled into complacency by the sight of the little green man on the walk signal. Displaying a troubling lack of awareness, Cyclist Two is somehow surprised by the right-turning Yukon (B) and must swerve to avoid contact. Passing behind the right-turner (A), this rider will be in a prime position to collide with Cyclist One.

Cyclist Three is able to avoid some of these problems by riding in the street but will not be immune to the normal hazards of busy crossings. The soccer mom in the Honda Passport (C), for example, might be overwhelmed by sheer excitement at the thought of shopping, and might try to sneak across prematurely. Cyclist Three will also be obligated to cross uncomfortably in front of the right-turner (A). In addition, Cyclist Three might draw the ire of impatient motorists behind, like the lane changer (F), while having to depend on the awareness and goodwill of these same motorists. Less than ideal.

Side paths and roads each bring their own sets of problems. Choosing one over the other often boils down to a matter of personal style. The side path might be the best option for a patient rider who is prepared to stop often—for dogs, pedestrians, left- and right-turning vehicles, other cyclists. . . . If time is an issue, and the rider hopes to keep moving, the road is probably the way to go. Unfortunately, in typical fashion, the local law bans cyclists from this particular boulevard. Even though the man with the dog (E) yells, "Get off the sidewalk!" at every cyclist he sees, the side path is actually the only legal option. Cyclist Three, therefore, is riding illegally.

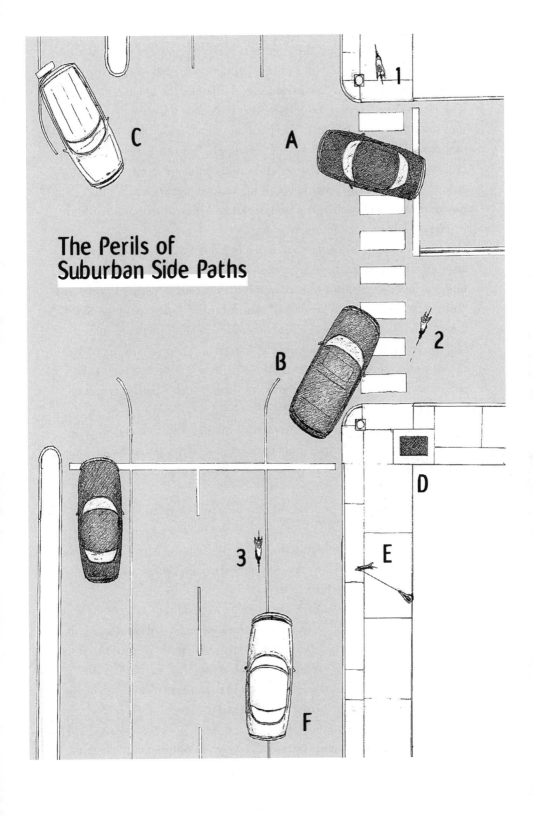

The Perils of
Suburban Side Paths

As the decades passed, the engineers corrected some of their mistakes, but not all of them. Bike lanes were repainted to the left of right-turn lanes, but some still lure inexperienced cyclists into the Door Zone (see The Door Zone, on page 116). Off-street paths, for the most part, evolved into smooth cement surfaces. The paths are much wider now—the typical modern bike path is a 10-foot-wide behemoth. But side paths still send cyclists awkwardly into the street and cause confusion at intersections. And the paths are still crowded with inattentive joggers and walkers, novice riders who can barely stay upright, and those distributors of four-legged chaos commonly known as dogs.

Modern-day urban riders are much better off than their old-school ancestors, because of a new generation of bicycle paths that flow right under or over streets, just like urban highways. Such a path is known as a "fully separated facility," and it's a beautiful thing. One is tempted to call these paths "bicycle highways," but since almost all of them are shared with pedestrians, joggers, and in-line skaters, and pedestrians in fact hold the all-time right-of-way on them, these paths still have much more in common with sidewalks than highways. Still, if such a path cuts across town and takes you reasonably close to where you need to go, use it. Use it because there will be no interactions with motors, and *no stop signs or red lights,* along its entire length. Judicious use of a fully separated bike path could reduce travel time and stress, even with the greater chance of minor collisions.

Experienced riders understand that they will be faced with hazards on bike paths that they would never see on the road. They know that they are more likely to hit something on the bike path than the street. But for some reason, many experienced riders still appreciate bicycle facilities, seek them out, and happily put them to good use.

Even the painted bike lanes are popular, although the riders who enjoy them may find it difficult to explain the attraction. The advantages of bike lanes are primarily psychological. Most of these lanes are painted on streets that are wide enough for cycling anyway, but the presence of the white lines gives cyclists an unmistakable territory of their own. This can be quite helpful around drivers who don't understand the law or don't respect cyclists as legitimate road users. Bike lanes might also serve as some legal protection for careful cyclists in case of a wreck—who can argue with a cyclist in the bike lane? There is an unfortunate corollary to this, that cyclists, conversely, might be legally compromised on streets with no bike lanes. Whatever psychological protection they might provide, bike lanes of course provide nil in the way of actual physical protection. Remember that bike-car wrecks usually involve vehicles that are turning or crossing, and a street rider will have to deal with these dangers, bike lane or no bike lane. Motorists smash into cyclists in bike lanes all day long.[7]

Admiration for bike lanes and paths is not universal among cyclists, to say the least. Led by John Forester, who was the first to mess up the program by pointing out the increased danger of separate facilities back in the 1970s, proponents of so-called vehicular cycling argue that bicycles belong on the roads, and only the roads. Although they can cite practical concerns, one gets the feeling that the vehicular cyclists are virulently opposed to separate facilities on principle alone. They argue to this day that bike lanes and paths represent the "ghetto-ization" of cyclists. The more dogmatic among them feel that riding on a bike path is a shameful act, and that riders who use separate facilities are unwitting dupes in a long-term plan to push cyclists off the public roadways for good.

Unfortunately, the vehicular cyclists' warnings about the insidiousness of bike facilities cannot be wholly dismissed. Indeed, a disturbing process seems to be at work that can be linked to the psychological implications of bike-path construction. As traffic increases on the roads, so does the frequency of conflicts. More people start to ask—what are those cyclists doing on the road anyway? Didn't we, the taxpayers, spend X-million dollars last year building the [insert name of path here] multiuse rail-trail? Didn't the bicycle people themselves beg to get this path built? So why are they still on the roads? Tantrums like this flare up from time to time among folks who have no understanding of the history of cycling in America or the needs of utility cyclists. But they find out soon enough that cyclists are entrenched on the public roadways. Cyclists are surly and politically connected enough as a group that bike-banning efforts are shouted down if they refuse to die quietly. In the future, we can expect more of these scattered antibike efforts to succeed, as motorists get angrier and more paths are constructed, and certainly we can expect future builders of major roadways to exclude the simplest on-street provision for cyclists, the wide curb lane, in favor of pushing cyclists onto off-street paths, even the dreaded side paths. In this way, the construction of separate facilities can lead directly to a decrease in cyclists' safety and options. So far, however, the fears of the bike path haters have not been realized. There is no widespread organized movement to remove cyclists from the nation's existing roadways, and, on the whole, the use of separate facilities is still voluntary.

The reality is that cyclists may be near the historical peak for access in urban areas, with nowhere else to go but down. Cyclists currently enjoy a unique, some might even say privileged, status in the transportation realm. With a few exceptions here and there, we are allowed to ride on pretty much any street that would be worthwhile to ride. When barred from a new boulevard (that we would likely try to avoid anyway), there is almost always a sidewalk, side path, or some other sneaky way to two-wheel it. We can ride streets with painted bike lanes if we wish, but are not required to. We can also ride on the separate paths, if we wish, but are (usually) not required to. With a legitimate place in both the vehicular and pedestrian realms, cyclists are having their cake and eating it too. *Cyclists have more freedom than any other class of road user.* Once the motor lemmings* figure this out, there could be trouble, so ssshhh. The best way for cyclists to conserve their already outstanding privileges is not to lobby for new bike paths, not to complain and blow up over every little lane conflict, but to continue riding the streets in a style that is smooth, quiet, and cooperative.

Streets, bike lanes, bike paths—even side paths—are all tools for the cyclist to use. The more tools the better. Just because a tool may be somewhat dangerous, like a bike path, does not mean it won't be a useful tool. If you went through the garage and threw out all the tools that could cause injury when misused, you wouldn't have much left over, except for maybe some tape. Let's say the most dangerous tool in the garage is the radial saw. Would you let your precocious three-year-old use the radial saw? Probably shouldn't let anyone clumsy or careless around sharp objects, no matter how old, fire up the saw. But the radial saw is still one of the handiest tools in the entire garage. You don't trash it just because it's dangerous. You reach for it every time you need to build a shed.

---

* *motor lemmings*: Not to be confused with Lemmy of Motorhead.

On the
Bike Path

The appearance of large numbers of novice cyclists on the paths is a good sign. It means that new cyclists are entering the ranks. It also seems to indicate that bike-path proponents are right when they assert that separate facilities will attract more citizens to the bicycle option in transportation. Beginning riders often express their hatred for the idea of cycling in traffic, but they seem to love the bike paths.

The beginner is his own worst enemy, of course, wherever he rides. His assumption of safety on the paths is undermined by his own presence there. Because beginners flock to the paths, the narrow paths become much more dangerous than they have any right to be. Inexperienced riders can be dangerous to themselves and others, just like teenage drivers after they've first gotten their licenses. They tend to weave around, misjudge distances and speed, and at times lose their balance on the paths. They often don't look where they're going, and sometimes don't know where they're going in the first place. When new bicyclists have to cross an intersection, they are often unappreciative of the level of danger that intersections pose. They are wide-eyed, hopeful, and innocent, and the accident numbers reflect that.

Let us not forget our own humble beginnings, and, while we're at it, let us bring some humility into our present. Give these new novices a break. Give them encouragement, if not the benefit of the doubt. When navigating an off-street path, cyclists should treat these riders the same way they treat questionable drivers, with polite mistrust and the proverbial "open mind." That is, don't rule out any possible movement the rider might make until the movement becomes physically impossible to make. Eventually road users will think of every possible movement, no matter how ill-advised, and execute it right in front of you. That's what people do. That's what traffic is.

The best way to avoid the missteps and bad decisions of others—drivers, cyclists, and pedestrians—is to leave plenty of physical space between you and them. In this regard, bike paths are troubling, because there is not much available space to escape into. Adjust for the lack of space by slowing way down around pedestrians and other path traffic. Commitment to slow riding around others requires patience. Patience is easy to come by on the path if riders can remember all the red lights they don't have to stop at. There will still be sections of path where discreet cyclists can stretch out and crank it up a bit.

When passing slower cyclists on a bike path, wait until there is plenty of space, and nobody coming the opposite direction, then pass on the left. Say, "On your left," without a hint of alarm, as you begin the pass. This lets slower riders know you're coming, so presumably they won't swerve left into you. It is also polite, and traditional among cyclists. In-line skaters, who take up a great deal of lateral space when they think nobody else is around, should get the same treatment. It may be useful and considerate, at times, to verbally warn pedestrians, but sometimes it is best for everyone if the cyclist can pass quietly, leaving a reasonable amount of space at a reasonable speed. Some cyclists use bells to good effect on the bike path; they warn pedestrians well ahead of time and don't have to slow down as much. "On your left" is a bike thing. Saying "on your left" to pedestrians is impractical, first of all, because they are moving too slowly and the cyclist is past them before they can process the words, and also because it causes about half of them to freak out and walk to their left, exactly the opposite of what you want.

Perhaps the scariest hazard on the bike path is the rider coming at you from the opposite direction. He's got his head down, he's pumping those pedals. He's drifting just a bit across the path. Bike paths are relatively skinny (11 feet wide for a full-size path, 6 feet wide for a thin one) so a little drift goes a long way. Prevent extremely violent, dangerous head-on collisions with other cyclists—literal head-on collisions—by hauling enough awareness for yourself and everybody else. And try not to ride on a bike path at night without a light, even though the surface, if it is the typical white concrete, will be easy to follow in the dark. The light isn't there for you to see where you're going, but so others can see you coming.

Like streets, the bike paths themselves can sometimes be dangerous, even when they're empty. Many paths are lined with soft grass on both sides, which is a nice inadvertent safety feature. Not so for Denver's Cherry Creek bike path, a fully separated concrete ribbon that is bordered for long stretches by fields of large, sharp rocks. Riders who wander off paths like this are sanctioned with serious injuries and broken bicycles. The obvious way to prevent these and other bike-path disasters is to keep the head up and eyes forward.

On the fully separated path, the increased danger of minor collisions could very well be offset by the elimination of car-bike interactions. Removing cars from the picture decreases stress along with the likelihood of deadly accidents. No cars . . . We really must stand back and admire these words for a moment.

While somewhat dangerous for inexperienced users, the fully separated path is the newest, coolest tool in the cyclist's toolbox. No cars, no stops. Seekers after the Holy Grail of Momentum need seek no further.

Sidewalks and
the Law

Observe any downtown area in any major city in America, and you will see bicyclists riding on the sidewalk. Most of these riders will be riding illegally, and they will do so even though they have some vague idea of the illegality of their actions. The pedestrians there will be occasionally perturbed, and occasionally terrorized by the sidewalk riders, but generally accepting of the situation. Sidewalk cycling, like rolling through stop signs, has gained some measure of legitimacy in American society that does not match the letter of the law.

The typical sidewalk law of a large American city bans bicycles outright from sidewalks in the central business district (CBD). Many municipal codes allow only children younger than age twelve or thirteen to ride on sidewalks outside the CBD, but many cities also allow adults to ride sidewalks outside the CBD—where the sidewalks are usually only 5 or 6 feet wide. The rider is always required to yield right-of-way to pedestrians.

That's the typical law, but there are some noticeable exceptions around the nation. Seattle has a very bike-friendly code: "Every person operating a bicycle upon any sidewalk or public path shall operate the same in a careful and prudent manner and at a rate of speed no greater than is reasonable and proper under the conditions existing at the point of operation, taking into account the amount and character of pedestrian traffic, grade and width of sidewalk or public path, and conditions of surface, and shall obey all traffic control devices."[8] Sidewalk surfers are required to yield right-of-way to pedestrians, and to give an audible signal when passing, but otherwise, if you want to ride your bike carefully on the sidewalks of Seattle, go for it.

The cities of Portland, Oregon, and Madison, Wisconsin, great bike cities that they are, have some of the most enlightened and reasonable sidewalk laws in the nation. In Portland, the rider may hop onto a sidewalk in the business district if he or she is "avoiding a traffic hazard in the immediate area." We can live with that. In Madison, "bicycle riding on sidewalks is permitted," except "where a building abuts the sidewalk."[9] These laws are the product of some careful, logical thought, rather than arbitrary antibike sentiment or the conventional dogma that classifies bikes as vehicles and leaves it at that.

Regardless of what the law in your city dictates, you will likely find yourself rolling on the sidewalk at some point. Realistically, unless you are a strict vehicular cyclist who shudders at the thought of riding anywhere but a street, any trip into the downtown area will put you on the sidewalk, perhaps just for a short while as you negotiate one-way streets or make your way to a destination at midblock.

It's conceivable that limited, selective sidewalk riding could be accomplished in a safe and courteous manner, but it always requires a good deal of special care. It must be accepted, first of all, that sidewalks always belong to the walkers. You are just visiting in their realm. On a sidewalk, slow to a near-walking pace. This is not enough, but it's a start. It's also easier said than done. Riding a bicycle under control at 3 mph or less is beyond the abilities of many bike riders. They can't come close to riding a straight line unless they are rolling quickly. Wild weaving, overcorrecting, on the verge of toppling over—please do not inflict your drunken clown circus act on the good citizens of your city. It is strongly recommended that those in the balance-challenged set spend a good deal of time practicing and honing skills in a neutral location before dicing it up in traffic or inviting disaster on the sidewalks. These riders will simply need to step off their bikes and walk 'em if they have to use a sidewalk.

It's not good enough to simply avoid peds while riding on a sidewalk—ride in such a way that you do not alter or disturb their intended path. *Allow them to walk the same direction, at the same speed, and in the same way they would if you weren't around.* This is achieved by passing behind pedestrians whenever possible, and otherwise leaving a somewhat melodramatically wide berth in front of any walkers, large enough that their inner alarms stay silent and they don't even consider slowing down or changing course. This is an example of zero-impact cycling. If everybody rode sidewalks like this, there would be no bans on riding sidewalks. Not only is this a very courteous way to move, it also greatly reduces the chances of collision. Obviously, this tactic could be ruined by a moderately busy sidewalk or pedestrians executing sudden flip turns, which they all do at some point—*I think I'll go to that open-air drug market on 15th before I go to the meeting on 18th.*

Municipal codes quite often require the cyclist to let loose an audible signal when passing pedestrians on a sidewalk or path. Some experienced riders harbor cynical feelings about the whole audible-signal thing. Voicing a warning or ringing a bell is sometimes quite useful, especially on bike paths where the rider is allowed to hold a bit of speed. On sidewalks an audible warning will often just gum up the works, especially when the rider is practicing a zero-impact style and can slip by a reasonable distance away from, and at a speed only slightly faster than, the walker. The audible signal may just confuse the ped, which defeats the purpose of this riding style. Audible signals have a way of startling small groups into stopping, turning, and roaming in random directions across the sidewalk. Best to just roll past gently, if possible. Do not disturb. If you're riding on a sidewalk, and a spread-out group blocks your passage, refrain from whistling, clicking your brake levers, or even saying "'scuse me." You will just have to wait. It's their world.

There is one way to continue practicing reasonable zero-impact cycling even on a fairly crowded sidewalk, and that is to ride the strip between the curb's edge and the parking meters and newspaper boxes. People rarely walk there. In fact, peds strolling down the sidewalk pretty much forget about this space entirely, although they infiltrate it when jaywalking, when entering and exiting vehicles parked on the curb, or when staring in a daze at the parking meter. This strip is usually between 1½ and 3 feet wide. It can be negotiated only at small speeds, and even this will require a somewhat advanced command of low-speed balance and straight-line riding. Riding here is much more difficult, technically speaking, than riding on the sidewalk itself. There is often a nasty longitudinal crack between the sidewalk slabs and the curb proper, and there are always hardened obstacles brushing the cyclist's shoulder and occasional car doors opening from the street side. Riding the strip remains useful, polite, and, like sidewalk riding in general, quite illegal almost everywhere.

Cyclists run into more trouble when riding on the other side of the sidewalk, next to the buildings. When a building directly abuts a sidewalk, people will be stepping directly out of the building onto the sidewalk. It also means, quite often, that the corners of the building will obscure the view of alleys or sidewalks lining intersecting streets. With respect to alleys, sidewalk riding necessarily reduces the buffer zone between the cyclist and alley intersections. Expect cars and trucks to roll out of the alleys, and expect pedestrians (and other cyclists) to come bolting out from the hidden sidewalks. Always expect the worst from an alley or a blind corner. Roll slowly at the far side of the sidewalk, away from the building, to avoid these hazards.

One of the strongest among many good reasons not to ride a bicycle on city sidewalks is the problematic interface between sidewalk riders and street traffic. Motorists who cross sidewalks or crosswalks will often swivel their heads in only one direction to check for traffic, the direction from which they expect traffic to come. So if you're on the sidewalk and rolling against traffic, don't expect these drivers to look your way, or to see you even if they do. Definitely don't roll in front of their vehicles. Roll behind them, or, if the sidewalk is completely blocked, put a foot down and wait.

Many cyclists are run down, perhaps deservedly so, as they roll off the sidewalk and into the street at the end of the block. This is pure kid stuff: failure to look, failure to appreciate common dangers or to stay minimally alert, general failure to pull the head from the arse. These are the types of riders for whom the vehicular-cycling principle would do a lot of good. They aren't ready to handle the available freedoms of cycling, especially sidewalk riding.

It should be noted that, in addition to legions of resentful pedestrians, a large contingent of serious cyclists are staunchly in favor of the sidewalk bans. Some of these are strict legalists with good intentions, and others are vehicular cyclists who claim they would like to see every last off-street bike path rolled up and crushed into gravel but are turned into hypocrites every time they have to go downtown. Lots of idealists in this group.

Riding in
Suburbia

Most Americans now live in areas that could be described as "suburban," and it is clear that much, if not most of American bicycling occurs in these areas. It is a mistake to think of suburbia as a monolithic, homogeneous entity as many do—endless rows of similar split-levels on curvy streets on the outskirts of town, the lawns, the mowers and blowers, the angst. These days the suburbs contain lots of apartment complexes for inhabitants of all incomes, parking lots, open space, retail conglomerations, parking lots, office parks and industrial complexes, parking lots, and some of the most cutthroat traffic anywhere. Did I mention angst? And parking lots. The structure of the 'burbs is all about travel by car. Unfortunately, a car can not be cinched up into a tiny stuff-sack when not in use, like a good windbreaker.

Probably the toughest, most ridiculous form of traffic exists on the big multilane arterial boulevards of suburbia. Invariably, these are the roads that are lined with the 'Marts and the malls and the chain restaurants, and the associated vast seas of parking. Vehicles zip in and out of these lots with furious abandon, the drivers dazed and drunk on entitlement. The sheer traffic volume can be immense. The drivers themselves may be somewhat more prone to fits of abject stupidity than drivers downtown, where there are a lot of professional drivers. And the ubiquitous messengers and commuters constantly pedaling through relatively cramped downtown spaces foster familiarity and effective, if not cordial, relations among road users, but no such familiarity is apparent out by the Old Navy parking lot.

The city centers were constructed for foot travel, horse-drawn carts, and streetcars. Automobiles have never been completely at home there. The suburban shopping centers and their access roads, on the other hand, were constructed just for individuals in their cars. The sight of a bicycle invading the dragon's lair of the car-centric universe is often surprising and unwelcome. In some communities it must seem downright outrageous. Developers and civic leaders have further thrown us under the bus by constructing most new suburban arteries without much thought for bicyclists—the right lanes of these roads are often too narrow to share and bicyclists are expected to stay on the sidewalk. Quite often, the cyclist is outright banned from using the roadway. But, due to the speed discrepancies, traffic volume, frequency of turning and crossing, and bad attitudes that are usually associated with these roads, many cyclists would just as soon find another route anyway.

Ah, yes, route-finding in the suburbs. It's not all it's cracked up to be. You'd rather not ride the hellish arterial boulevard that would take you directly to your destination, so you make a foray into the land of quiet side streets. But soon you find this street you're on does not seem to want to take you where you assumed it would take you. You used to be going north, now you're going west. All the other streets seem to do the same thing. It's a very curvy neighborhood. Soon you are looping back to a point very near where you started. What's this—back to the same arterial boulevard you were trying to escape! A half hour's riding has produced about a quarter mile of actual progress toward your destination. This is a typical suburban cycling adventure, at least for those who are unfamiliar with the territory and all its little tricks and shortcuts. A good map is much more useful for navigating the suburbs than the city centers, where streets tend to be laid out in predictable, orthogonal grids.

Once a good route is located, perhaps using sections of multiuse path along with quiet, hospitable streets, the suburbs can provide much more relaxed and carefree riding than the dense city centers. It is true that the width and curviness of suburban streets can tempt some people into aggressive driving, and the speed-matching which comes easily while bicycling downtown is a rare commodity on suburban side streets. Here, you're getting passed, but the road is generally wide enough to facilitate easy coexistence with drivers, and there aren't that many drivers to worry about anyway. On suburban side streets, where citizens loll about in ultra-low-density housing, there is much less on-street parking, and there are far fewer pedestrians to account for. With all those flat green lawns, sight lines are longer and clearer, and there are fewer places where you have to look. The lowest *intensity of traffic* in any municipality is generally to be found on its suburban side streets, while the highest is likely to be found on the sub-urban shopping frenzy arterials—downtown streets would fall somewhere in the middle, in my opinion. Finally, the pavement structures of suburban streets tend to be in much better shape than those near the city center.

While riding in quiet sections of suburbia can safely be said to allow for a less acute level of concentration than riding elsewhere, successful suburban cyclists nonetheless have the same basic, untrusting mindset of their downtown counterparts.

Riding at Night

Night riding is an important component of the cycling experience. This is especially true in North America, where the winter months bring early darkness for commuters.

Discussion of night-riding techniques can often be quite interesting, as it can reveal the underpinnings of one's whole cycling philosophy, and per-haps other personality traits as well. Some will say, for instance, that a cyclist need only gear up with the proper lights and reflectors, and stick to classic traffic-law principles, to be able to ride safely on the busiest streets on the darkest nights. Others will insist that no amount of lights and reflectors will completely solve the problem of cyclists' being overlooked on the roadways. This is just an extension of the ongoing debate about proper technique for riding in daylight. As with the larger debate, the truth is somewhere between these two extremes.

Night cycling looks very dangerous on paper. In 2001 about half of cyclist traffic fatalities occurred between 6:00 P.M. and 6:00 A.M.[10] This

amazing stat is even more impressive when you consider that relatively few cyclists ride at night. Many of these riders were run down from behind by drunks or sleepers on high-speed roads and never stood a chance. Some of these victims, however, as with their daylight counter-parts, were riding irresponsibly and erratically, without proper equipment, and had only themselves to blame. At night the garden-variety bonehead mistakes of cyclists are compounded massively.

It stands to reason that some of these cyclists-turned-statistics would not have been hit at all if they had been using proper lights and flashers. Ideally, a night rider will have a helmet light as well as a handlebar-mounted light, and at least one bright red flashing reflector to clip on the back somewhere. In most jurisdictions, this equipment is legally required for night cycling (although the law is rarely enforced). But will the lights and flashers be enough? Echoing the helmet debate, it must be said that attitude, style, and experience are more useful and important for cyclists than safety equipment. Undoubtedly some of these victims could have saved themselves by drastically altering their route and technique to make up for their lack of lighting.

Although one hopes that cyclists will keep their lights charged and blazing, they should also take a lesson from those who have learned to ride in the dark without any lights at all. Is it possible to go lightless safely, and if so, how? Riding at night without a light is not only possible, it can also be a very instructive drill. That's not to say we should make a habit of it! But—even those who are religious light users, the true believers wor-shipping at the altar of Visibility, would probably benefit from at least con-sidering the implications of this alternative, just to gain a partial under-standing of it. (And, realistically, a dedicated cyclist will be forced into this less-than-optimal situation from time to time anyway.) The style that is required to safely pull this off is a zealous version of what has been called the "invisible style." It is, by necessity, extreme antisocial cycling. The rider starts by choosing the quietest route within reason, to minimize interactions with cars. Then, whenever cars are encountered, the rider proceeds as if he or she is totally invisible—which is probably the case, frankly, if the rider is out at night with no light. This means slipping behind cars at intersections, adjusting speed to avoid situations where the rider is dependent on being seen by a driver, et cetera. There is an undeni-able element of sneaking and creeping to this style that is very unpalatable

In Traffic

to the vehicularists. Indeed, it is an extremely defensive, conservative, and patient style. It is a style that requires constant engagement, constant thinking ahead.

Now, let's keep our jerky knees firmly lashed down for just a bit here as we acknowledge some of the more interesting advantages of using the invisible style at night. From one point of view, the night rider's lightless paranoid-invisible style is extremely liberating. There is no pretense of being seen, and no dependence on it. It is all up to the cyclist to avoid the moving "obstacles," rather than up to the drivers to see and avoid the cyclist. The rider thus seizes control of his or her own destiny, in theory. Some riders who are devoted to this style claim that their visibility to motorists is occasionally a complicating factor—a disadvantage—in car-bike interactions. Some veteran night riders have been known to switch their lights off from time to time, for precisely this reason.

A rider utilizing a reasonable vehicular style, on the other hand, well-lit and dedicated to riding in a predictable manner, will enter situation after situation that should rightly be characterized by a gnawing uncertainty: *Does that driver really see me?* Guesswork. The invisible cyclist is not plagued by this question. The invisible cyclist has gotten inside this question, and has beaten it from within.

OK, you can unstrap your knees now and let 'em fly. The problems associated with the invisible style are well-known and probably outweigh the advantages. It is a style that could be criticized as selfish, and even unfair to other road users—because, even if the rider is shrouded in darkness, there will still be a few drivers here and there who will notice, and who might be confused or startled by the rider's presence. It is true that some drivers will not notice a cyclist on the street, but it is also true that many drivers will notice. As cyclists, we must somehow respect and reconcile these two opposing facts of life, whether it be day or night. For this reason, the invisible style is not practical for use on busy streets, or with other riders in close proximity.

Riders who practice the no-lights method will likely have some serious trouble with the city surface, even if they avoid all car trouble (see The Great American Pothole, on page 45). Lights don't reveal surface anomalies with flawless precision, but they are far superior to flying blind. A true samurai master of cycling, theoretically, would be so perfectly acquainted with the route that he or she would be able to pick a path around any potholes in complete darkness, with eyes closed. Good luck with that.

There are important elements of the invisible style that we should master and adopt for everyday riding. On the other hand, it is not always suitable or effective. The same could be said of the vehicular-cycling principle. Enlightened cyclists achieve an artful blend of these two styles, the end result of which could be called a *modified invisible style*, or a *modified vehicular style*, depending on one's point of view. Their method in fact shifts fluidly along this continuum between the vehicular style and the invisible style, as they adapt to a multitude of variables. It is no different for night riding.

Due to the presence of potholes, and the practical unavoidability of at least occasional encounters with motor vehicles—not to mention other cyclists—the author must insist in no uncertain terms that night-riding cyclists use proper lighting whenever possible. This means using at least one bright, illuminating headlight (a light that not only makes the cyclist more visible to other road users but also illuminates the road ahead) and at least one flashing red blinker for the rear. Lights are effective, necessary equipment (and ungodly expensive). But they are not enough. The night rider must artfully adopt the cynical mind-set, vigilance, and flexibility of the invisible cyclist, even while flashing like a UFO.

Riding with
Others

The cyclist in traffic is shadowed by a tricky dualism: the need to take precautions against drivers who may not see, and, at the same time, ride predictably for those who do. Unfortunately, these demands are not one and the same. In fact, they often pull and tug against each other, and the cyclist must decide how the balance should be tipped.

Every move that the cyclist makes in traffic is subject to the perceptions of other road users nearby. There is usually an audience, although that audience doesn't always pay much attention. Whether we like it or not, this adds another degree of complexity to our decisions. Will they be able to react to what we're doing, and, if so, how will they react? Will they freak out? Will they back off? Will they be calmed and assured? Or maybe they won't even notice.

Accounting for the perceptions and reactions of others is one of the cyclist's primary tasks. This is true concerning motorists and pedestrians, but especially so for other cyclists riding in close proximity.

The "organic" method of riding described in the previous pages is a method for the singular rider, alone in a flow of cars and trucks. It is a somewhat selfish style. It is not always suitable when two or more cyclists are riding together through town. An individual rider can take a few liberties here and there in the interest of personal safety—moving well out into the street to avoid getting hit from the right, for instance, or stopping sharply on a green light in anticipation of a vicious left-turner. These same moves, however, could surprise the hell out of an unsuspecting riding partner. When in the company of other riders, it may be necessary to abandon most of the free-form anticipatory moves in favor of a more structured style, falling back to something akin to a strict vehicular style, with accompanying hand signals no less.

In traffic it becomes glaringly obvious when two riders are practicing different styles. But even two riders who are totally in agreement on style and are seeing and anticipating the same things can still come into conflict with each other. If both riders are very experienced in traffic, they will both feel compelled to occupy the same space on the road, and they will have to share the safe zones. The position of one rider determines the available maneuvering space of the other, and mobility is necessarily limited for both. By riding more robotically than one otherwise might, it is possible to find relative safety in city traffic in the company of other cyclists, but there is always some degree of compromise involved. That is why some highly experienced riders will express a preference for riding alone.

Bike-bike wrecks are not uncommon and are of two basic types. The first type is that which results from the sort of conflicts described above, two or more experienced cyclists are out for a ride, together, and run into each other. Pace-line mishaps and misunderstandings at intersections are common in this genre.

In the other major type of bike-on-bike accident, one or both cyclists are beginners who are practicing the most primitive and dangerous form of cycling, "absentminded anarchy," and they randomly come together, often at a blind corner. They are hauling ass on the sidewalk, or cruising in the cycling space on the wrong side of the street, things like that. They are tumbling through your city like meteors looking for a planet to hit. They will eventually find the trouble that they appear to seek. In the meantime, there is not much that we can do or say that will keep these people from their appointment with destiny. The best we can do is know they're out there, and watch out for 'em. Be prepared to swerve when the time comes. Let's not become part of some other rider's learning process.

bicycle accidents and injuries

The
Statistical Quagmire

You would probably like to see solid statistical evidence to back up the claims made here about accidents and injuries, and the author would like to oblige. Just one problem—it doesn't exactly work that way. Using statistics to quantify the danger of cycling is like trying to trap a mouse under a taco shell.

Statistics fail to paint an accurate picture of the overall risk of cycling. The biggest reason for this failure is simple: The vast majority of bicycle accidents never get reported, written down, or noticed in any official way. Researchers can't count the numbers if the numbers aren't there. You see, when a cyclist gets smashed by a car, there is usually a police report saying so; when a cyclist visits an emergency room, there may be some record of the visit with a general description of the accident. But when a cyclist wipes out in a dime-a-dozen solo wreck—the most frequent sort of bike wreck by far—even though that cyclist may be hurt, she or he will usually not seek medical attention or file any kind of report, and therefore leaves no paper trail. Cyclists do the bulk of their suffering in silence. They tend to limp home, tough it out, and chalk it up to experience—all without notifying the Department of Transportation.

Paper chasers have estimated that about half a million cycling-related injuries are treated in American emergency rooms each year, with an additional half a million seeking treatment in doctors' offices.[1] That's a substantial bloody mess of significant injuries. But this number (which, remember, is still only an estimate) is just a drop in the bucket.

Experienced riders will tell you that they hit the ground, smash up their bikes, and actually hurt themselves many times for every time they are forced to visit a doctor or emergency room. This leaves more questions than answers. If one million or so cycling wrecks require emergency or outpatient treatment each year, then how many injuries go *untreated*—three million? Ten million? More? We can only guess. And how should we define "injury" anyway? When we expand our concept of danger to include not just the ER-worthy mishaps, but also the more common injuries—the cracked ribs, sprained shoulders, deep bruises that hurt for weeks, the saucer-size pavement burns, and so on—then cycling suddenly looks like a very dangerous activity.

Clearly, the pain and danger of cycling has been underrepresented in many statistical surveys. Adding to the confusion, the danger of cycling has also been *overreported* in many influential research studies, because these studies lump the cycling accidents of children together with those of adults. As most of us can remember, kids do silly things on bikes, like riding out of driveways into the street without looking, or jumping ditches on Kmart specials. They stack it up with far greater frequency than adult cyclists, which is part of what makes a kid a kid. Their accidents are imbedded in the statistics and become distracting, misleading clutter when we try to quantify the danger of cycling for adults.

The rise of mountain biking has thoroughly jacked up the stats as well. Most of the recent studies of emergency room data fail to differentiate between off-road and road bicycling accidents. Some of these studies have a designation for "nonroadway" wrecks, but this category can include parking lots, playgrounds, driveways, and other nonpublic thoroughfares, in addition to the local BMX tracks and homemade vacant-lot jumps.

Even if we could somehow account for every single cycling mishap, sort out all the kids' wrecks and the off-road wrecks, and obtain perfectly detailed information about injuries, the true nature of the urban bike wreck would still elude statistical analysis. You can't qualify or quantify a bicycle accident. Every wreck is a mystery wrapped in an enigma, born of multiple factors not completely recognized or understood even by those who experience the incident firsthand. Every accident is as unique as a snowflake.

Fear not! Using *(manipulating)* accident statistics is not a totally hopeless endeavor after all. Continuing a great American tradition, the author of this book will gleefully include statistics wherever they suit his purpose. Simultaneously, he'll be employing top-secret selective amnesia techniques to deal with the fundamental problems in doing so. See how that works? We will pick out numbers here and there like picking out fruit at the market. It won't be that easy, because even our favored studies are booby-trapped with problems—they come from foreign countries, attempt to draw broad conclusions from few subjects, or include children in their data. Some were produced at a time when "The Hustle" was sweeping the nation and Jimmy Carter was president. We'll use them anyway, because we like the numbers.

The key to escaping statistical tyranny is to not strain your brain too much about it. One must realize and accept that there will be more art than science to this enterprise. Beware of engineers, cycling advocates, spokes-models, and authors who come at you spewing official-sounding statistics about cycling accidents. Numbers are not the ultimate authority here.

Rather than searching for answers in piles of paper, let us seek knowledge from the cyclists themselves, those with literally hundreds of thousands of miles' worth of experience and decades of truck dodging behind them. These men and women have plenty of stories to tell. We are wise to listen to them well, and to read their scars with a careful eye, while taking the stats with a grain of salt.

The
Stats at a Glance

After bad-mouthing accident statistics for the past several hundred words, it should be noted that the statistically evident phenomena described below are confirmed by cold, hard experience. Without getting too specific or excited about criticizing the various studies, it is possible to pick out some undeniable patterns in the accident statistics. Some of these patterns may be quite surprising to beginning riders.

The most important lesson to be learned here is a bitter pill to swallow: *There is no greater danger to the cyclist than the cyclist's own incompetence.* As a whole, it turns out, cyclists are not an entirely smooth and skillful lot. The majority of cycling accidents are embarrassing solo incidents, with the cyclist sliding out on turns, stacking it up after ramming potholes, curbs, and other obstacles, or just generally losing control.

Collisions with motor vehicles are potentially more damaging but account for no more than about 15 percent of all cycling accidents. About half of car-bike accidents are instigated by cyclists who ride into traffic without looking, ride on the wrong side of the street, blow lights and stop signs, or otherwise ride in an unpredictable and lawless manner. This means that about half of car-bike collisions could be prevented if cyclists would simply follow traditional traffic-law principles. (Most of the rest could likely be prevented with a little experience, preparedness, and respect for the perils of the road.)

Admitting it is the first step toward moving beyond it. That surly looking character in your bathroom mirror is often your worst enemy out on the street.

Most experienced adult cyclists who are involved in a collision with a motor vehicle are found not to be at fault. Dissecting the subset of car-bike wrecks that can be *legally* blamed on motorists, we find that the most frequent of these involves the driver turning left into the cyclist. Collisions caused by drivers running stop signs, and turning right into cyclists, are also among the most common in this subset.

About 90 percent of all car-bike accidents in urban areas involve turning or crossing. Parallel-path collisions (in which a car sideswipes or hits a bike from behind) are relatively rare in city traffic but are much more common in rural areas, and on rural-style roads within cities, where they are disproportionately deadly.[2]

Cycling
Fatalities

Researchers concerned with bicycle accidents have focused much of their attention on fatalities rather than injuries, probably because the fatality numbers are so much easier to deal with. Unlike the murky injury stats, crunching the fatality numbers involves relatively little guesswork. A fatality, after all, is a fatality, while nobody seems exactly sure what an injury is.

Just because these fatality stats are easy to obtain does not mean drawing conclusions from them will be a straightforward matter. Because fatal cycling accidents are rare, focusing on them alone gives an overly rosy impression of the risks of cycling. While it is a sketchy enterprise to estimate the total amount of cycling that occurs for a given unit of time, and thus to conjure an estimate for the danger of cycling in terms of fatalities-per-hour or fatalities-per-mile, it's clear that your next bike ride is relatively unlikely to end in death.

By any estimation, the chance that any of your bike rides will kill you is infinitesimal—somewhere under one death per million hours of riding.[3] These happy, reassuring numbers do no justice to the overall danger of cycling, as its rate of ER-worthy injury is roughly *600 times* the fatality rate.[4]

The stress on fatalities leads naturally to a narrowing of focus, with the spotlight placed on a specific type of injury at the expense of all others. Cycling fatalities are most often the result of head injuries resulting from car-bike collisions, but head injuries actually represent a relatively small portion of all injuries from car-bike crack-ups, and car-bike collisions are a relatively small slice of the pie when considering all painful bicycle accidents. Overall, head injuries account for less than 5 percent of all bicycle accident-related injuries.[5]

There is another more specific way that the attraction to cycling fatality statistics has fostered misconceptions. Studies show that a substantial percentage of cycling fatalities result from cyclists getting hit from behind by a vehicle. This type of accident, however, is actually very rare among *urban* car-bike accidents. The hit-from-behind scenario is typically a rural phenomenon. It usually occurs on high-speed roads, with drunk driving as a common factor. Still, the common fear of hit-from-behind collisions has been used as justification for numerous policy changes and traffic engineering decisions in urban areas.[6]

The annual tally of bicycle accident–related deaths has declined steadily since 1975. In 1975, there were about 1,000 fatalities, and in 2006, if the trend holds, there will be around 700.* To what should we attribute this welcome decline? Nobody knows for sure, but we can theorize. It seems unlikely that the drop in fatalities would be related to any sea change in drivers' attitude or disposition toward cyclists. It's more probable that the decline is due to a corresponding drop in the number of cyclists on dangerous roads, or a dwindling usage of bikes by kids. According to the U.S. Department of Transportation, the portion of total cyclist fatalities involving children under 16 years of age fell from roughly 1-in-3 in 1998 to 1-in-5 in 2004, while the number of adult victims has basically held steady.

---

* The number of bicycle-related traffic fatalities is around 1.7 percent of the total yearly number of traffic fatalities, reported at 42,636 for 2004. (National Highway Traffic Safety Administration)

The Paradox of
Experience

Another thing the stats confirm quite clearly is the value of *experience* to cyclists. The more experience a cyclist has, the fewer wrecks he/she has per mile or per hour of riding. This effect is dramatic. A decade of experience will reduce a cyclist's accident rate by about 80 percent.[7]

It's important to understand that this does not mean experienced cyclists have fewer total wrecks—they have far fewer wrecks *per mile* or *per hour* of riding than beginning riders, but they tend to ride far more. In the end, beginners and vets tend to have about the same number of serious accidents per year.

Bicycle-fitness-guru Ed Burke has written that "careful cyclists crash . . . every 4,500 miles on the average."[8] Of course, we don't know exactly what he means by "careful" or exactly what he means by "crash," and Burke does not cite his source for the number. If Burke is referring to the bulk of crashes, even those that do not send the cyclist to the ER, then his number sounds about right.

In a 1976 study involving members of the League of American Wheelmen, riders reported logging an average of 2,400 miles per year, while suffering a bicycle accident–related injury about once every 9,000 miles. A similar survey of British Cyclist Touring Club members in 1984 showed that these riders, cycling under quite different cultural conditions than their American counterparts, suffered injury-causing wrecks about once every 15,000 miles. A 1996 update of the LAW study found riders with an average of 14 years experience wiping out hard every 30,000 miles or so.[9]

The numbers are inexact at best, and the confounded definitions of "injury" are all different, but when you put it all together, it means that an average cyclist with some years of experience in heavy traffic can expect a good, solid wipeout about once per year, and a more serious injury-causing wreck about once every three to five years. More importantly, it means that accident rates decline big-time as experience is gained.

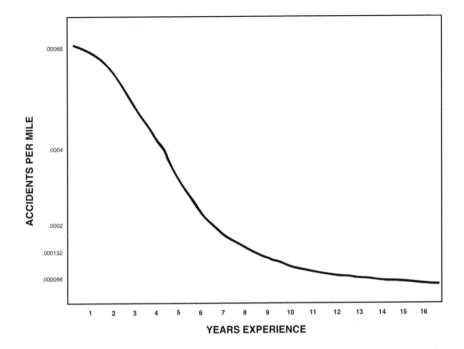

As the cyclist accumulates years and miles on the bike, the clumsy floundering is weeded out of the repertoire. The city has to cook up increasingly bizarre and complex scenarios to get the better of a quick-learning cyclist. The total number of wrecks per mile will decrease, while the percentage of the total wrecks that involve collisions with a car or truck will increase. The accidents become much less frequent, but more serious, over time.

The Accident

Immune System

There is a painful catch-22 involved in cycling—the best way to avoid wrecks is to wreck. By God I wish it weren't true, but pain is the best teacher. You never forget what Professor Pain tells you.

After you've been on the bike for many years, it becomes difficult to escape the notion that you're *collecting* one of each type of wreck. There will be one wipeout on diagonal railroad tracks, one loss of control after unseen pothole, one slide-out on gravel, one door, and on and on. Once you get clipped by a stop-sign-busting delivery truck, you will forever onward think of stop signs, and delivery trucks, in a different light. All it takes is one time. Call it the Accident Immune System.

Unfortunately, there is no shortage of different accident types to collect. Like viruses, they seem to mutate in response to our defense mechanisms. They become less frequent, and less, how you say, Mickey Mouse, as time goes on, but the wrecks keep on coming, surprising you with their endless variety.

The badge of experience is the scar. Experience hurts. Are you sure you want it? Some don't. They suffer one good fall and stuff the bike into the back of the garage behind the WetVac. Can't really blame them too much, but this book is for the rest of you.

Road
Rash

Road rash is the cyclists' term for the most common bicycle-related injury, the abrasions that result from falling onto the pavement and sliding across it. A little bit of road rash is just the cost of doing business.

Road rash is a precious gift. Road rash is your friend. Bask in it, appreciate it, love it. Above all, learn from it.

The time-release pain of road rash, a constant companion for a week or so after any decent tumble, serves to remind the victim of What Not to Do. Don't fight it. Listen to what the road rash is telling you: "You're not that great of a cyclist. Maybe you should try a Segway. You're dangerous to yourself and others. You need practice. . . ." Allow the *humility* of road rash to enter your consciousness, where it will displace malignant pride* and help keep you out of the ER through your cycling career.

---

* Cyclists are no more susceptible to this disease than any other group, but are more vulnerable to its side effects, especially the false sense of security that leads to a decrease in vigilance.

Abrasions result from almost every type of bicycle wreck, even car-bike collisions, because almost every type of bike wreck involves hitting the tarmac at speed. Road rash leaves its mark anywhere the body meets pavement. After a really action-packed wreck, the victim is often surprised to find pavement burns on both sides of the body—hips, knees, ankles, elbows, wrists, shoulders, back, and elsewhere. There may not be any memory of rolling like that, but the road rash record proves that it happened.

Road rash laughs at Lycra clothing. A short slide on the road surface can rip a pair of Lycra cycling shorts halfway off, leaving the haunches bloody and raw, a fairly common sight at the local amateur races. This type of injury can show up beneath layers of heavy clothing as well, quite insidiously, even on skin that was "protected" by jeans and jackets. This is a sobering indicator of the destructive power of sliding on the street.

Treatment for all but the worst road rash is fairly simple and do-it-yourself. The least enjoyable part of treating these abrasion-type injuries is cleaning them. It's important to remove the debris from the wound, and this is usually a bit painful. Use antibacterial soap and water, then treat the wound with a topical antibiotic ointment, and cover it with a sterile dressing. A nonstick bandage is best. Lately, pro racers have been using a special type of dressing that is water-based, designed to keep the wound moist so it will heal faster.[10] Uncovered road rash can be repeatedly irritated by layers of clothing, which impedes healing and hurts like hell.

The only ways to prevent road rash are to ride with humility and intelligence, and perhaps to cover your skin with leather the way motorcyclists do. In any case, wear gloves on every ride, along with your helmet. When you fall properly, the hands make first contact with the street.

Collarbones

"I didn't hear it," says Christie, "but other people did."

What Christie didn't hear, and what ruined the appetite for lunch in the pedestrians around her, was the sound of a collarbone breaking as her body hit the pavement. She had wrecked hard after riding over some severe waves in the asphalt that she hadn't noticed (see Waves, on page 49). The unseen waves twisted her bike out from under her and threw her down so quickly and violently that she had no chance to duck, roll, or otherwise prepare for the impact.

Although Christie didn't hear the actual *snap,* she understood immediately what had happened, because her arm had been rendered suddenly and completely useless. There was no moving it. That, and the tremendous pain that flooded the area about ten seconds later, made for an obvious diagnosis. When a collarbone goes, it's not subtle.

Faced with the knowledge that one of the biggest bones in her body had broken clean in half and was trying to poke out through the skin,

Christie quickly began to go into psychogenic shock.* She lay down and put her feet up on a snowbank. Cell phones were put into action and the paramedics were on the way.

The collarbone, or clavicle, is the bone at the top of the chest running from the shoulder to the sternum, or breastplate. There is one collarbone on each side. These are the prominent bones that you can see in the mirror and grab with your hand. Clavicles are broken quite often in bicycle accidents, usually due to a serious impact with the street, when the cyclist is thrown down directly onto the shoulder (like Christie), or hits the ground with an arm held out stiffly (see How to Fall, on page 171).

"All I got was four pain pills and a sling," Christie says of her hospital experience, which she insists was decidedly unpleasant, especially when the doctors had to cut her favorite sweatshirt off and then abandoned her to wait half naked and helpless on a gurney for hours while they attended to more critically injured patients. Nonchalance in the ER is a fairly typical reaction to this painful but relatively nonthreatening injury.

A fractured clavicle is usually pretty straightforward stuff, but it's not an injury that can be handled without professional treatment. If you snap a clavicle, head to the emergency room. (If nobody is around to drive you, you have earned a trip in an ambulance—don't attempt to ride with a broken collarbone.) The docs will want to look you over, take an X-ray or two, and make sure that none of the major blood vessels or nerves in the area of the fracture has been damaged. Beyond that, immediate medical treatment will involve little more than strapping you into a sling or specially designed "figure-eight" harness, giving you some pain pills and words of encouragement, and sending you out the door. Installation of

---

* *Psychogenic shock* is a fear reaction that rapidly dilates the blood vessels and causes decreased blood flow to the brain. Fainting is the extreme form of this most mild version of shock, which is usually "self-correcting." The general public tends to confuse psychogenic shock with other forms of shock that are far more serious. Severe bleeding is the major cause of "real" shock *(hypoperfusion)*, during which the body's cells and organs are starved of blood. In response to a hemorrhage, the body sends signals to the heart to pump more juice. The heart rate is increased, causing additional blood loss. If this downward spiral is not interrupted, it will end in cardiac arrest and death. The first outward signs of this deadly form of shock—restlessness, anxiety, pale skin, rapid heart rate—mimic the symptoms of psychogenic shock and, sometimes, life itself. Paramedics are taught to watch carefully for and treat signs of shock if there is the slightest possibility of internal hemorrhage. (J. David Bergeron and Gloria Bizjak, *First Responder* [Upper Saddle River, N.J.: Prentice Hall, 2001], pp. 322–24.)

Bicycle Accidents and Injuries

metal plates or pins (surgery) is almost never necessary. You will probably be asked to return in about six weeks for a follow-up.

Adults usually require about six to eight weeks, maddeningly slinged up, to heal their snapped collarbones. After the pain goes away, the patient should start some physical therapy to regain strength and range of motion. Even with a good rehabilitation regimen, however, the arm and shoulder on the side of the break may never function quite as well as they did before the accident. There will likely be some funky lump or other minor deformation left over in the area of the break—total badge of honor and usually quite inconsequential.

Six weeks is probably not enough time for a clavicle to heal to the point that it could withstand another hard blow, so when you get back in the saddle, be patient and ride conservatively. Christie understands this all too well: About six *months* after her accident, she was surfing the city streets again on her bicycle, and, yes, she hit pavement again. This time, a minor tumble was caused by her chain slipping off the big ring. Her clavicle snapped at the exact same spot of the original injury. Back to the hospital, another sling, a few more pain pills, and the whole deal all over again.

Even after her two collarbone incidents, Christie continues to ride through the city every day. She says the experience has made her a more vigilant cyclist, and left her with a physical reminder in the form of a minor deformity known as a "winged scapula" (one of her shoulder blades poinks out).[11]

The fractured collarbone, painful and frightening though it may be, is really just the extreme version of road rash. Call it a warning from the streets. The crash victim left with a broken collarbone as the most severe injury is actually a lucky individual who has been granted a reprieve of sorts, because any crash violent enough to cause a fractured clavicle is a crash that could quite easily have caused, with just a bit more speed or an inch here or there, serious head trauma. And while collarbones magically stitch themselves back together over time, a damaged brain may stay that way forever.

Some have suggested that cyclists might be able to prevent collarbone fractures, and other fractures, by eating foods rich in calcium and vitamin D. The best way to avoid such injuries, of course, is to avoid falling, or to fall correctly. . . .

How to
Fall

"The ship was turning gradually on her nose—just like a duck that goes for a dive. . . . The band was still playing. I guess they all went down."[12]

—HAROLD BRIDE, survivor of the *Titanic*

Many painful and debilitating injuries, especially the collarbone fractures and severe road-rash incidents detailed above, could be avoided if cyclists would apply more finesse to their crashes. There is a right way and a wrong way to fall off a bicycle.

Crashing is a crucially important skill for cycling. Some do it well, and some cyclists are hopeless crashers. Unfortunately, it's a skill that seems to require innate athletic talent, or perhaps it is learned early in life—in roughhousing, peewee football games, and such—and not one that can be easily acquired as an adult. It may be possible to practice this skill, by heading to the local park or soccer pitch and taking some dives off the bike. Everyone around will think you've completely lost it, which is always a nice bonus. In our current litigious environment, however, guys can't go around recommending that people should fall off their bikes on purpose.

The key to a good crash is to roll with it, and thus distribute the force of the impact. This is not always possible, even for a skilled crasher, because some crashes are just too violent and sudden. This is precisely the difference between a "good" crash and a "bad" crash.

The process of crashing begins with a frightening flash of realization: "I'm going down." This is a moment that really pumps the adrenaline, a moment of complete raw fear and life, without distractions. It is pure action combat with the street at that point.

The talented crasher recognizes this point of no return—which will be different for each rider in any given situation—at the earliest possible moment and abandons fruitless attempts to avoid the inevitable, leaving more precious time to set up for the fall. The first thought is for the hands—get them off the bars and out. Separate from the machine. Some really poor crashers maintain a death grip on the bike and ride it right down into the pavement. Not good. If the ship's sinking, don't start rearranging the deck chairs.

So you're falling away from the bicycle with your arms out, checking out the landing zone. That's not to say you should try to absorb the whole impact with the hands—far from it. But the hands should make the first contact with the street. For this reason, gloves are among the most important bits of safety equipment, along with attitude and helmets. Much better to lead with the hands than with the shoulder or head. If the crashing cyclist is able to get the arms out, half the battle is won.

The idea is to minimize the force of the impact, and to keep the head from smacking pavement. Don't hold the arms out stiff—you'll break your wrist or your collarbone that way. It might seem silly to suggest, but deliberately try to relax your body while falling, and, as the blacktop rises quickly to meet you, think consciously about how you can soften the encounter. *Hello, street. It's me again.*

Upon touchdown, the outside arm collapses, absorbing as much of the fall's energy as possible. First with the hand—a tender touch, like Cary Grant reaching for Audrey Hepburn—then the forearm, rolling onto the back of the shoulder and over. A perfect roll is harmless to a gloved hand. Lucky for us, most falls naturally send the rider off to the right or left, which begins the rolling process nicely. Complete the crash by getting the heck out of the street. When executed correctly, the worst you'll end up with is some minor road rash on the forearm and shoulder and a wicked adrenaline rush followed by an overwhelming sense of relief.

The sequence outlined above is a rather optimistic scenario. It assumes that the crash has been "telegraphed"—that you can feel it happening in time to execute the roll. This is simply not the case with many types of bicycle accidents. Even the most talented and cat-quick bike handlers can get slapped down awkwardly and hard more than a few times in their lives. Their shoulders will be torn up, their helmets cracked open like raw eggs, before they realize what happened. For these violent falls, by definition, there is no magic technique that can help. The only answer is *prevention*, in the form of a conservative, defensive, and very focused attitude in the rider.

Even after a successful tuck-and-roll maneuver, the cyclist is left with a discomforting sense of the terrible force involved with hitting the street. Longtime cyclists know it well: a sudden, gripping panic that is perpetually justified by the shocking violence of the collision. The pavement is not soft. You never say to yourself, "Man, I want to try that again."

For those among you who have yet to experience this little joy and are wondering what it's all about, try this simple exercise: Tomorrow, when you're out riding, get up to about 20 to 25 mph, then visualize your body with, suddenly, no bike underneath it. Falls are not very pleasant, but if we ride well enough to make them infrequent occurrences, and know how to fall correctly, a few crashes are a small price to pay for the great privilege of riding a bike through the city. The injuries to the head and face described below, however, make the transaction far less favorable.

Facial
Injuries

Due to the face-forward position and high center of gravity of cyclists (recumbent riders being an exception here), we are vulnerable to having our faces smashed in sudden, violent wrecks. Bicycle helmets are wonderful for protecting the top of the head and therefore the brain, but offer scant protection for the lower face. The average cyclist rarely considers this particular vulnerability, which is why it is being given so much attention here. Allow me to enrich your paranoia.

Serious facial injuries, as with brain injuries, often result from impact with motor vehicles, either moving or stationary. These are wrecks where the bike is suddenly stopped cold in its tracks, while the rider continues forward. With the front wheel blocked, the rider flies forward and tends to catch his or her legs on the handlebars, which forces the head and upper body to pivot downward and slap against whatever immovable object is there.

Facial injuries also occur from particularly nasty versions of solo crashes, especially slide-outs from high-speed cornering and wrecks caused by sudden displacement of the front wheel. Slide-outs and slap-downs.

In the mountain of bicycle accident statistics on the desk here, the term "head injury" usually refers to any injury above the neck. Got a bloody nose? Head injury. Knock some teeth out? Head injury. In this way, the numerical incidence of head injuries, as we traditionally think of them, is overstated, while the incidence of facial injuries is forgotten. Circumstantial evidence suggests that cyclists are more likely to suffer an injury to the face than a concussion or other brain injury, but the facial injuries are lost in the statistical purgatory.

Many dedicated cyclists can confirm having had teeth knocked out at some point, or fracturing one or more of the fourteen irregularly shaped bones of the face. These events provide some the least-beloved memories of their entire lives.

Unfortunately, traditional road-cycling helmets provide no protection against these common injuries.[13] Full-face mountain-bike helmets, like those used in downhill racing, should be considered for use by riders who like to take a lot of risks in heavy traffic but want to stay pretty.

Head Injuries

Head trauma is the grizzly bear of all cycling disasters—rare but deadly. Although head injuries account for a very small percentage of all cycling-related injuries, they are implicated in about 85 percent of cyclist fatalities.[14] Across the board, severe head injuries result in death for about half the victims who suffer them.[15]

A cyclist who smacks his or her head in an accident will, if lucky, escape with only a concussion. Concussions cause confusion, headaches, sleepiness, and short-term memory loss. Recovery is usually quick, but the victim may be left with a particular vulnerability to repeated concussions, a "syndrome" that is a bit of a mystery to the medical community.[16]

A more serious accident may bruise the brain below the site of the impact, or bruise both sides of the brain if it "rattles" in its hard case (a *coup-contrecoup* injury). A violent blow may fracture the skull. In these cases, it is not the contusions on the brain or even the skull fracture that pose the greatest danger. Such injuries may involve broken blood vessels that bleed into the space around the brain, and the swelling caused by this bleeding is the most dangerous and deadly complication of head trauma. In extreme cases, a hematoma (collection of blood) around the brain can compress and destroy brain tissue, or it can push the brain through the opening at the base of the skull. Such severe swelling is immediately life threatening.

Because intracranial hematomas can grow slowly, victims of accidents involving the head need to be watched closely even if they seem fine. Symptoms of brain swelling may mimic intoxication. "Raccoon eyes" are an ominous sign of intracranial bleeding. An even more ominous sign is bleeding from the ears.[17] Any victim of significant head trauma should be immobilized due to the danger of spinal injury, and, of course, professional medical help should be summoned immediately. For severely injured victims, every minute is critical. For the walking wounded, MRI will reveal any hidden hematomas and damage to the brain.

To prevent head injuries, the cyclist should strap on a certified crash helmet for every ride. Bicycle helmets provide significant protection against such injuries but are no magic bullet. The most effective safety device is not the helmet, but that hunk of rock it is supposed to protect.

Other
Injuries

Road rash, busted collarbone, smashed face, and cracked skull are, unfortunately, not the only injuries common to cyclists. Falls from the bike cause all manner of damage to the upper extremities. Broken or dislocated fingers; broken or sprained wrists; cracked elbows; and sprained, strained, or dislocated shoulders are all familiar. (Muscles get strained and ligaments get sprained.)

Damage to the rib cage is a typical result of various types of sudden drivetrain failures, in which the rider is thrown violently into the stem and handlebars (see Drivetrain Maintenance, on page 236). Catastrophic mechanicals are also known to cause painful contusions around the knee.

Cyclists who get hit by cars often end up with broken legs from the initial impact with a low bumper. The cornering slide-outs so popular among beginners often cause a broken or badly twisted ankle on the inside leg. Occasionally, these same wrecks can fracture a hip.

"Soft" injuries, such as saddle sores and knee pain, are extremely common, but they result from poor bike fit and other issues, not from accidents. These problems will be treated in a later chapter.

Disclaimer

First of all, right off the bat, let's get one thing straight. *Cyclists should wear a certified bicycle helmet whenever they ride.* There.

This needs to be stated first because, without it, the information contained in the following sections could get the author thrown from a high place. This helmet stuff tends to get folks all riled up.

If you are like most cyclists, the information below will probably make you feel uneasy and will challenge most of what you think you know about helmets and their effectiveness. Please read the entire section with an open mind before freaking out. The information is important and, in the end, learning it will probably provide more protection than the helmet itself. Remember, knowledge is power.

The Helmet
Controversy

. . . no falsehood is so fatal as that which is made an article of faith.[18]

— THOMAS PAINE

The first hard-shelled bicycle helmets for mass consumption appeared in the late 1970s. Twenty years ago, only a small percentage of cyclists wore them. Today, however, the use of helmets is thoroughly entrenched in cycling culture.[19]

From the racers to the commuters, it is almost taken for granted that cyclists should wear helmets on every ride. You buy a bike, you buy a helmet to go with it. Cyclists who choose not to wear them suffer pangs of guilt and are widely considered to be nuts. In Australia, New Zealand, and parts of Canada, adult cyclists are required to wear helmets.* In America, many state and municipal codes require children to wear helmets, and the parents are held responsible if they don't. These laws are becoming more popular. While helmet use is still voluntary for almost all adults in this country,** American cyclists purchase millions of bicycle helmets each year and wear them religiously.

So, what's the controversy? The push for helmets is supported by solid and incontrovertible evidence, right? Well, it depends on who you ask. Those untiring preachers of helmet usage—like the U.S. Consumer Products Safety Commission, the National Center for Injury Prevention and Control, the Snell Memorial Foundation, the Insurance Institute for Highway Safety, and dozens of other private and government agencies—rely on just a handful of research studies to make their case. These groups seem quite happy with the available research. But the studies they cite are not immune to the pitfalls that have plagued other studies of bicycle accidents and injuries, and so the studies have attracted critics like thrashing, injured fish attract sharks.

If you spend any time at all looking at this issue, you'll quickly and repeatedly come across the claim that "helmets reduce the incidence of serious head injuries by 85 percent," or something similar. This figure is derived from a series of studies that gathered data from Seattle-area emergency rooms in the late 1980s and early 1990s. The researchers simply looked at the injuries of cyclists who wore helmets versus the injuries of those who did not, and they found that the helmeted riders treated in the ER suffered fewer and less-severe head injuries.[20]

Critics of these Seattle studies are quick to point out that severity of injuries could not be pinned on helmets alone. As the studies' authors themselves acknowledge, riders using helmets tend to be more experienced and safety conscious than riders who don't, and therefore may suffer less-severe accidents and injuries. Helmeted riders—being more affluent, in general, with much better

---

* After a few high-profile deaths, racers in the European pro peloton are now required to wear helmets in every race. The only exception is for races with mountaintop finishes, during which racers are allowed to remove the helmet for the final climb.

** Those in Dallas and large portions of Washington state, including the otherwise great city of Seattle, being notable exceptions.

access to health care[21]—might be more likely to seek treatment for less-serious injuries, which would skew the results in favor of helmets. Likewise, helmet-wearing children tend to have more concerned parents who might rush their kids to the hospital even after minor falls—just to make sure. All of this would result in helmets looking more effective than they actually are. By what amount, it's impossible to say. The Seattle studies, though enticing, have assumed an authority in the helmet debate that is not justified by the studies' methodology.

If helmets are the lifesavers they are advertised to be, then we should expect to see a significant drop in cyclist fatalities as helmet use rises. On the face of it, the correlation seems to be there: Helmet use has gone drastically up in the United States and fatalities have dropped (by about 25 percent) since the late 1970s. When we use pedestrians as a control group, however, helmets don't look so good. The number of fatalities among pedestrians has dropped right along with cyclist fatalities, both in the United States and Canada.[22] Since helmets have never been very popular with pedestrians in either country, it could be argued that the decrease in deaths is due to other factors—for instance, traffic-calming measures, tougher drunk-driving laws, the construction of off-street facilities for pedestrians and cyclists, and a general decrease in the number of cyclists on high-speed roadways.

In a possible preview of legislation coming to the United States sometime in the future, the Australian states of Victoria and Western Australia enacted mandatory bicycle helmet laws for adults in the early 1990s. The data has been fairly inconclusive so far, but years after the laws were implemented there was no indication of any statistically significant reduction in the rates of head injuries or fatalities due to vastly increased helmet usage.[23] Even before a similar law was passed in New Zealand in 1993, there was a great increase in the number of cyclists there who voluntarily donned helmets, and yet no corresponding decrease in the rate of serious head injuries could be found. The only trend that has been associated with these mandatory helmet laws is a general decrease in cycling.[24] The statistics from Down Under have not been helpful for the arguments of those favoring mandatory helmet laws for adults.

The obsession with bicycle helmets seems particularly irrational when the danger of cycling is considered alongside the danger of driving and walking. Compared to the danger faced by other road users, there is nothing special about cycling that is particularly likely to cause a head injury. Statistically, an hour of driving seems to be in the same range of deadliness as an hour of cycling, and it is about as likely to cause a serious head injury.[25] Driving and walking helmets—hypothetically speaking—would prevent many times more deaths and brain injuries than would bicycle helmets. But if someone were to seriously suggest that a law should be passed forcing all drivers, passengers, and pedestrians to wear helmets, that poor someone might be burned at the stake. Many of the same people who think unhelmeted cyclists are completely insane would consider any helmet-wearing drivers and pedestrians to be, well, completely insane.

When a bareheaded cyclist suffers a head injury, everyone shakes their collective head and sighs: "Shoulda been wearin' a helmet." But when a helmeted rider suffers a head injury, nobody seems to doubt the effectiveness of the helmet. Instead, there is an automatic assumption that the injury would have been worse without the helmet. In fact, there is rarely any evidence to prove that an unhelmeted rider's brain injury could be blamed on the lack of headgear, or that a helmet would have made any difference at all. We just assume. There is a great deal of hopeful superstition behind our faith in bicycle helmets.

What Are
Helmets Built For?

Some emergency room doctors have seen firsthand the limitations of bicycle helmets. What these doctors know, the rest of us should try to understand: Bicycle helmets are built to soften relatively minor blows to the head, like those that can result from falls, but are unlikely to save the bacon of a cyclist in a high-speed collision with the road or a car.

If you look on the inside of a new helmet these days, you should find a sticker stating that the helmet meets the standards set by the Consumer Products Safety Commission (CPSC).* If you have yet to buy a helmet,

---

* The CPSC has certified all models of bicycle helmets sold in the United States since 1999. Prior to that, helmets were certified by the American National Standards Institute (ANSI), the American Society for Testing and Materials (ASTM), or the Snell Memorial Foundation. Snell's were the most rigorous among all the standards, including the current CPSC rating.

make sure the CPSC sticker is on any helmet you purchase. But don't get too excited about it.

Helmet models are tested by strapping them onto fake heads and dropping them straight down onto anvils of various shapes. If the so-called headform slows down gradually enough, as measured by a device called an accelerometer, the model passes. The CPSC sticker means that the helmet is certified to protect your head in an 11-mph impact with a jagged surface like a rock or curb, or a 14-mph impact with a flat surface.[26]

Fourteen miles per hour? Obviously, the CPSC's testing conditions are exceeded regularly by any decent cyclist on the way to the grocery store, and absolutely blown away during other common cycling scenarios—fast descents, for instance, or some car-bike collisions when the speed of the rider is compounded by the speed of a vehicle. That CPSC certification is not going to keep your skull together in a really bad crash. It's no surprise that many of the most vocal helmet boosters are pediatricians, as bike helmets are designed to provide effective protection in the kind of low-speed accidents suffered so often by kids.

Adult cycling consumers don't want anything on their heads that might slow them down. They want helmets that are slick-looking, lightweight, and well-ventilated. These demands create a conflict with safety concerns. If manufacturers wanted to produce a much more protective and safe helmet for adult cycling, they could do that. In fact, such a model has already been created. You can get one if you want. It's called a *motorcycle helmet.*

Bicycle helmet manufacturers have done a remarkable job within the confines of the market. With the tension between safety concerns and consumer demands to guide them, bicycle helmets have been designed to gradually slow the rate of the head's deceleration in a wreck, not so much to protect from the blunt force of the impact. The term "hard-shell," when applied to today's bike helmets, is a complete misnomer, an anachronism left over from the 1980s. Built to collapse and break apart, the modern bike helmet consists of a layer of polystyrene foam covered with a literally paper-thin sheet of plastic. Its apparent solidity is an illusion.

Most skateboard helmets can withstand repeated blows, but bicycle helmets become compressed and unusable after a single impact and therefore need to be replaced. You could wear a good skateboard helmet and it would protect you just as well for all your cycling needs, but your head would get hot, and people would always be asking if you can do a 720.

Torsion
Injuries

At 8:15 A.M. on July 28, 1998, Robert strapped on his helmet and started riding his bike to work. At 8:30 A.M., he rode head-on into a Mercedes SUV and was knocked out cold in the middle of one of the busiest streets in the city. A few homeless guys dragged him onto the sidewalk so he wouldn't get run over again. About an hour later, he woke up in the hospital, surrounded by doctors, technicians, and beeping medical equipment. He was lucky to be alive.[27]

On a monitor by his bed, a strange scene was unfolding. He couldn't quite figure out what he was looking at. It looked like a scene from *Aliens*. "That's the inside of your carotid artery," someone explained. A tiny camera had been inserted into the large artery in his groin and was threaded all the way up to his neck, allowing the medical team to observe a life-threatening blood clot in the artery feeding his brain. "Cool," Robert said, and fell back to sleep. The pharmaceuticals were really kicking in at that point.

Later on, the doctor came to Robert's room and explained how he might have received such a dangerous neck injury. The helmet may have saved your life, the doctor told him, but it almost killed you at the same time. He had seen this type of injury before in cyclists and had a theory for it. Due to the wide, oblong shape of most bicycle helmets, an off-center impact on the helmet's surface can translate into a violent twisting of the head and neck. Furthermore, the "sexy, high-performance vents"[28] of the typical high-end helmet can catch in a wreck and twist the victim with disastrous results. This is particularly scary news for loyal helmet wearers, because torsion-type head injuries, in which the brain stem and the blood vessels in the neck can be torn, are among the most deadly of all injuries.

It is certainly very disturbing to think that a bike helmet, due to design features based on aerodynamics, ventilation, and style, might actually cause more harm than good in some crash situations. Not enough case control studies have yet been produced to clarify this. Keeping this frightening complication in mind may cancel the false sense of security that some cyclists feel when wearing a helmet, and that can only be a good thing.

Robert, for what it's worth, has weighed the consequences and continues to wear a helmet on every ride.

The
Helmet Verdict

As humans, we are attracted quite naturally to easy answers. Quick fixes. To cyclists, the bicycle helmet can seem like the easiest answer of them all. It is not.

The purpose of the previous sections has not been to disparage use of helmets, or to suggest that they shouldn't be worn, but simply to inject a needed dose of sobriety into a microculture that has come to revere the bicycle helmet as some kind of magic force field against head injuries. In reality, bicycle helmets should be recognized as a compromise between safety, style, ventilation, and weight.

Considering the limitations, and the fact that some are so light and comfortable they are barely noticeable when worn, bicycle helmets do a remarkable job protecting heads in most falls and low-speed impacts. Violent collisions are another matter, but—you never know—a bike helmet's 1 inch of expanded foam could be the difference between a nasty concussion and a lifelong handicap. Legions of cyclists have pieces of broken helmets stashed away somewhere, to remind them of what might have happened to their skulls. Experience, not some spotty research study, has made helmet believers out of them. Others without helmets will be launched head first toward the street, and, just before impact, a single thought—perhaps the clearest thought they will have for some time—will flash into their minds: "I sure wish I had a helmet on right now."

The brain is too important and vulnerable to forgo this easily applied preventive measure. Strapping on a helmet won't make us immune to accidents or injuries, even brain injuries. But, while we dismantle some of the claims made by the pro-helmet groups, we must emphasize that bicycle helmets provide a significant net gain in safety for cyclists who wear them. Use a helmet and wear it properly, low on the forehead, securely fastened. If you're unsure how to properly adjust your helmet, any local bike store should be happy to help you properly fit and secure your helmet to your head. After all you just gave them an assload of cash for it.

Cyclists should wear helmets and ride like they don't. Wear a helmet, but don't let it go to your head.

air pollution and the cyclist

A Historical
Reality Check

When you get a minute, climb into your time machine and go back to New York City, 1890. It's educational.

Of course you can expect, in addition to seeing plenty of ladies in funny hats, a notable absence of cars and trucks. A total lack of highways and overpasses. No diesel-spewing buses, and not a single parking garage in sight. Sounds great, right? But hold on—before you get all romantic about the old-fashioned unmotorized city, realize that the first thing you're likely to notice about the hundred-year-old New York is its godawful *smell*. Be prepared for that.

"Ack!" you say to yourself as you emerge from your time machine, carefully avoiding a gang of Irish toughs, "what is that stench?" It's unpleasantly familiar . . . a combo of rotting garbage, sewage, coal smoke, and, of course, horse dung. To the intrepid time traveler visiting the most-overcrowded city on earth,* it becomes painfully apparent that exhaust comes in many forms, and it originates from sources other than motors. The nineteenth-century cities were so heinously dirty that living within them was considered (especially by ladies in funny hats) to be a grave threat to human health.

Much of the blame for this pollution was placed on the popular transportation technology of the era—the horse. New Yorkers in 1890 had to contend with a frightening yield of horse exhaust. Deposited on the city's streets each year were tens of thousands of gallons of urine and two-and-a-half-million pounds of manure, which created clouds of dried dust or, depending on the weather, green puddles. The buildings lining the streets were stained by splash from the pools of excrement. The draft horses themselves were so overworked that they would frequently drop dead in the streets, to the tune of some 15,000 per year in New York alone.[1] That's an estimate of course—it's doubtful that anyone was out there weighing dung or counting horse carcasses. In any case, don't forget to bring your fenders along in the time machine, because cycling through the nineteenth-century city without them will put a nice greenish-brown stripe up your backside and pretty much ruin your knickers.

It's no surprise that the automobile's arrival into this stinking, soupy environment was celebrated by affluent city dwellers. They figured it would bring a vast improvement in terms of cleanliness and health, in addition to a revolution in mobility. The ladies in funny hats were all about it. The danger of motor-vehicle exhaust was the furthest thing from their minds. Newly motorized Americans enjoyed several decades of blissful ignorance until the insidiousness of the internal combustion engine wafted into the national consciousness from the left coast.

Around 1950 the air over Los Angeles, the world leader in all things automotive, had achieved a shocking density and brown hue. A new word was born: "smog." No matter how much folks wanted to, the strange new cloud could not be blamed entirely on industry. Angelinos weren't about to give up their cars at that point—nor could they, one could argue, as the city's rapid-transit system had just been torn out in its entirety—but they demanded that their elected officials pay attention to the region's air quality, or lack thereof. With a cloud like that, something had to give.

---

* New York's Lower East Side, near the turn of the century, housed more than 300,000 people per square mile. Today the most densely packed areas of Manhattan hold about 100,000 people per square mile.

Decades of regulatory experiments in California set an example for the whole nation, culminating in the tough federal Clean Air Act of 1970. This legislation eventually forced a significant cleanup of industrial pollutants and emissions from new vehicles.

The Good News about
Air Pollution

Going through the long list of poisons that hang over our streets and pump in and out of the lungs of city cyclists is a scary exercise that tends to make horse crap sound pretty nice, so let's start with some good news.

Due to government regulations and advances in technology, a new car today produces about 10 percent of the pollutants produced by the typical 1970 model.[2] The use of the *catalytic converter,* a device attached to a vehicle's exhaust system that changes harmful pollutants into such benign substances as oxygen and carbon dioxide, is the primary reason for this massive improvement. Basic catalytic converters were introduced in 1975, and more sophisticated "three-way" converters (which reduced emissions of carbon monoxide, hydrocarbons, as well as nitrogen dioxide) were mandated by law in 1980 and today appear on all cars sold in America.* The 1990 amendments to the Clean Air Act brought still more stringent emission controls.[3]

---

*Catalytic converters force the exhaust stream through a tight honeycombed structure made of ceramic material. The ceramic honeycomb is coated with precious metals, such as platinum, rhodium, and palladium that *catalyze* the pollutants into nonpollutants. Platinum, for example, strips the nitrogen atom away from the noxious nitrogen dioxide molecule (NO_2) and "holds" it, leaving oxygen (O_2); the leftover nitrogen atoms then bond to form harmless N_2. *Voila!*

The catalytic converter was the American auto industry's response to the stringent mandates of the 1970 Clean Air Act. It's worth mentioning that the American car companies did not go gently into this new era. In fact, they put everything they had into fighting it, claiming that the new laws would cause a "business catastrophe." Their full-court press of lobbying swayed Washington for a few years, until foreign competitors such as Volvo, Honda, and Mercedes showed they could exceed the new U.S. guidelines years before they went into effect, and the American companies were shamed into action. For a decent account of the fight over the Clean Air Act, see Jack Doyle, *Taken for a Ride* (New York: Four Walls Eight Windows, 2000).

The gasoline used today is not your father's gasoline. In the cities with the worst pollution, "reformulated" gas is used. This new fuel contains additives that boost its oxygen content to make it burn more completely, reducing harmful emissions.* Federal laws have also tamed diesel fuel by removing most of the sulfur content. In city buses and maintenance fleets, conventional diesel is being phased out in favor of cleaner-burning fuels, from propane to recycled cooking oil.[4] And lead has been gradually phased out of gasoline over the years, so this extremely toxic ingredient has been virtually eliminated from air in America (not so for many developing nations, where leaded gas is still in use).

Smokestack emissions from factories, refineries, and power plants have also been cleaned up significantly. Generally speaking, about half of our man-made air pollution comes from these "fixed sources," although this percentage has been rising steadily as auto pollution has been reduced.

Even when we take into account the vast increase in the number of cars on the road, and the increase in miles driven, air quality in America has actually improved throughout the past two decades.[5] The early 1980s were probably the worst years for air pollution in the United States, due to the combination of the total automobile population and the relatively high number of older, unregulated vehicles that remained in service. The attrition of older vehicles is still the best thing to happen to lungs (with the possible exception of wind).

There could be more good news on the horizon. It seems possible that the nation's vehicle fleet will, at some point in our future, run on hydrogen instead of petroleum. Hydrogen fuel-cell emissions consist entirely of water vapor. If all that hypothetical hydrogen is generated from clean sources such as solar or wind power, as opposed to burning petroleum,

*It could be argued that the use of oxygenated fuels has produced an unfortunate, frying-pan-into-the-fire situation. Although it is being phased out as we speak, until recently almost 90 percent of oxygenated fuel contained MTBE (methyl tertiary butyl ether). MTBE has been detected in drinking water supplies throughout the country, especially in areas where reformulated gas is mandated, where it has a nasty habit of leaking from underground storage tanks. MTBE is particularly frightening because it doesn't break down easily under natural conditions and persists for years. While we know that MTBE is toxic to humans, and is a likely carcinogen, it is not yet known what level of contamination is safe, if any. In effect, we have all been guinea pigs testing the dangers of MTBE, in the air and water. As of 2006, a surge of public consternation about MTBE has led nineteen state legislatures to ban or phase out the additive, in favor of ethanol, which is made from domestically grown corn. (Blewett and Embree, *What's in the Air,* pp. 61–65; see also the EPA's MTBE homepage at www.epa.gov/mtbe.)

from which it can also be derived, the nation's air pollution problem will cease to exist as we know it. Perhaps there will be a revolution in urban air quality and some of us will live to enjoy it. Some would say this is an overly optimistic and naive outlook.

What Am I Breathing and What Does It Do to Me?

Okay, hope you enjoyed that good news, because this next section can be a bit frightening. The fact remains that cyclists are still subjected to dangerously high doses of a multitude of poisons, despite the improvements in air quality. Here are the main pollutants we should be concerned about.

CARBON MONOXIDE. Carbon Monoxide (CO) is a poisonous product of the imperfect, incomplete combustion of gasoline and other hydrocarbon fuels. (During complete combustion, the carbon in the fuel is fully oxidized into carbon dioxide [CO_2], a nontoxic gas.) Back in the day, CO was the most obviously toxic of all the tailpipe pollutants, and the first to catch the world's attention, because of its uncanny ability to knock folks out and put them to sleep—forever. Even with the improvements in engine technology and fuel composition, and the addition of catalytic converters, CO gas still reaches dangerous concentrations in American cities on a regular basis.

Breathing CO reduces the flow of oxygen in the bloodstream. The national standard for CO dictates a maximum allowable concentration of 9 parts-per-million over an eight-hour period (the U.S. National Ambient Air Quality Standard—NAAQS), but readings have been taken among groups of idling cars at about 1,000 parts-per-million![6] If you were to hang out for too long in that much CO, you would pass out and die. Luckily, such concentrations do not last for long, as cars eventually move, the air mixes up in the breeze, et cetera.

CO concentrations vary wildly and depend on many factors, so it's difficult to say for sure what kind of dose urban cyclists receive in their day-to-day travels. That said, an average of 10–20 parts-per-million is probably a safe estimate of a cyclist's exposure during a spin through the typical large American city, with the occasional spike far in excess of those levels.[7] At these concentrations, cyclists often notice the more subtle effects of CO, in the form of headaches, light-headedness, and general blah. Although CO is odorless and tasteless, it comes as a package deal with other ingredients of exhaust that you can detect, so if you're smelling that nearby traffic jam, you're also sucking down a good dose of CO.

HYDROCARBONS. Hydrocarbons are molecules made of hydrogen and carbon atoms in various combinations. The volatile hydrocarbons in gasoline are what explode and make engines turn. Unfortunately, because there is no such thing as perfect combustion, a portion of these hydrocarbons remain unburned and come out in the exhaust. A large portion of the hydrocarbon molecules in fuel don't even make it that far, evaporating into the air from engine compartments and gas tanks. This is a very bad thing for cyclists, because hydrocarbons cause cancer. Perhaps the most notorious of these hydrocarbon molecules is benzene, which has been found to increase cancer risk at very low levels of ingestion. Benzene constitutes about 2 percent of American gasoline.[8]

Hydrocarbons cause additional problems by combining with nitrogen oxides (NO_x) in sunlight to produce ozone (O_3), another harmful irritant.

NITROGEN OXIDES. In the combustion chamber of an engine, extremely high temperatures cause oxygen and nitrogen atoms—the main ingredients of pure, lovely air—to form nitrogen oxides (NO_x). The most notorious of the nitrogen oxides in exhaust is nitrogen dioxide (NO_2). The complete catalog of effects of NO_2 on individuals has not been pinned down, but scientists have shown that breathing lots of it can damage one's immune system and cause injury to the lungs. Normal exposure levels in urban areas could decrease lung function and exacerbate such existing problems as asthma and bronchitis.[9] Nitrogen dioxide is a key ingredient in acid rain, and teams up with hydrocarbons in sunlight to form "photochemical oxidants" such as ozone.

OZONE. Ozone (O_3) causes a lot of confusion. On the one hand, we're supposed to be worried about the destruction of the ozone layer, because it protects us from the harmful rays of the sun. On the other hand, we're told that ozone is a harmful pollutant and an indirect product of automobile exhaust. In fact, both are true.

Ozone is the three-atom version of oxygen. It exists naturally in the environment and forms a thin layer high above the earth, where it intercepts ultraviolet radiation. Ozone molecules are also created by a photochemical reaction when nitrogen oxides and hydrocarbons from motor-vehicle exhaust and industrial emissions are cooked in the sunlight. Cyclists should be concerned about this man-made brew because ozone is an oxidant that attacks the body's cells and tissues, especially in the lungs.[10] Inflammation and damage to the immune system have been shown to result from ingestion of ozone. At low levels it makes you cough, wheeze, and ache. It constricts the airways and wrecks lung function. Damage from ozone may be cumulative, progressive, and irreversible, but this has not been proven.[11]

In short, ozone is bad news unless it stays in its place: about 30 miles up in the stratosphere. An expanded awareness of the health effects of O_3 led the U.S. EPA to recommend tightening the standard for this pollutant in 1997 to an eight-hour average of just .08 parts-per-million, down from .12 parts-per-million.[12] The new standard survived a concerted challenge from industry and a long period in legal purgatory, and today most major American metro areas stand in violation of it. Many cities still struggle to meet the older, more lenient standard.

PARTICULATE MATTER. This broad category includes many different types of pollutants, including some of the hydrocarbons listed above, which emerge from tailpipes as solids that float in the air. Black hydrocarbon-filled clouds of diesel exhaust are the most obvious culprit in terms of suspended particulate matter (SPM). But suspended particulates come in many other forms and from many other sources.

Regulators have turned their attention to particulates in the last fifteen years, primarily because of a number of case control studies that have shown a causal relationship between SPM and what the scientists call "morbidity." Simply put, researchers found that people in areas with high levels of SPM die sooner than people in other areas; perhaps even more frightening, they found that more people die on specific high-SPM days. Turns out that particulate pollution has a way of pushing folks with existing conditions, such as heart disease, right over the edge. Not to mention the fact that many of the particles in question are known to be carcinogenic. So if it doesn't get you now, it might get you later.[13]

You may have heard, at some point, someone jabbering on about "PM-10." PM-10 is the favored term for particulates 10 microns in width or smaller. A 10-micron particle is about one-fifth the width of the typical human hair. Such particles float around all day and can be breathed deeply into the lungs, where they are likely to stay. The PM-10 scare gave birth to the PM-2.5 scare. The 2.5-micron-and-under specks appear to be even more sneaky and dangerous.

In addition to exhaust particles, SPM consists of a multitude of other ingredients. Some of the most common of these include pulverized sand and gravel, masonry dust and dirt from construction sites, and, my personal favorite, *tire dust*. A single vehicle tire, as it wears down, can lose several pounds of rubber each year; some of this rubber stays on the streets, but some of the particles are fine enough to become SPM. Allergists have identified tiny black specks of rubber in the mucus coughed up by their patients.[14]

Breathing Strategies for the
Cyclist

As with crashes and traffic accidents, there is no way for the cyclist to completely eliminate the danger of air pollution—it's just part of the game. But we can employ a multitude of strategies that will help *minimize* the risk.

BREATHE THROUGH THE NOSE. Breathing through the nose, rather than the mouth, is the easiest and one of the most effective ways to minimize ingestion of harmful pollution, especially particulates. The human nose has evolved over millions of years to function as a high-tech air filter. When you inhale through the mouth, there is a good chance that unwanted particles will end up buried deep in the lungs, but if a particle is to make it all the way through the nasal passages and into the lungs, it must somehow pass through a gauntlet of defenses to get there. The much smaller size of the nasal airways, first of all, makes it more likely that pollutants will get snagged against the side. The nasal passages are lined by mucus membranes that secrete, of course, mucus (also known as snot in some circles). Nasal mucus moistens inhaled air before it reaches the lungs and also traps unwanted particles in its slimy grip. The other defenses include the obvious and visible nose hairs, but also the equally hardworking *ciliated cells* that lie deeper in the nasal cavity. Each of these cells sprouts what is essentially a microscopic hair made of protoplasm. The trapped particles, caught in the pleasantly named "mucus blanket," are constantly swept out of the airways by the movements of the *cilia* and usually end up in the stomach, or back in the street, perhaps after a farmer blow.[15]

EASE UP. During strenuous exercise, we obviously consume more air, and we tend to breathe through our mouths in an effort to suck in more oxygen, so consequently our lungs can be exposed to much higher levels of pollution.[16] When the air gets nasty, slow down enough to keep your breathing steady and your mouth closed on the inhale. Slower riding is usually safer riding anyway.

REJECT BAD AIR. Micromanage your breathing. No two puffs of air are created equal. If you are about to pass through a cloud of dust or diesel exhaust, hold your breath for a few seconds. When you catch the unmistakable whiff of hydrocarbons entering your nose, there is no law that says you have to inhale that junk deeply into your lungs. Blow it out! Reject it! With any luck, 10 or 20 meters down the road you will find a relatively crisp, clean volume of air for your breathing pleasure.

CHOOSE A CLEANER ROUTE. Studies using personal dosage-monitoring devices show that pollution concentrations vary quite a bit from place to place within any given area. The distribution, however, is not random, and can be predicted to some extent. The concentration of auto-sourced air pollution is governed largely by a few simple rules: (1) High-traffic areas tend to be about twice as polluted as quiet residential neighbor-hoods. (2) Downtown areas, with streets packed tight into concrete canyons between tall buildings, tend to hold higher concentrations of pol-lution than open areas with the same traffic patterns, because of restricted airflow. By the same token, air in tunnels and parking garages is the most polluted air in the city. (3) Stop-and-go driving produces more emissions than highway driving. Not only do cars on the highways spew less exhaust, their speed churns the air and thus disperses toxins. That's not to say you should be out riding on the highway—it's probably illegal any-way—but you might want to think about avoiding the lurchy, stop-and-go routes. (4) Finally, on a smaller scale, there is more pollution hanging around in the middle of the street than off to the sides; the farther away from the cars, the cleaner it gets. Air around an off-street bike path will be cleaner than air in the street.[17]

Looking at these factors—especially number (1)—you can see that the cleanest routes in terms of air pollution might correspond nicely with the cleanest routes in terms of traffic. What luck! Once again, a little patience goes a long way. Charting a route through residential areas, away from busy arterial streets, can save you a lot of headaches (literally), although it might cost you some time.

AVOID RUSH HOUR. Schedules often demand that the cyclist be right out there in the mix with the twice-daily flood of auto commuters. If you have the luxury of doing so, ride during off-peak hours and significantly reduce your exposure to air pollution.

AVOID RIDING ON HIGH POLLUTION DAYS. Most major cities have pro-grams that notify residents about high pollution days, usually in the local paper or on the cheesy morning faux-news program. Forget about all that. Your nose and eyes are probably better detectors than the remote meters set up by your local health department (which may have placed their monitoring stations well outside the high-traffic areas to avoid viola-tions of the federal clean air standards, as such violations may cost your city precious millions of federal highway dollars under the Clean Air Act). If you walk outside in the morning and immediately smell the pol-lution, or see it hanging in the trees like fog, it's probably a good day to use the public transportation system if it's available.

High pollution days take on a whole new meaning in areas that are prone to *temperature inversions,* such as Los Angeles and Denver. A temperature inversion is a topsy-turvy meteorological phenomenon during which cold air becomes trapped beneath a layer of warm air. An inversion will trap pollution below the warm layer as surely as if a Plexiglas dome had been placed over the city. Avoid riding on such days, if possible.

USE A MASK. Wearing a mask with a carbon filter will keep the particulates and ozone out of your body, although it does nothing to stop carbon monoxide, the density of which is very similar to air itself. Aside from the material benefits, some of these masks give a very eerie postapocalyptic look to the wearer, an effect that seems to shake a lot of people out of their comfort zone. Such masks make drivers, at least for a second or two, think about the poisons they're producing. Making a point through fashion—this fits in nicely with the passive-aggressive tendencies of many cyclists.

Does Air Pollution Cancel the Health
Benefit of Cycling?

Who knows? Opinions are divided. The truth is that nobody knows for sure. It's a rather complex issue when you try to sort through the science.

The concern is that cyclists—by virtue of their being out in the air and at times breathing more of it, more deeply, than other folks do—might be doing themselves undue harm. On the other hand, cyclists are able to escape many traffic jams and other high-pollution situations in which drivers have no choice but to sit and stew. And cyclists, thanks to the physiological effects of exercise, tend to be healthier than average people and their immune systems tend to be more robust. What pollution they do breathe in may be more effectively neutralized. (So, a better question might be: Do the health benefits of cycling cancel the negative effects of air pollution?)

You don't have to travel too far out on a limb to claim that cycling is plenty healthy, *given the alternatives*. Let's be realistic—if you're not going to ride your bike what *are* you going to do? Never leave the house? Ride the bus? Walk? Or sit on your bum in a car, breathing slightly less of the same bad air, while suffering at stoplights, in traffic jams, dying of frustration and stress? *Come on!* Any real cyclist already knows the answer to these questions.

Given the availability of the defensive strategies mentioned above, the choice is clear. Ride your bike and be happy.

punctures and flat tires

Flat Repair
Equipment

Flats are common enough that cyclists, to achieve any semblance of self-sufficiency, must be able to repair them anywhere they occur in a reasonable amount of time. This means that all the necessary tools—a pump, patch kit, and two tire levers—must be carried on every significant ride. Consider this equipment part of the bicycle, and take it wherever the bike goes. Some experienced riders would consider an extra inner tube and cab fare to be included on the essentials list.

Having experienced a host of problems with self-adhesive, or "stick-on," patches, I recommend using the traditional-style patch kit with glue. These kits work wonders when the directions are followed. Make sure your pump matches the style of valve stem on your bicycle (*Presta* valve stems are the thin type with the locking pin, and *Schrader* valves are the old-school type, like those on car tires). Many pump heads can be set up to fit either type of valve stem.

Fixing Flats:
A Primer

Like sands through the hourglass, so are the flats of the cyclist. It may be glass, or a thorn, or some random piece of metal that does the deed. It may be a pinch flat, or the dreaded blowout. Chances are you will collect several of each type of flat as time marches on. These occurrences should not send you into fits of frustration, nor should they send you into the bike shop for assistance. Flats should not even raise your eyebrow with the slightest hint of surprise. The inconvenience of dealing with them is easily overcome by knowledge and experience. Fixing flats is no big deal.

Readers with a good working knowledge of flat repair can skip this next section. For the rest of you, here is an opinionated how-to in fourteen steps:

1. Remove the wheel from the frame. (If you aren't completely proficient in this operation, become so by removing and reinstalling the wheels until you get it down cold. The rear wheel can be quite tricky to remove and install, but with practice it becomes a piece of cake. Many of the fork dropouts on late-model bikes have "safety tabs," a ridiculous product of our lawsuit culture, which undermines the concept of quick-release wheels.)

2. Inspect the outer surface of the tire to see if you can locate the puncture. There may be a visible thorn or shard of glass sticking out, or an audible hiss of escaping air. If you can locate the point of puncture before actually removing the tube, this will make your job a little easier (because it will give you advance knowledge of where the hole is and what may have created it). If not, no worries.

3. If the tube is still holding some air, release the air by using the valve.

4. Use the tire levers to pry the tire off the rim. (This step takes a little bit of practice, but it's not rocket science. The best way to learn is to try it. With the first lever, gingerly crowbar one side of the tire out of the rim in one spot, and hook the back end of the lever around a spoke to hold it in place. Then use the second lever, a few inches away

from the first, to continue prying one side of the tire off the rim, section by section, all the way around. Be careful not to "pinch" the tube, which would create an additional hole.)

5. Pull the tube out of the tire, but leave the valve poking through the rim. There is no reason to completely remove the tube unless the puncture happens to be right above the valve stem, or you can't locate the hole and need to submerge the tube (see Step 7 below).

6. Very carefully, *run your fingers all the way around the inside of the tire to find any objects poking through it.* What you are looking for is probably very small, and very sharp. It's quite possible that there will be nothing at all to find, or there may be several offenders, so be thorough. Remove the objects from the tire and note their location, which will help you find the hole(s) in the tube. At this point, become an active learner. Observe the perpetrator. What is it? Where did it come from? How did you pick it up and how can you avoid it in the future? Refrain from tossing the little beast, whatever it is, back into the street.

7. Use the pump to put about fifteen or twenty pumps of air in the tube. This should give the tube enough air pressure to cause the puncture to reveal its exact location with a hiss. If pumping up the tube fails to give the tube any shape, the hole is quite large—probably caused by a blowout or a pinch flat–type event (see Pinch Flats, on page 213). If you still can't find any hole after doing this, remove the tube entirely, submerge it in water while inflated, one section at a time, and look for telltale bubbles. Obviously, this baptism method might be problematic while out on a ride. The problem of mystery punctures is a great reason to carry an extra tube.

8. Once the puncture is located, use the *sandpaper* in the patch kit to rough up an area of about 1½ inches in diameter around the hole. This removes the shiny substance that coats the tube. This is residue of a chemical that keeps the tube from sticking to the mold during the production process, and, if left unmolested, this substance will also prevent any patch from sticking well.

9. Using the glue in the patch kit, spread a thin layer of glue around the puncture point, enough so the area covered by glue will be easily bigger than the area of the patch.

10. *Let the glue dry,* long enough that it no longer feels tacky to the touch. This usually takes a few minutes.

11. Peel the patch away from the foil backing and press it over the hole. Press hard all over the patch to make it stick. There should be no bubbles or loose edges. It is not necessary to remove the clear plastic. Repeat Steps 8 through 11 for any additional holes in the tube.

12. Stuff the tube back into the tire—some folks like to add a few pumps of air to the tube to give it some shape prior to this—and work the tire onto the rim with your thumbs. More so than tire removal, reinstallation can seem difficult, especially if the tire is quite stiff. Avoid using tire levers to install a tire. If the last bit of tire refuses to go on the rim, pump up the tube a bit, then let the air out completely and try again.

13. Pump the tire back up to the desired pressure. Make sure it's properly seated, with no sections of tube caught between the tire bead and the rim (see Blowouts, on page 214). Be careful with your pumping action if you are using Presta valve stems, because vigorous, uncivilized pumping will break the valve or tear it away from the tube at the base of the stem.* Don't seriously tighten the bolt that holds the Presta valve where it comes out of the rim until you're done pumping.

14. Does the tire feel like it's holding air? Put the wheel back on the bike.

Whatever you do, don't skip Step 6, 8, or 10. These steps are absolutely crucial to a successful flat repair, but few cyclists give them the respect they deserve.

It's a good strategy to carry a spare tube (or two) while cycling, especially in thorn-prone areas (see Tribulus Terrestris, on page 208). That way you can just slap the new tube in and save a lot of time. Fix the bad tube later, and make that your spare tube. If you employ this strategy, don't forget Step 6!

◆ ◆ ◆

A note on RIM STRIP: "Rim strip" is the piece of rubber, plastic, or cloth that covers the inside of the rim. Its purpose is to protect the inflated tube

---

* Any tearing of the stem from the tube is very difficult to repair and effectively ruins the tube. However, if the Presta valve stem's pin is broken off, the tire can still be ridden as long as there is good air pressure already in the tube. The air pressure in the tire will hold the valve closed, but you won't be able to add air once the valve pin is broken. Replace the tube as soon as possible.

from the sharp edges of eyelets and spoke nipples on the inside of the rim. The cloth strips are best because they stay in place and last. The rubber strips can move and expose the edges they're meant to cover, and plastic strips fall apart. Here's a hint: Use cloth tape. Usually, rim strip is a no-brainer and demands very little, if any, attention. But if you find yourself suffering multiple flats on the underside of tubes, suspect a disintegrating or improperly seated rim strip.

Broken
Glass

Nationwide, broken glass is the most time-honored and feared perpetrator of punctures for cyclists. It's evil powers, however, are much overrated.

There are two general types of broken glass to be found in American cities: *tempered glass,* and what I will call *bottle glass*. Tempered glass is hardened by forced cooling during the manufacturing process. The faster than normal cooling compresses the surface of the glass, leaving it much more resistant to breaking than nontempered glass. This kind of glass is used in the rear and side windows of motor vehicles.* When fractured, a car window made of tempered glass collapses into a pile of soft-edged pebbles. The pieces usually aren't sharp and rarely puncture bicycle tires. Feel free to ignore it. Bottle glass (and the glass from automobile side mirrors) is another matter entirely. It shatters into jagged pieces, any one of which has the potential of causing a flat.

On the street, it's possible to distinguish broken bottle glass from broken tempered glass, even while riding. Along with the obvious difference in appearance, location can provide additional clues. Tempered glass is generally confined to streets and parking lots, and, due to car break-ins, is often found in piles in the gutter or just outside the parking lane on narrow streets. Bottle glass, on the other hand, is found everywhere. If there's

---

* Windshields are made differently, with a thin sheet of plastic sandwiched between two panes of tempered glass. This "laminated glass" is not supposed to shatter at all.

glass on a bike path or anywhere else that is off-limits to motor traffic, it's almost always bottle glass. Bottle glass is occasionally green or dark brown, a dead giveaway, or has beer-related writing on it, also a dead giveaway.

Avoid the bottle glass if you can. Steer around it if no other vehicles are present, but please keep your priorities straight—flats are the least of your worries as a cyclist. Pick a new route rather than ride over batches of bottle glass each day.

Tire
Wiping

The consequences of rolling directly across a pile of bottle glass are somewhat less than dire. No truly scientific analysis has ever been completed on this, but it seems that the rate of flats versus the total number of nasty bottle glass fields encountered is somewhere around 1 in 20 for lightweight road-racing tires. (Heavy riders on thin rubber will pick up slightly more glass flats than light riders on thin rubber, and cyclists using knobby mountain tires don't have to worry that much about glass flats at all.)

Some cyclists believe they can further reduce this rate by wiping their tires after inadvertently crunching through a patch of glass. With the bike still rolling, these cyclists typically reach down and hold one gloved hand against each tire for a few revolutions, hoping to remove any bits of glass that may be stuck there.

There are a few problems with this whole tire-wiping enterprise. For one thing, it can be hazardous. Especially for beginners, attempting the act can lead to supreme disaster. Until an unconscious knowledge of the exact position of the tires is gained, the tire wiper might accidentally reach into the spokes of a revolving wheel, which could result in a hand injury and, most likely, an awkward fall from the bike. A careless tire wiper could also get a finger caught between the frame and the tire. Furthermore, removing one hand from the bars is generally bad policy, especially when combined with the leaning forward and reaching involved in the tire-wiping action. It would be very ugly to hit a massive pothole at the same moment you're reaching forward to wipe the front tire.

An alternative, perhaps superior, method is to use the feet rather than the hands. Unless you are worried about keeping your shoes in pristine condition, move one shoe against the rear section of the front tire, down low, not up next to the frame where it could get jammed between the frame and the tire with disastrous results; then swing your foot back and place it against the rear tire, either on the top, or on the lower-front section, beneath the chain. Due to the position of the crankset and chain, the left shoe is preferred. Use the top or the side of the shoe rather than the sole. The shoe method has one major safety advantage over the glove method in that it allows the rider to keep both hands on the handlebars. But the danger of putting a body part into the spokes is still there.

Some cyclists pull over and stop to wipe their tires, spinning the wheels by hand. This frequent stopping defeats the ultimate purpose, which is, of course, to avoid stopping. Learn to wipe the tires safely while rolling, or skip it entirely.

Actually, the earth will continue to rotate on its axis should you decide to forget about tire wiping altogether. There are eminent figures in the cycling world who claim tire wiping is a complete waste of time. The essence of their argument is that glass shards enter the tire rubber to near-maximum depth upon first contact, and the ends protruding from the tire are sheared off within the first few tire revolutions, long before the tire wiper can reach them. Jobst Brandt, author of *The Bicycle Wheel*, explains: "Before you can get to wipe the tire, it has made about ten revolutions. If [the glass] isn't thoroughly embedded by then it won't be."[1] Any faith in tire wiping as a preventative measure, the skeptics claim, comes from assumptions that cannot be verified.

The anti–tire wipers have a point there—it's true that the evidence in favor of tire wiping is entirely circumstantial. But the circumstantial evidence is hard to ignore: (1) Rarely does an encounter with broken glass on the street lead immediately and directly to a puncture. And yet, many cyclists can recall running over a patch of broken glass, then, hours or even days later, having to deal with a sudden, mysterious, glass-caused flat. This would seem to indicate that small glass shards stick in, or on, the tire for a time before finding their way into the tube. The skeptics concede this point but insist that embedded shards could not be removed with a glove or shoe. (2) When the streets are wet, you may notice debris sticks more readily to your tires. If the wipers are correct in their assumptions, more glass flats will occur during and after wet conditions, and indeed, this seems to be the case. This phenomenon might also be explained by the water's softening of the rubber, however. (3) Perhaps the strongest bit of circumstantial evidence in favor of tire wiping is that many tire wipers report having actually felt the forceful dislodgement of small pieces of glass from smooth road tires while using both the glove and the shoe methods.

The whole issue of glass flats is mired in uncertainty and pseudoscience. Despite the legions of cyclists who compulsively employ this method at the first sight of broken glass, it's quite possible that tire wiping amounts to little more than superstition. In any case, flat prevention is only a matter of convenience—when the principle of *safety first* is applied, the inherently dangerous practice of tire wiping must fall way down the list of priorities, or off the list entirely.

Glassphalt

Don't be afraid. It's only "glassphalt."

"Glassphalt" paving material can cause hopeless glassophobes to suffer flashbacks and convulsions. This special asphalt sparkles in a way that mimics very closely the appearance of a biblical amount of glass shards scattered on the road. If it looks like crushed glass, well, that's because it *is* crushed glass. "Glassphalt" incorporates a small percentage of recycled glass, called *cullet,* into the aggregate mix.

Decades ago, the use of "glassphalt" was driven by economics. There were so many sources of cullet around that it was considered a useless waste product. It was being given away, and those responsible for paving and resurfacing streets had the bright idea that it could be used in the road mix as a way to cut expenses. Today, however, with the widespread use of plastic bottles and the general decrease in sources of glass, asphalt containing crushed glass costs more than regular asphalt. Even with the added expense, it is still used occasionally as it significantly increases the durability of the road surface.[2]

Like some sort of cruel prank, the sparkly bits of embedded glass disappear as you ride toward them, while still more come into view beyond, flashing like mad. Even knowing that "glassphalt" won't cause flat tires, it's hard not to experience a tiny panic attack while gazing upon what appears to be a vast sea of broken glass.

Tribulus
Terrestris

Puncture Vine, Goathead, Sandbur, African Devil Weed . . . call it what you want, it doesn't matter. The thorny seeds produced by *tribulus terrestris,* as it is known in the science books, are the number one cause of punctures for urban cyclists in some cities in the western United States. Thorns in the west, rust in the east.

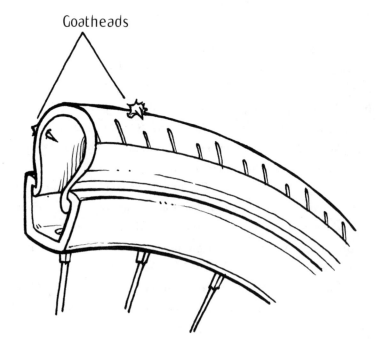

Goatheads

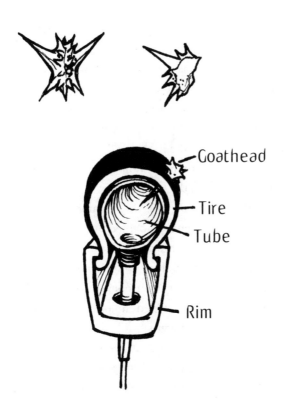

Goathead

Tire

Tube

Rim

Tribulus terrestris forms a mat along the ground, with tough vines that sprout very small, dark green leaves and nice-looking little yellow flowers, in addition to the spiked seeds that start out green and soft but mature into thorns as solid as hardwood. The fruit is the pointy part of this plant, not the stems (such as a rose bush), or the leaves (such as thistle). The mat formed by one *tribulus* plant, from a single tap root, can easily grow 6 feet across, and it can produce several thousand seeds. *Tribulus* seeds fall away from the plant and some of the lucky ones go off to see the world.[3]

Strangely enough, hopeful weightlifting-type guys have been buying supplements said to contain extracts of the *tribulus terrestris* weed, which is supposed to give them bigger muscles and more serious erections, you know, the usual. To just about anyone else, *tribulus* is considered to be a noxious weed, an invasive species, and a major source of frustration. Accidentally introduced with a load of Mediterranean livestock some time in the 1800s, low-maintenance *tribulus* is now fully living the American Dream. It thrives in so-called areas of disturbance, the sandy, infertile, chemical-soaked soils where other plants fail. That's why it loves cities so much—a city can be described as a vast area of disturbance, and cities are full of rolling rubber, which is *tribulus*'s best friend.

In the early years of the automobile, tires were essentially the same on cars and bicycles, so goathead thorns frequently stranded motorists along with cyclists. In California, where the Mediterranean-like climate is particularly friendly to *tribulus,* the highway department used to douse the roadsides with diesel fuel hoping to vanquish the evil weed, to no avail. Making very thick tires was the only answer.[4] Ironically, *tribulus* was the mortal enemy of the rubber car tire, yet the rubber tire was the best thing ever to happen to *tribulus*. Having adapted over millions of years to stick in the fur and paws of passing beasts, the patient *tribulus* plant was gifted one of the greatest windfalls in all of evolutionary history with the near-simultaneous inventions of the rubber pneumatic tire and the automobile. Together, these technologies provided the perfect mechanism to transport *tribulus*'s seeds across the continents.

Once confined only to the dry southwestern states, *tribulus* has now been found in all states except Massachusetts, New Hampshire, Vermont, and Maine. We can only assume that New England is next on its list. The various agencies responsible for controlling *tribulus* have failed primarily because of the remarkable properties of the thorns. Not only do goathead seeds hitch rides cross-country and around the world, they can lie dormant in the ground for many years, perhaps decades, before sprouting—spiky little time bombs. Back in the 1960s, the government recognized, for a moment, the futility of dumping chemicals on Puncture Vine and imported *tribulus*-eating weevils into the States. The success of this plan has obviously been limited, although the weevils seem to be enjoying their new home.

Tribulus terrestris is the most well-known member of the Caltrop family *(Zygophyllaceae)*. In medieval warfare, a caltrop was a small iron device composed of four spikes. It was designed in such a way that it could be tossed on the ground in front of advancing cavalry and, no matter how it landed, one of the spikes would always be sticking up.

Tribulus thorns work much the same way. With one impaler always pointed skyward, those little caltrops cut right into your rubber, effortlessly. Tubes advertised as "thorn-resistant" should be looked upon with a healthy degree of skepticism, as should tubes that are supposed to patch themselves with green goo. The thick knobs of mountain-bike tires, by simple virtue of their being thicker than the thorns themselves, can keep the thorns from making contact with the inner tube. But since the knobs cover only part of the mountain-bike tire, protection is incomplete. Some brands of touring tires are said to be thick enough to foil thorns, and some cyclists report good results from protective plastic strips, but these exact a significant toll in increased weight and rolling resistance.

Technology probably won't save you from thorns, but a little bit of common sense might. The most effective strategy for avoiding thorn flats involves using the thorn's own frightening power against it—thorn jujitsu. Since the thorns are collected by any tire or soft-soled shoe that presses down on them, simply ride where other bicycles, cars, or pedestrians have gone before. Ride near the center of bike paths, and away from debris fields that collect in the least-used areas of streets, when possible. If you find yourself cruising through a vacant lot or across some random dirt patch, find the most established path and don't stray from it.

It's time we started giving this plant the respect it deserves after a century of royally kicking our ass. Hail *tribulus!* We surrender! Those living and cycling in the thorn zone should get to know the plant that produces the thorns. Learn not only what *tribulus terrestris* looks like, but also where and when it likes to grow. Where it now lives, it's there to stay. Where it doesn't live, it's probably on its way.

A Thorny
Dilemma

Let's say you look down at a stoplight and notice a nice-looking goathead thorn stuck in your front tire. Despite your consistent practice of thorn jujitsu, you've been stung. This presents a dilemma—to pluck or not to pluck. Eyeing the disposition of the goathead, you ask yourself a tough question: Has that damn thorn pierced the tube? Probably, but maybe not.

There is the small chance that the thorn is askew and somehow failed to penetrate the inner tube. There is also the nagging possibility that the thorn has yet to puncture but will do so if it is not removed. You reach down and press on the tire with your thumb. Seems full enough, but that still doesn't answer your question. If the thorn has already pierced the tube, the leak of air caused by the perforation could be quite slow or non-existent—thorns, you see, have a way of nicely plugging their own holes. In such a case, pulling the thorn out would only open the hole and allow the tube to deflate rapidly.

Do you feel lucky? It takes a confident and experienced cyclist to roll the dice and pluck away, happily and fearlessly, knowing that deft tube-patching skills will handle whatever consequences await. Those more fearful of having to fix a flat on-site will want to leave the thorn in the tire for as long as possible, where it serves as the perfect custom-sized plug for any hole it makes.

These painful dilemmas become more urgent when the cyclist's tire is stuck with multiple thorns, a demoralizing but fairly common occurrence in thorn country. Two extra tubes, one for each wheel, provide some peace of mind when nothing else will.

Random
Sharpies

Goatheads and bottle glass can be blamed for the vast majority of cyclists' punctures, but certainly not all of them. A small percentage of flat tires will be caused by a rogue's gallery of random debris. Among this group, nails, screws, and tacks of various kinds form the most common family of objects: the construction-grade fasteners. There are also staples, pop tops, pins, campaign buttons, busted CD covers and other shards of plastic, dress shoe taps, pieces of wire, broken pencils, lawless twigs, valve cores, and an endless variety of unidentifiable machine parts lurking on the streets, waiting for unlucky cyclists to roll over them at just the right angle.* It is quite useless to prepare for random encounters with random objects, aside from learning well how to patch a tube.

The punctures caused by this wreckage are generally violent and obvious and result in a rapid loss of air from the tube. In the case of nails and other tough, elongated pieces, the foreign object tends to penetrate all the way to the rim, leaving two big holes in the tube. Punctures of this sort can usually be patched in the normal way, provided there are enough patches left in the kit. If the object punches a hole in the tire casing that is large enough that the tube balloons out of the hole when inflated, the tire itself will have to be patched (see Blowouts, on page 214).

An interesting aspect of random object punctures is that these punctures almost always occur in the rear tire rather than the front. With a little thought, we can guess why. Most of these objects are lying flat on the street and are harmless in their sleeping position. But when a tire rolls over an object like a nail or shard of plastic, the object can snap to attention, popping up off the ground. With two tires rolling over the object in quick succession, the front tire causes the object to stand up straight, and the rear tire receives the brunt of the attack.

Pinch
Flats

In general, pinch flats occur when a tire is underinflated for the conditions at hand. This type of flat is often associated with mountain biking on rocky trails, but it can occur in the urban setting. Skinny tires are especially vulnerable to pinch flats when striking curbs, railroad tracks, potholes, or rocks in the road. Because they are associated with underinflation, pinch flats are symptomatic of a prior undetected slow leak, or simple negligence on the part of the cyclist. The occurrence of pinch flats on well-inflated tires calls into question the handling skills of the cyclist—fast, furious, and clumsy.

---

* All of these items have been stuck in the author's tires at one time or another.

An experienced rider can feel a pinch flat at the exact moment it occurs. The tire "bottoms out" as it strikes an obstacle, and the wheel's rim impacts solidly with a sickening *clunk*. This impact causes the inner tube to be pinched harshly in the tire casing as it comes together. Pinches like this cause a small but significant slit to open in the tube, or two matching slits arrayed in the familiar double-fanged snakebite pattern—which is why pinch flats are often referred to as "snakebites." When patching a pinch flat, always search for a second hole, usually about 1 centimeter apart from and parallel to the first. But don't stop there. If the cause of the underinflation leading to the pinch flat is a mystery, then search for a *third* hole, and carefully grope the inside of the tire for the cause of a possible slow leak.

Pinch flats can be easily prevented by maintaining proper tire pressure (very firm to the thumb test) and by riding in a less than reckless manner. Keep your eyes up and watch for objects and potholes in the road. Latex tubes, lighter and more expensive inner tubes favored by racers and other performance mongers, are less vulnerable to pinch flats when properly inflated. These tubes don't hold air nearly as well as regular butyl tubes do, however, so users of latex tubes often suffer from chronic tire hypo-inflation and, ironically, pinch flats.

Blowouts

The frightening term "blowout" can be used to describe a few different types of events. Most commonly, when a cyclist claims to have had a blowout, it means that the tube has exploded due to improper installation of the tire. Sometimes, when a tire is worked onto a rim, a section of the tube is stuck between the rim and the tire bead. The faulty installation may go undetected even after the tire is pumped up hard. The unsuspecting cyclist goes out to ride, the tube steadily works its way to freedom, then *blam!* With nothing holding it back, a section of the tube explodes (contrary to popular belief, a tube can't explode spontaneously inside the tire). If the blowout occurs while the cyclist is cornering fast, there could be painful consequences. Blowouts like this can also occur when the bike is just sitting there in your house, which can cause heart attacks. *Blam!*

To prevent this most-common form of blowout, simply exercise some care when installing a tire. Make sure the tire is seated properly, with no sections of tube visible. As a way of insuring good tire positioning, some like to inflate, deflate, then re-inflate the tube after they install a tire, but this is really not necessary.

Another form of blowout occurs at the local gas station, when the recreational cyclist attaches the air compressor built for automobile tires to the Schrader valve on his or her bicycle. Damn, that thing fills up fast, don't it? *Blam!* Remember, if you are tempted to do this, that the gas station compressor is designed to fill tires with vastly more volume than bicycle tires hold. The same source that requires a minute or two to fill a car tire could blow out your bike tire in about fifteen seconds.

A third type of blowout event is associated with excessive tire wear. And I'm talkin' *excessive*. When a tire—a rear tire, let's face it—is so absolutely finished that its rubber is completely gone, and even the inner casing is totally worn away in spots, there is nothing left between the inner tube and the road. The tube pokes out of the opening, grinds onto the road surface, and *blam!* (Actually, this sort of blowout sounds more like a *pifft!* than a *blam!*) Obviously, flats of this sort can be forestalled by replacing the bad tire. If gross tire wear looks likely to cause a flat in the immediate future—say, while you're out on a ride—switch the front tire to the back and you will probably make it home, or to the nearest bike shop. If the tube has already popped—*pifft!*—you must *boot* the tire in addition to patching the tube, or the tube will flat repeatedly. Ideally, use a small piece of rubber or denim and fit it on the inside of the tire to cover the worn-out spot. Some cyclists claim success using folded-up dollar bills for this application, but paper products will not last long. Hey, you could always use duct tape.

chapter seven

equipment

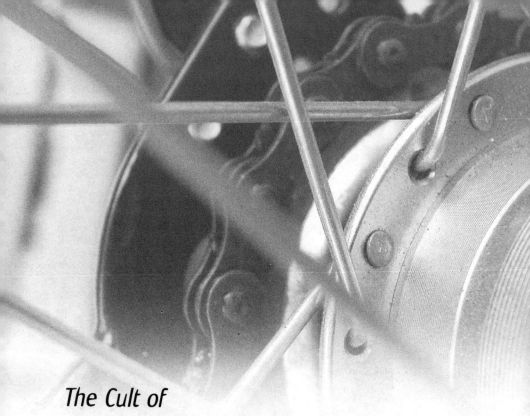

The Cult of
Equipment

It is not really the place of this book to dole out too much detailed advice about equipment, clothing, maintenance—these sorts of things. Plenty of books out there already do a fine job with these nuts-and-bolts issues of cycling, of which there are many.[1] If there is one point that consistently gets lost in the shuffle and should be reasserted here, it's that very little special equipment is required for most trips by bike in the city. To any new cyclists out there: Don't think you have to acquire hundreds of dollars worth of gadgets and flashy clothing items before you can live the dream.

In addition to the bike, it is recommended that the rider obtain a helmet (of which the cheap models protect just as well as the fancy ones),[2] gloves, pump, patch kit, and tire levers to start out. Maybe a water bottle. Basically just a bike and the tools to fix a flat. You can wear regular clothing, for the most part. Many a happy mile has been ridden in tennis shoes.

Soon you might decide to try out special pedals and shoes, padded shorts, and on like that, and the fat will get burned off of your bank account right quick. Or you may just decide that the add-ons are not helpful for your needs, in which case you will save quite a bit of money. However, you will miss the reassuring feeling that comes from joining a cult, which, to many cyclists, is actually their favorite part of the whole bicycle experience.

It is important to recognize that bicycle equipment choice is often based on personal superstition and arbitrary preferences. People hold zealous views about bikes and bike parts they've never seen. Many cyclists are convinced their Way is the best, even though they have never tried any other. Their Way, whatever it is, works for them year after year, and they like it, so maybe some mental gymnastics are effected to reassure the fragile self that this Way is the only true Way. Cyclists become quite testy about their equipment choices. Criticizing the equipment choices of another rider can be as personal as calling them out on religious or family issues.

In fact, many very different Ways will work. A mind-boggling number of equipment choice combinations are possible. There are many different paths to paradise. But there are also some dead ends.

In general, the cyclist buying equipment gets what he or she pays for and should look with a cynical eye at ridiculously cheap equipment. Cheap parts generally don't work as well or last as long as the expensive stuff. As the saying goes, choose any two: light, strong, cheap. There's a lot of truth in that. However, just because something is ungodly expensive doesn't mean it's important, or well-made, or a good idea to buy it. Faddish parts have been an annoying problem in the bike industry from the beginning. The latest thing that everybody must have, forgotten three years later. Cyclists have only themselves to blame for this, having swallowed hook, line, and, sinker many blatant gimmicks over the years. Many of us have had experiences with such parts that we're still trying to forget.

At this late date, there's almost no fancy idea that hasn't been conceived, fooled around with, and discarded. There is very little uncharted territory in bicycle technology. The most significant improvements of the past one hundred years have been materials related. New carbon frames, for instance, show much promise in terms of weight and strength. Especially in the past few decades, new materials and alloys have helped bikes become lighter and stronger—nicer—than ever before. But bikes are

Equipment

still bikes. Most contemporary cyclists will never own a bike as nice as Major Taylor's ride in 1900, an eighteen-pound rocket. No doubt if steel was discovered tomorrow, it would be touted as the "greatest thing since carbon," or some such BS.

There have been some improvements in bicycle components, but few radical ones. An example of a very nice, and fairly recent, improvement in componentry is the incorporation of the shifters into the brake levers on road bikes. The mechanism allows the rider to keep both hands on the bars—on the brake levers, no less—while shifting and to shift easily while standing out of the saddle. This innovation is an important safety enhancement for city riders on road bikes. Another improvement enjoyed by everyday cyclists is the mountain-bike clipless pedal (not to mention the mountain bike itself). Wearing mountain-bike shoes in the city allows the rider to enjoy the power transfer and control of clipless without having to click around and waddle like a duck when off the bike. Don't be afraid to throw some freedom-enhancing MTB pedals on your road bike. While these and other pieces of equipment improve the cyclist's overall experience, they should not be labeled as necessities.

The sad fact is that some of the components that appear on today's new bikes are there only due to rather irrational market forces. What the consumers want, the consumers get. Their preferences are usually not based on experience. The beginners, for instance, decide quite naturally that they want shocks on their bikes, even if they never want to ride an inch of dirt. So now it has become somewhat difficult to find a solid, cheap bike that doesn't have some toy version of a suspension fork on it. Everybody suffers, even those who think they're getting what they want, although they don't know it.

Considering that the bike industry literally invented the concept of planned obsolescence,[3] it is surprising how much punishment the higher-end components can withstand, day after day. But everything man-made wears out eventually, except maybe war. Your bike parts will wear out after a while and you will need some more. At which point your local shop will be more than happy to suck every last dollar out of your wallet.

When choosing equipment, watch out for components that are designed specifically for racing unless that is what you plan to do with them. If something is made as light as possible it may not stand up to the rigors of everyday riding. Beware of titanium bolts, for instance, as they are known to snap. Remember that when a pro racer's bike fails, a fresh one appears as if dropped from the clouds by the hand of God. Sure would be nice if all cyclists could enjoy such fancy service.

When choosing bikes and equipment, know that what everybody else rides or what everybody else does will probably not be the best guideline for you personally. Beware the sales associate at the bike shop who informs you of things you "need." Just get out and ride, and you will find out soon enough what you need and what you don't.

Bike
Choice

Which type of bicycle you choose to ride depends on convenience, style, personal priorities, what routes you ride, and what you need to carry. Three speeds, cruisers, BMX bikes, track bikes, cyclo-cross bikes, mountain bikes, recumbents, and straight road bikes have all seen extensive action in America's cities, and all work well for certain purposes. Each has its own advantages and disadvantages. (Riders should shy away from ultracheap department store bikes, some of which are known to disassemble themselves spontaneously at the most inopportune time.)

Lately the question of bike choice tends to boil down to mountain versus road bikes. Since they hit the mass market a few decades ago, mountain bikes (also known as all-terrain bicycles, or ATBs) have been the most popular choice for buyers, but most people who buy them are beginning cyclists who don't really intend to ride their bikes on actual mountain trails. The popular appeal of the mountain bike has to do with fashion, the more upright position, which attracts many beginners, and the fact that mountain bikes are just plain awesome machines.

Many old-school purists wouldn't dream of putting a mountain bike into regular service on the city streets, but ATBs bring some real advantages over their lighter, faster road cousins for this application. For instance, a real mountain bike enjoys potholes, a real road bike does not. Some of the most brutal drainage grates, those that eat road wheels for breakfast, can be tamed by a mountain bike. Curbs are less threatening to a mountain bike. And, since mountain-bike tires put more rubber between the pavement and the inner tube than road tires, they are less prone to flatting from glass and thorns. Light ATBs with rigid forks work especially well in the city. Knobby tires are unnecessary on pavement until it snows, but big tires can be helpful all year long. Full-suspension downhill bikes, built to jump off cliffs, are overkill for street riding, but many cyclists enjoy them anyway and put them to good use. Many riders like a fully suspended trail bike with slick tires pumped up hard. Whatever works.

In general, road bikes are faster and roll farther with less effort, but they are somewhat more vulnerable to the city's little obstacles. It is natural for riders to gravitate to the road-bike option as their skill level and confidence grows. Road bikes are for pavement, and the city is paved, no denying it. It becomes more obvious with each ride. Get down and bang your head against it if you still don't believe. Most longtime riders who have tested many different types of bicycles in the urban setting come to prefer classic, lightweight road machines.

Bicycle manufacturers have created new marketing categories that mix the trendy look and plush ride of the mountain bike with design features that are specific to the needs of commuters, or beginners who like to cruise slowly on the paved roads and paths. These bikes have been marketed as "hybrids" and "city bikes."*

Most recently, the market has produced something called a "comfort bike," which is usually just a generic bike that caters to the typical beginner's desire to sit up straight on a wide saddle. These bikes are often just inexpensive bikes with flat bars, wide tires, wide, cushy saddles, and sometimes suspension seatposts and forks. Comfort bikes are apparently for folks who want to ride a bike but nevertheless want to make it as much like sitting on the couch as possible.

---

* Some riders would say that the real "hybrid" bike is actually the cyclo-cross bike, a beefy style of modified road-racing bike with cantilever brakes and clearance for wide tires. Invented long ago, these bikes are designed for a punishing form of off-season racing, cyclo-cross, but turn out to be quite suitable for everyday use in the urban setting. Some riders find a good "cross bike" to be the ultimate ride, especially in winter.

An advantage that touring-style bikes, and some of the hybrid/comfort family of bikes, have over their sleeker cousins—they have *eyelets* brazed onto the frame near the dropouts. This feature greatly eases the installation of effective front and rear fenders and racks. Anywhere outside the desert, fenders are extremely important tools for everyday commuters because they keep rainwater and oily road grime from splattering all over the rider's clothing. A rear rack, when combined with panniers or some other container, allows the rider to avoid hauling a backpack, and thus to avoid a sweaty back, theoretically. (The sweaty-back issue becomes part of the backpack-versus-pannier debate. See Messenger Bags, Backpacks, and Panniers, on page 234.)

Other than the rack and fender mounts, possibly, there is little real reason to buy a bike that purports to be specially designed for city riding. In general, don't believe the hype. Road bikes are great, and honest trail bikes work very well in this setting, too, especially with some slight modifications.

Whether one rides a mountain, road, or hybrid model is not all that important. What is most important is that the bike should be reasonably well maintained, so that the bike itself does not cause an accident, and it should fit the rider very well.

Track
Bikes

It's possible to ride a fixed-gear track bike with no hand brakes in a crowded city. Thousands of messengers do it every weekday. A more-reserved and watchful style is used—a much slower style—because the lack of brakes pretty much eliminates the possibility of the full panic stop (see Panic Stops, on page 130). A skilled rider can stop a fixed-gear bike pretty well, but not as quickly as a rider on a freewheel bike with hand brakes. For this reason, many fixed-gear riders slap a front brake on their bike to add significant stopping power, although this cancels some of the cool.

The use of no-brakes, fixed-gear bikes by messengers has a lot to do

Track bikes have changed very little in the past century.

with the peculiarities of the subculture. It used to to set them apart from the civilian population, although that's not so true anymore. Track bikes and fixie-converted road bikes are not necessarily the most practical machines for delivering packages in a crowded city and are limiting in many respects. Like the other bicycle types, however, the fixed-gear track bike has its own set of advantages. Fixed-gear riders report having a more precise control of the machine at low and moderate speeds. The simplicity of the bike is also a major plus: It's cheaper than a regular road bike and can be built up in about twenty minutes. In the winter the track bike has no gears or cables to freeze up, and the bike's "brakes" still work in wet conditions. This is a big deal for messengers, who never get days off for bad weather. A track machine is also usually lighter and quicker than a road-racing bike. An added bonus of the fixed-gear, no-brakes bike is that not many dimestore hooligans know how to ride one. This greatly reduces the chance that a bike thief will successfully pedal away on it. If someone tries, it could provide the afternoon entertainment.

Track bikes are very smooth, elegant machines. Riding one well in city traffic makes you a high priest in the Cult of Equipment.

Bike
Fit

No matter what type of bike you use, the most important consideration will be the fit of the bike. Does it feel comfortable? Does it feel right? Do you like it?

If you purchase a new bicycle and have no idea how it should feel, scope out the local shop's most-experienced and helpful employees and have them set up the bike the way it generally should be before you roll it out the door. Some shops have a special system of fitting bicycles to customers in a meticulous way, but some will just eyeball it and that will probably work out just fine.

Like many things in the bicycle world, there is no real consensus on the subject of bike fit. But there are lots of old cycling coaches, racers, and self-appointed gurus out there who would love to tell you what they think about it. This proselytizing would seem to be a dubious exercise, as bike fit and position eventually boil down to matters of personal preference. Attempts to make a science of bike fit are frustrated by the unique physical proportions of each cyclist.

Even with all the differing opinions and differing body types, there are still a few areas of common ground. When the pedal is in the six-o'clock position and the ball of the foot is over the pedal axle, the leg should be slightly bent. The saddle should be set just below the point where the rider's hips rock back and forth during pedaling. That loosely covers seat height, which is arguably the most important aspect of bike fit, and perhaps the easiest. From this baseline, tweak the remaining adjustables until the bike "disappears" beneath you. The level of the handlebars will probably be an inch or two below the level of the saddle, although some of the aforementioned gurus have been advocating higher handlebar positions. Some riders will want to feel more stretched out, others will prefer to be a little more upright. Saddle fore-aft position is another topic that inspires a lot of heated arguments. The idea is to get the most out of your pedal stroke, but the best position will vary depending on the type of seat and the type of pedaler. You may find that you like to have your saddle pointed ever so slightly downward, that you prefer a shorter top-tube and a longer stem, or any number of personal eccentricities. Most important, the bike should feel very good to you.

There is one possible exception to this if-it-feels-good-do-it rule. A lot of rookies have the seat way too low and the bars way too high, and it somehow feels right to them. They don't like the classic road-cycling position, wishing that their bicycles were chairs instead of bicycles. These position-challenged riders—while they represent a huge chunk of the bicycle-buying public, and so have the manufacturers and retailers down at their feet kissing their socks—have it all wrong. One shouldn't sit so heavily on the bike seat. While this is the position prescribed by the "comfort bike" setup, it will lead, ironically, straight to discomfort and bad attitude. This terminally faulty positioning is the reason for many novices' lack of love for bicycling. They will never love it until they get their seats up and learn to distribute the weight.

Comfortable, efficient cycling means that the feet, the hands, and the butt all share the load. Even while "sitting," one is really standing on the pedals, while using the hands and sitting bones to ease the burden. The saddle is something on which to prop yourself up. Cycling is not a passive activity for heavy sitters. The rider should make very frequent adjustments on the saddle, easily sliding back or forward to keep the muscles fresh. Absorb road shock with the arms and legs rather than through the seat.

Poor bike fit typically leads to some common ailments. Setting the handlebars too low results in the rider's putting too much weight on the hands, and therefore pain and numbness in the hands. Improper seat height is more serious, causing various types of knee pain, and also some very annoying crotch-oriented problems. Seats that are pointed up too much are known to cause numbness of the package in men and excessive chafing in women.

There is some evidence that cycling could cause fertility problems in men. Research in this issue is ongoing, and there is currently much uncertainty surrounding it, but men would be wise to take extra care of their nether regions—try to sit and pedal in such a way that you're not crushing the plumbing in the perineum area. Circumstantial evidence suggests that most avid cyclists are doing just fine in the fertility department, but it's easy to imagine how a feller might damage himself. Any kind of serious pain and numbness in the genitals is not a normal, acceptable feature of cycling.

Micro-adjust seat height and angle until it feels perfect—half a centimeter up or down can make a huge difference—and carefully choose a seat that matches your particular, unique backside. Once you find a setup that is very comfortable for long rides, don't mess with it.

Tools

To achieve complete self-sufficiency, a cyclist must have an awesome set of tools,* in addition to a grip on mechanical reality that few of us will be able to attain. Many devoted riders opt out of total self-sufficiency and settle for a substantial, but ultimately incomplete, level of control. Lacking full sets of tools, they are happy to retreat to the bike shop for some of the more involved fixes, overhauling the bottom bracket, for instance. There is no shame in this. Many riders eventually learn to perform every possible mechanical operation on their bike but still go to the old-fashioned, barely surviving local shop to get frames tapped and straightened, and to get headset cups removed or installed, which requires even more special tools than the other special tools.

Tools can be dauntingly expensive. One way to ease the pain is to accumulate tools slowly year after year. For example, one might buy a tire on sale and get a pedal wrench with that extra ten bucks. Tools are the gift that keeps on giving. Tools are an investment. This sounds cute, but on a

---

* *awesome set of tools:* Apologies to Spiccoli.

strictly financial level it holds true. The avid rider who spends on tools and knows how to use them will save money in the end.

When accumulating tools, one should discriminate between tools that might be needed today or tomorrow, and tools that will be needed down the line. Decide which are more likely to be needed early and get those first. Beginning riders have some fairly urgent tool purchases to make. The proper order of tool accumulation might look something like this:

1. **PUMP, PATCH KIT, AND TIRE LEVERS** are tied for number one. These should go along on pretty much every ride. To achieve the minimum level of self-sufficiency, the cyclist must be prepared to fix a flat.

2. Number two is pretty close, but we'll have to go with: set of **ALLEN WRENCHES**. Allen wrenches are also known as "hex wrenches" or "hex keys" because of their hexagonal cross section. Perhaps a Y-shaped three-way wrench at first. Later on, accumulate all the little ones, some of which will eventually be needed, and also the big daddy 8-millimeter crank bolt wrench (see page 229). Allen wrenches with really long handles are nice to work with but impractical on rides. If you're riding an older bike with older bolts, you'll need older wrenches.

3. **GREASE AND CHAIN OIL.** A controversial choice—is lube really a tool? Not necessarily something to take with you,* but you'll need it early and often.

4. **SPOKE WRENCH.** Wheels aren't what they used to be. Most of the wheels these days are built by drunken robots, and sometimes the spokes chronically get loose and just plain need to be tightened. Often it is just a single spoke that is the culprit. In these cases there usually isn't much fancy trueing involved, but you still need the wrench. Get a spoke wrench that matches the spoke nipples on your bike, or get one that fits lots of different sizes.

   Wheel trueing is a bit of an art but anyone can do it. Find where the rim is bent out of alignment. One way to do this easily is to turn the bike over and watch the rim spin past the brake pads. Look at the rim and not the tire. If the rim is bent to the left, find a few spokes around the bend area that connect to the right side of the hub and give 'em a small twist to tighten. Just remember that, to tighten, the

---

* Lip balm makes a decent emergency lube when out on a ride.

spoke nipples are turned counterclockwise with respect to the visible surface of the rim. Just a quarter turn or so at a time. This will pull the rim slightly to the right. Then loosen a few of the spokes there that go to the left side of the hub. This has the same effect as tightening the right spokes, but the combination of loosening and tightening keeps the rim round, as well as straight. If you just tighten one side without loosening the other side, the rim will develop a flat spot. There is an art to knowing which spokes to mess with, and how much to mess with them. Spin the wheel and check your work. Then readjust with more twists of the wrench if needed. It doesn't have to be perfect. Be careful not to overtighten. A classic rookie mistake is to tighten, tighten, and tighten the spokes over the course of a few months until the spokes begin to pull through the rim.

5. **CHAIN TOOL.** Take it on every ride? An interesting question. If you're out in the middle of nowhere, you want the chain tool, and the ability to use it.

6. You probably already have a **LITTLE PHILLIPS HEAD SCREWDRIVER.** Keep it with the bike tools. You will need it to adjust your derailleurs.

7. **CRANK WRENCH.** To remove but also to tighten the crank bolts, which often come loose. It's good to give the crank bolts a little twist every now and again. Crank wrenches come in the form of huge 8-millimeter Allen wrenches, or more standard-looking wrenches.

8. **PEDAL WRENCH,** although many pedals can be removed/installed with an Allen wrench. Remember that the left pedal has reverse threading. Right is right, left is wrong.

9. Those with old-style threaded steer tubes and headsets should purchase a set of **HEADSET WRENCHES** at some point.

10. **CONE WRENCHES.** The hubs depend on strangely shaped bolts known as cones. Adjusting the cones can be a somewhat delicate operation, and the rider may do well to consult a maintenance manual or experienced colleague. Or you might just learn to do it yourself. Banzai!

11. **BOTTOM BRACKET TOOLS.** Now we're starting to get into territory beyond the everyday adjusting tools. These are tools that are used for building up bikes and cracking open their vital organs. To get the bottom bracket apart you will need the crank wrench (see above), the crank puller, a violent little tool that slowly yanks the crank arms off

the bottom bracket spindle, and tools to remove the bottom bracket itself. Different brands of newer bottom brackets require different splined tools for removal or installation. Older, classic-style bottom brackets require a two-sided wrench to remove the fixed cup (which is reverse threaded like the left pedal) and lockring, and a separate tool to hold/move the adjusting cup.

12. **CASSETTE TOOLS**. As with most bottom brackets, a special splined tool is required to remove the cassette body. A chain whip is indispensable for removing the cassette.

13. Going along with the bottom bracket tool and the cassette tool is the **BIG-ASS CRESCENT WRENCH** that is used to turn them. Problem is, bottom brackets and cassettes are supposed to be tightened to within a specific range of torque. A torque wrench is a nice addition to any home, but people get along without them easily enough.

14. True bicycle lovers own their own **CABLE STUFF**. This includes cable cutters and something to cleanly cut the housing, easier said than done, and little needle-nose pliers to pull the cable to the proper tension. It's also good to have plenty of extra cable and housing around, and ferrules to cover the cable and housing ends.

15. **REPAIR STAND**. Grips the bike and holds it steady so it can't get away.

Beyond this basic set, some riders accumulate still-more-specialized tools. Jigs, headset presses, wheel-building stands (formerly known as trueing stands), spoke tensiometers . . . When the Revolution comes, they'll be ready.

There is some other stuff, depending on what specific parts you run, and not everyone will agree with the order above. And just owning the tools does not automatically give the owner the knowledge to fix the bike. For that there are many other fine books and knowledgeable mechanics who can help. Among the how-to books, there are many offerings, from very dry and detailed shop manuals to more condensed, user-friendly pocketbooks. Lennard Zinn is probably the most respected and trusted of the current crop of author-mechanics.

Experience, of course, is the best teacher. Good luck.

Clothing

Many people believe, even some relatively experienced riders believe, that certain clothing items are an absolute necessity for cycling. For instance, it is often stated that skintight cycling shorts are almost mandatory. While these shorts do have substantial advantages that many riders greatly appreciate—superior aerodynamics, padding, and enhanced package disclosure, to name a few—a necessity they are not. And as far as the storied comfort of padded cycling shorts goes, you won't have to look too hard to find experienced riders who find these shorts to be less comfortable than regular shorts, even for long rides. These riders don't appreciate the bike shorts' extra, er, grip. Millions of riders, on the other hand, swear by them and can't imagine riding in anything else. The issue of cycling clothing, you see, just like most of the other equipment concerns, in large part boils down to cultural norms and personal bias. This is true even for some of the sacred cows of cycling equipment, shorts included.

Especially if the rider is making a short trip to the office or store or something, the undeniable practical benefits of special shorts or jerseys may be canceled by the extra time spent changing into them. Everyday trips through the city can be accomplished in just about any garb within reason. Lots of riders have great success wearing jeans and T-shirts, for instance. Some women even wear long skirts. Naked cyclists have been reported in certain western states and in Vermont. Really the only clothing items that might approach the grand mantle of necessity are gloves and a helmet, and cleated cycling shoes for those with clipless pedals. Out in the cold rain and snow, of course, jackets and other items become very important even for the shortest trips.

For longer rides, clothing choice becomes much more important, especially so when bad weather threatens. One of the most unpleasant sensations in cycling is getting sweaty, or otherwise wet, on a cold day. A base layer composed of a wicking fiber—polypropylene, for instance—will keep the skin dry and prevent the rider from going hypothermic. Cotton kills, so they say. Up on the Continental Divide, this is a much more important concern than it is down in so-called civilization, where keeping warm and dry is more about comfort. But the fact remains that a single polypro undershirt or a nice wool-blend jersey could be the difference between the perfect ride and a slimy hell. You gotta really appreciate anything that saves you from a slimy hell. Beyond the wicking layer, the cold-weather cyclist does well to carry something warm for the top half, like a wool sweater; a decent waterproof breathable jacket, preferably with side zippers; waterproof, lined gloves; waterproof pants; thermal tights; two pairs of nice wool-blend socks; and a hat of wool or fleece. Polypropylene skull caps and balaclavas work well under helmets. This getup will fend off pretty much anything the lower forty-eight can dish out. The trick is not so much to stay warm, but to balance the outer cold with the inner warmth. This is one of the most difficult tricks in cycling.

Commuters who hope to arrive at work in *clean,* nonsweaty clothes have special equipment needs—*fenders,* is really what it boils down to. Fenders are key for keeping greasy road splatter and black puddle splash away from the Dockers. But keeping one's cycling clothes clean while riding is not a simple matter of slapping on some fenders and rolling up a pant leg. The primary reason for this is that well-used bicycles have on them multiple sources of grunge. Bike seats, for instance, often will transfer some of their pigment onto the pants or shorts of the rider—one of the best arguments in favor of black cycling shorts. This problem is greatly exacerbated by moisture. The cables, especially near where they disappear into the housing, are often the culprits for mysterious, suddenly appearing stains around the thighs and crotch. The bike frame itself can cause the same problem if it's dirty. Bicycle tires are some of the dirtiest things within reach of you at any given time, which becomes evident every time you have to repair a flat. Touch your tire or rim to your khakis as you wheel the bike out of the house in the morning, and you might have a nasty spot staring at you all day long. And then of course there's the drivetrain, which must be avoided like the dark pestilence that it is. A greasy drivetrain is almost as good a reason to wear shorts as any other. Your bike hates pants.

Until this problem is completely figured out, cyclists can mitigate the damage by keeping the bike very clean, by wearing dark clothing, or clothes that can be terminally dirtied with an easy mind, and by keeping some fresh shirts and pants at the office, if possible. And of course the

Equipment

seekers after cleanliness should mount a good set of fenders and deal with the right pant leg (the one next to the drivetrain), which is the biggest trouble spot. Roll it up far enough that any contact of the pants with the drivetrain will only soil the inside of the garment, or lash it firmly around the calf and ankle, or both.

If we can forget about the problem of greasy stains for a moment, the thought of cyclists pedaling around in their standard everyday garb is heartening. The more riders who do this, the more obvious it will be to the general public that cycling is about straight utility in addition to recreation and exercise, an important point that has yet to penetrate the thick skull of American society.

Messenger Bags,
Backpacks, and Panniers

So you've got some stuff. How do you carry it?

Well, hopefully you won't have to carry it in your hand as you ride along. This maverick hauling method is a traditional wreck causer for cyclists, often because the rider is unable to properly operate the brake levers and carry at the same time. Other times, a rider will attempt to haul a bag in one hand as he holds onto the handlebar with the same hand; the bag inevitably tries to swing into the spokes and cause a wreck. If you find yourself hauling something, keep one hand on the *front* brake lever, usually the left hand. Carry the bag or object in the other hand, and prepare yourself for the possibility that you may have to jettison the cargo. Obviously, to carry lattes and sacks of tacos and things like this, one must possess a solid command of front-brake modulation and an ability to maneuver the bicycle with one hand on the bars. Some riders have enough trouble using two hands.

Any city rider worth half a damn will eventually have to haul enough stuff around to necessitate the acquisition of a backpack or set of *panniers*—panniers are saddlebags that hang over a rack, commonly used by cycle tourists. In deciding what type of system to go with, the rider will have to make a fateful decision: to haul the goods on the body, or on the bike.

For decades the conventional wisdom on this issue has been in favor of racks and panniers. Putting the weight on the bike is said to be physically easier on the rider, who puts all energy into powering the bike and is not fatigued by weight hanging on the upper body. Panniers also allow the rider to avoid the slimy, sweaty back that often comes from wearing a pack, and lowers the center of gravity of bicycle and rider.

But not everything is so wonderful over in pannier land. Some riders try panniers and detest the new handling characteristics of their weighted bicycle. With a loaded backpack, though the rider's neck and shoulder muscles may be struggling mightily, the quick road bike still feels like a quick road bike. Another problem with panniers is mobility. Let's say you just purchased some expensive new *chichi* bike parts at the local shop, and you're carrying them home in the panniers. But you want to stop at the grocery store on the way home. Are you going to detach the panniers from the rack and carry them into the store with you to protect those expensive parts from being lifted? Some types of panniers are quite difficult to deal with in these situations. The backpack solves this dilemma. Also, it can be difficult to fix racks to the racing-type bikes that many riders use and prefer. The fastest bikes don't have rack mounts.

Newer generations of backpacks have been specifically designed to hold the pack itself away from rider's back. This helps with the sweat problem, although it does not solve it completely. The panniers still own that point.

Antipannier sentiment has been mounting, and just maybe the backpack is taking over in the conventional wisdom department. The use of panniers for everyday riding is becoming the badge of the seriously old-school commuter.

Among commuters, the popularity of messenger bags probably has more to do with fashion than anything else. Messenger bags, with a strap slung over one shoulder, are designed so the wearer can remove packages from or place packages in the bag without actually removing the bag. It's a nifty feature if you need it. The messenger swings the bag into the front to deal with deliveries, then throws the bag around onto the back and rides. The messenger bag's versatility is also its big problem, though. When well-loaded, the bag has a tendency to swing uncomfortably around the rider's neck any time the rider stands out of the saddle. Unless the rider has multiple deliveries to get off, the messenger bag is probably not the best choice. Many working couriers have replaced their traditional, single-strap bags with special messenger backpacks with large openings at the top.

There are a few other methods of carrying substantial amounts of loot. Among these, the large seat-mounted bag is promising for small loads. Some riders use a rack, but instead of panniers, they simply lash their backpack or a gym bag to the rack using bungee cords. And don't forget the ever-trusty milk crate. One problem with the milk-crate-on-rack system is that your stuff will fly out in a wreck.

Drivetrain Maintenance

Drivetrain maintenance is a crucial *safety* matter for cycling.

A chain skip can be disastrous if it occurs, as it often does, when the rider is pushing heavily on the cranks. The sudden disconnect of a slip-ping chain can throw the rider violently into the stem and handlebars. These impacts are usually absorbed by the knees, thighs, groin, or chest, where they are known to cause broken ribs. Such an event could also lead to a heinous secondary collision with the city surface and/or a motor vehicle, a possibility that should not be taken lightly.

A very dirty, gooped-up drivetrain can cause the chain to skip, as can a poorly adjusted derailleur or stiff link in the chain. Another common cause of a skipping chain is excessive wear. With use, bicycle chains elongate slightly as the plate holes and rivets wear. After the chain "stretches" by a certain amount—about ⅛ of an inch over 1 foot of chain length—the elongated chain begins to round out the cog teeth on one side, and eventually the chain begins to skip dangerously. The worn-out teeth assume a distinctive shark-fin appearance.

All new bicycle chains have half-inch pitch, pitch being the distance from pin center to pin center. Ideally, the chain should be replaced when twenty-four pins' worth becomes noticeably longer than 1 foot, but before it reaches 12⅛ inches. (This can be checked by holding a ruler up to a chain under tension.) Beyond this point, the cog teeth have begun to change shape to match the worn chain, and a new chain will not mesh properly with your old gears. This means you will have to replace the cassette/freewheel and chainrings in addition to the chain. At the first sign of skipping on a worn but clean, properly adjusted drivetrain, replace them all. It's expensive but it's worth it. Take it from any cyclist who's ever wiped out after smashing a knee into the stem.

In the meantime, keep the chain and the rest of the drivetrain clean of excess buildup, and keep it lubricated. There is an ongoing argument about what is the best method of cleaning a chain, if any, and what sort of lube works best, if any—"dry" lube, Teflon, motor oil, chainsaw oil, wax. Many cyclists are insistent that a chain should never be oiled on the bike. They believe this casual lubing washes fine grit into the workings of the chain and accelerates wear. So they remove the chain, submerge it in solvent, and give it a good bath before applying any lube. Others think this is a silly overreaction to chain wear. These arguments are based largely on superstition and won't be solved here.

# of bicycles and cities

Unreal City,
Under the brown fog of a winter dawn . . .

— T.S. ELIOT, *The Waste Land*

When I tell people that I ride my bike on weekends, for fun and fitness—in addition to riding all week at work and using a bicycle for almost all my transportation needs—they tend to give me a funny look. They want to know: "Don't you get tired of it?"

The answer is no. More precisely, the answer is *hell no*. And I think I know why not.

Riding a bike allows a person to pack more life into a day. As Americans, we know all too well that the car driver often finds himself caught in a void, a void of dead space and time. The time spent driving to the store, to work, caught in traffic, attention vaguely drifting from the road ahead to the radio and back, is so nondescript, so forgettable, it is lost forever. Did the driver really live these minutes spent in motorized transit? Technically. On the bike, it is vastly different. This is *actual* living. Blood and oxygen pumping, muscles straining. There is a sense of being a true part of the world, a participant in one's own life, rather than simply watching it pass by on a big screen.

If cycling makes cyclists happier, it's not because cycling is easy. Cycling requires a high level of engagement, mental and physical. Cyclists have much that they must attend to out there, starting with the constant scanning of the road surface itself, watching for potholes, sand, expansion joints—things that drivers don't have to notice. And negotiating traffic is a whole different ballgame for cyclists. In contrast to motorists, who are enclosed, cyclists are exposed. Completely exposed in a stream of heavy machinery, and exposed to the sky above, feeling whatever weather is coming down. The cyclist's exposure, although it is a source of fear and trouble, turns out to be an even greater source of joy, as it makes the experience of cycling that much more colorful and intense. Even the most ordinary errand becomes a memory-maker. Although the trip may take longer, time spent on the bike is never wasted. The journey becomes an end in itself. That, my friends, is what life is all about.

There are many other important reasons, of course, why cycling is an attractive mode of travel. It's nearly pollution- and petroleum-free, cost-effective in many ways, et cetera. You've heard it all before. Yawn! These are not the reasons that cause me to stare lovingly at my bikes at night when they're leaning against the wall in the living room. These bicycles, I swear, are possessed of an indescribable magic.

Bicycling is better. Life is too precious to spend it in a car.

It's more than likely that you, reading this book, already know this. I'm preaching to the choir here, and, as a firm believer in the different-strokes-for-different-folks philosophy—whatever turns your crank—I try to resist proselytizing to noncyclists. Who am I to tell someone who doesn't ride a bike that they should ride a bike? I possess no desire to be the pied piper of cycling, leading fat American motorists down the wide curb lane to freedom. This is a book for folks who are already aware of the bicycle's magic.

But even those of us who understand and appreciate bicycles have trouble understanding the cities and suburbs in which we ride them. All that is obvious about these places is that they are imperfect and, from a cyclist's perspective, could be improved. So we bang up against our cities, clash with them, flail about, and try to change what might not be changeable, wasting precious riding time. Today's Real American City, in all its grungy glory, is already rockable on two wheels. Though it is not nearly as hospitable to cyclists as the emerald cities in our utopian fantasies, the Real American City can be dealt with in style. Sure it takes awareness, intelligence, a modicum of skill. It requires a healthy dose of compromise. Perhaps above all else, it takes patience. With patient observation, the truths of the city are revealed.

As the layers of paint and mystery are pulled away, it becomes apparent that unpredictability, chaos, and madness are some of the most important cogs in the city's machinery. The deck is stacked with jokers. There is a ghost in this machine, and it appears to be stupid and/or drunk. This situation will not change, because the human condition is its source. Accepting this reality is the first requirement of the cyclist in traffic.

The patient observer will not fail to notice that the messy reality of the Real American City does not coincide with the tidy vision of it that has been offered over the decades by some of the grand, old wise men of cycling. Theirs is a city governed by order: white lines, laws, and foregone conclusions. In their city, cyclists need only obey a few simple principles to get along successfully. Theirs is just another dream city, and not a very exciting one at that.

The Real American City marches to the crazy beats of millions of different drummers. The masterful urban cyclist finds him- or herself in a strange sort of dance, moving to all those drummers. There is no single principle that will see us through. But we have much more powerful tools at our disposal: timing, flexibility, and flow. Freedom. A successful, safe ride through American traffic is not an exercise in rule following, but a beautiful piece of interactive performance art.

Good luck out there, fellow cyclists. Keep your eyes open, your heads up, and the rubber side down. Be considerate to other road users, especially the noncyclists, poor fellows. Ride with fear and joy.

chapter notes

CHAPTER ONE: *Frankenstein's Monster*

1. Augusto Marinoni, "The Bicycle," in Ladislau Reti, ed., *The Unknown Leonardo* (New York: McGraw-Hill Book Company, 1974), pp. 288–91.

2. The arguments against Marinoni's claim are summarized in Jonathan Knight, "On Yer Bike, Leonardo," *New Scientist,* October 18, 1997, p. 28.

3. The drawing of the chain link can be seen in Reti, ed., *The Unknown Leonardo,* p. 291. See also Vernard Foley, "Leonardo and the Invention of the Wheellock," *Scientific American,* January 1998, pp. 96–100. The Leonardo bicycle appears to be nonsteerable as drawn. This was a great strike against the sketch's authenticity—why would Leonardo design a nonsteering bicycle? But Foley writes that he and his students "integrated additional sketches—from the 1490s and in da Vinci's own hand—that enabled us to reconstruct a sophisticated steering system for his bicycle." They also built a working model based on the lost sketch and diagrams from the *Codex Madrid,* one of several functioning replicas that has been built over the years (p. 99).

4. The account of the *draisienne,* boneshaker, and high-wheeler eras is a meld of information found in a wide range of sources, but primarily from two works: James McGurn, *On Your Bicycle: An Illustrated History of Cycling* (New York: Facts On File Publications, 1987), pp. 14–50; and Robert Smith, *A Social History of the Bicycle* (New York: McGraw-Hill, 1972), pp. 3–6.

5. McGurn, *On Your Bicycle,* pp. 51–73; and Smith, *A Social History of the Bicycle,* pp. 7–13.

6. McGurn, *On Your Bicycle,* pp. 86–100; and Smith, *A Social History of the Bicycle,* pp. 13–14.

7. McGurn, *On Your Bicycle,* pp. 89–90.

8. Ibid., p. 130; Smith, *A Social History of the Bicycle,* p. 33.

9. Cyclists' role in the smoothing and paving of American roads, prior to the arrival of large numbers of automobiles, is well appreciated by historians of automobility. For example, see James Flink, *The Automobile Age* (Cambridge: MIT Press, 1988), p. 5. Flink notes: "At the national level, a petition to Congress drafted by the LAW [League of American Wheelmen] resulted in 1893 in the creation of the Office of Road Inquiry in the Department of Agriculture." See also Ashleigh Brilliant, *The Great Car Craze* (Santa Barbara: Woodbridge Press, 1989), p. 15. Brilliant includes a quote, dated 1895, from a surveyor of the newly formed California State Bureau of Highways: "The influence of the bicycle upon this agitation for improved highways cannot be overestimated. Millions of dollars have been invested in the manufacture of these easy and graceful machines of locomotion and this agitation for better roads is due more directly to the efforts of the wheelmen than to any other one cause. . . ."

10. Smith, *A Social History of the Bicycle,* pp. 215–19.

11. Ibid., p. 13.

12. Ibid., p. 61.

13. John B. Rae, *The Road and the Car in American Life* (Cambridge: MIT Press, 1971), p. 28. In 1971 Rae called the bicycle "a device whose significance in the history of transportation has never been properly appreciated."

14. Flink, *The Automobile Age,* p. 5.

15. Ibid., pp. 5–6.

16. Peter Nye, *Hearts of Lions* (New York: W.W. Norton & Company, 1988), pp. 42–73.

17. ". . . an engine on four wheels, a machine in which brute strength and a disregard for nearly all the essentials of modern automobile construction are embodied." "How It Feels to Drive Under the Minute on a Circular Track," *The Automobile,* August 1, 1903, p. 116.

18. Ibid.

19. Flink, *The Automobile Age,* pp. 6–10.

20. Barney Oldfield, as reported to William Sturm, "Wide Open All the Way, Part One," *Saturday Evening Post,* September 19, 1925, p. 54.

21. *Horseless Age,* an early auto-booster publication, described the typical crowd reaction to Oldfield in their edition of July 29, 1903: ". . . he could be seen skidding around the curve at the quarter in a manner so obviously dangerous as to draw a spontaneous groan from the crowd." "The Races at the Empire City Track," *Horseless Age,* July 29, 1903, p. 124.

22. "A Carnival of Sport at Yonkers Track," *The Automobile,* August 1, 1903, p. 99.

23. Barney Oldfield as reported to William Sturm, "Wide Open All the Way, Part One," *Saturday Evening Post,* September 19, 1925, pp. 56, 61.

24. Ibid.; also Barney Oldfield as reported to William Sturm, "Wide Open All the Way, Part Two," *Saturday Evening Post,* September 26, 1925, pp. 20–21, 129–134, 137, 140.

25. Barney Oldfield as reported to William Sturm, "Wide Open All the Way, Part One," *Saturday Evening Post,* September 19, 1925, p. 56.

26. Wilson was then president of Princeton. Rae, *The Road and the Car in American Life,* p. 43.

27. Henry Ford's letter to *The Automobile,* January 11, 1906, p. 107. Cited in Rae, *The Road and the Car in American Life,* p. 55.

28. Rae, *The Road and the Car in American Life,* p. 41. Rae describes the rush to the automobile as proof of its necessity: "If necessity is the mother of invention, presumably the speed with which an invention is adopted is a fair measure of the degree of necessity, and by this standard the need for a workable motor vehicle was urgent." Personally I don't buy it. Other factors, such as laziness and fashion, should be considered along with necessity.

29. Flink, *The Automobile Age,* pp. 24–38.

30. Ibid, pp. 129–30.

31. Rae, *The Road and the Car in American Life,* pp. 73–74.

32. Flink, *The Automobile Age,* p. 359.

33. Ibid., pp. 140, 300.

34. Matthew Wald, "One Vehicle on the Road, Two Others in the Garage," *New York Times,* August 29, 2003.

35. Flink, *The Automobile Age,* pp. 326–27.

36. Ibid., p. 250.

37. National Bicycle Dealers' Association statistics.

38. I include the "comfort bike" category among the "knockoffs." True mountain bikes were clinging to about a 33 percent market share in 2004, the lowest in many years. Comfort bikes have declined to about 15 percent, as have youth bikes. Road bikes are coming back into style but accounted for no more than 10 percent of bicycle sales in 2004. National Bicycle Dealers' Association.

39. Michael Hugo-Brunt, *The History of City Planning* (Montreal: Harvest House, Ltd., 1972), p. 34.

40. Flink, *The Automobile Age,* p. 3.

41. Joel Garreau, *Edge City* (New York: Doubleday, 1991), pp. 120–21.

42. This view is borrowed from Garreau, *Edge City.*

43. Kenneth Jackson, *Crabgrass Frontier* (New York: Oxford University Press, 1985), p. 170.

44. Scott Bottles, *L.A. and the Automobile* (Berkely: University of California Press, 1987), pp. 3–17.

45. As Kenneth Jackson puts it, "Americans taxed and harassed public transportation, even while subsidizing the automobile like a pampered child." *Crabgrass Frontier,* p. 170.

46. Le Corbusier, *The City of Tomorrow and Its Planning* (London: J. Rodker, 1929), pp. 116–18.

47. Rem Koolhaas, *S, M, L, XL* (New York: The Monacelli Press, 1994), p. 961.

48. Lewis Mumford, *The City in History* (New York: Harcourt, Brace and World, 1968), pp. 218–19.

49. Anthony Downs, "Might As Well Enjoy It," *Washington Post,* January 1, 2001.

50. Jane Jacobs, *The Death and Life of Great American Cities* (New York: Random House, 1961), p. 351.

51. Steven Johnson, *Emergence* (New York: Scribner and Sons, 2001), p. 74.

52. Art Buchwald, "How Un-American Is That," *Have I Ever Lied to You?* (New York: Putnam Press, 1968).

CHAPTER TWO: *The City Surface*

1. Clay McShane, "Transforming the Use of Urban Space: A Look at the Revolution in Street Pavements, 1880–1924," *Journal of Urban History,* May 1979, pp. 282–83.

2. New York City Department of Transportation Press Release 03-44, "D.O.T. Exceeds Goal During Pothole Blitz," May 5, 2003.

3. Nai C. Yang, *Design of Functional Pavements* (New York: McGraw-Hill, 1972), p. 17.

4. E. J. Yoder, *Principles of Pavement Design* (New York: John Wiley and Sons, 1959), p. 506.

5. Corey Kilgannon, "Tons of Hot Asphalt Make a Day's Work of 1,600 Potholes," *New York Times,* February 23, 2003.

6. Any ranking of surface hazards suggested here is based on circumstantial evidence alone, and there exists no study to confirm or deny it.

7. Correspondence with the author's cousin, July 1, 2003.

8. Yang, *Design of Functional Pavements,* pp. 159–60.

9. See Peter Blake, *The Master Builders* (New York: Alfred A. Knopf, 1960), for a discussion of both Le Corbusier and Mies van der Rohe and the close relationship between the two men.

CHAPTER THREE: *In Traffic*

1. Ambrose Bierce, *The Devil's Dictionary* (New York: Dover Publications, Inc., 1993), p. 106. Originally published in 1911 as part of Volume VII of *The Collected Works of Ambrose Bierce* (New York: Neale Publishing Company).

2. This version of the statement actually comes from Forester's *Bicycle Transportation: A Handbook for Cycling Transportation Engineers* (Cambridge: MIT Press, 1994), p. 3.

3. *The Analects of Confucius,* translated and annotated by Arthur Waley (New York: Random House, 1938), Book IV, no. 12, p. 104.

4. "It gives the motorist superior rights and status over the cyclist . . ." writes Forester. Forester, *Effective Cycling* (Cambridge: MIT Press, 1984), p. 154.

5. Brilliant, *The Great Car Craze,* pp. 89–90.

6. Forester, *Bicycle Transportation: A Handbook for Cycling Transportation Engineers,* p. 9. Forester cites Jerrold Kaplan, *Characteristics of the Regular Adult Bicycle User,* National Technical Information Service, 1976. Kaplan studied the accidents of LAW members for his master's thesis at the University of Maryland.

7. There is a smattering of statistical evidence to suggest that bike lane stripes are somewhat effective traffic-calming devices. For instance, see William Moritz, "Adult Bicyclists in the United States," a survey of League of American Bicyclists members from 1996. On www.bicyclinglife.com/library/moritz2.htm. Moritz used a "Relative Danger Index" to reach the conclusion that "streets with bike lanes have a significantly lower crash rate than either major or minor streets without any bicycle facilities." Over in facility-friendly San Francisco, the city has come to embrace a different approach—the "sharrow," a sort of bike-arrow glyph on the street which tells drivers

to share the road while encouraging inexperienced cyclists to ride with traffic. Other cities are dabbling with these as well. It is hoped that "sharrows" will bring the advantages of bike lanes without the problems associated with a confining stripe. Clearly, the psychological effect of these markings will depend largely on where they are placed in the street—that is, how far left. The current standard is a minimum 11 feet from the curb for a street with on-street parking. See http://sf-now.com/sf-bike/Sharrow_docs.pdf.

8. Seattle Municipal Code.

9. Exact wording from the municipal codes of Portland, Oregon, and Madison, Wisconsin.

10. Insurance Institute for Highway Safety.

CHAPTER FOUR: *Bicycle Accidents and Injuries*

1. These numbers are estimations from the U.S. Consumer Product Safety Commission (CPSC), and are based on the CPSC's National Electronic Injury Surveillance System, a statistical sampling from multiple emergency rooms around the country.

2. The numbers in this section are approximations derived from numerous studies of bicycle accident rates. The studies include Chlapecka, Schupack, Planek, Klecker, and Driessen, *Bicycle Accidents and Usage Among Elementary School Children in the United States,* National Highway Traffic Safety Administration, 1975; Kenneth Cross, *Causal Factors of Non-Motor Vehicle Related Accidents,* Santa Barbara Bicycle Safety Project, Santa Barbara, 1980; Kenneth Cross and Gary Fisher, *A Study of Bicycle/Motor-Vehicle Accidents: Identification of Problem Types and Countermeasure Approaches,* National Highway Traffic Safety Administration, 1977; Jerrold Kaplan, *Characteristics of the Regular Adult Bicycle User,* National Technical Information Service, 1976; Schupack and Driessen, *Bicycle Accidents and Usage Among Young Adults: Preliminary Study,* National Safety Council, 1976; and Watkins's survey of the British Cyclists' Touring Club (1984). All of the above are cited by Forester, *Bicycle Transportation: A Handbook for Cycling Transportation Engineers,* pp. 41–61. The studies are all more than a bit long in the tooth, but they are among the best available. Various additional publications from the National Highway Traffic Safety Administration and the U.S. Consumer Products Safety Commission were also used.

3. It is easy to count deaths. But decent data on fatality *rates* is virtually impossible to come by. There have been some apparent stabs in the dark, however. For instance, see the well-known chart, purported to have originated from the risk analysis firm Failure Analysis Associates, that first appeared in an article about car fires in *Design News* magazine ("Comparative Risk of Different Activities," *Design News,* October 4, 1993). The chart pops up in every Internet debate about helmets or the danger of cycling, but is effectively useless for any serious purpose because no methodology is provided, and therefore no way to check the work. The chart made the claim that cyclists suffered .26 deaths for every one million hours of riding. In other words, the chart also made the claim, although it was unstated, that cyclists rode about three billion hours total per year in the United States—a number which is perhaps in the realm of possibility, but is certainly on the high end. This chart appeared in the first edition of this book, but I have decided to remove it from the text due to its terminal uncertainties and general sketchiness.

4. Based on known fatality statistics and the U.S. Consumer Products Safety Commission's National Electronic Injury Surveillance System.

5. This number is necessarily an estimation, based on the U.S. Consumer Products Safety Commission's National Electronic Injury Surveillance System, which estimates about 500,000 cycling-related ER visits each year, and estimates about half of these are related to head injuries. The total annual number of cycling injuries, as stated earlier, is unknown and unknowable, but five million is a conservative estimate.

6. Forester has been especially exasperated on this point. He devotes much of his energy to debunking the popular fear of this type of accident. Forester, *Bicycle Transportation: A Handbook for Cycling Transportation Engineers,* pp. 9–13, 46–47.

7. Ibid., p. 41.

8. Ed Burke, *Serious Cycling* (Champaign, Ill.: Human Kinetics, 2002), p. 86.

9. Forester, *Bicycle Transportation: A Handbook for Cycling Transportation Engineers,* pp. 41–44. The update of the 1976 Kaplan survey is William Moritz's, "Adult Bicyclists in the United States" (1996), and can be viewed online at www.bicyclinglife.com/library/moritz2.htm. The accident rates for highly experienced riders found in Moritz's survey are nicely corroborated in Ken Kifer's "September 2001 Bicycle Safety Survey," which is only available online at www.kenkifer.com/bikepages/survey/sept01.htm. About 10 percent of respondents in each survey reported suffering a "real injury" or a "serious" accident in the previous year.

10. Burke, *Serious Cycling,* p. 88.

11. Conversations with Christie M., winter 2002–2003.

12. John Carey, ed., *Eyewitness to History* (New York: Avon Books, 1987), p. 435. Mr. Bride's account originally appeared in the *New York Times* of April 19, 1912. The *Titanic* went down on April 15.

13. Thompson, Nunn, Thompson, and Rivara, "Effectiveness of Bicycle Safety Helmets in Preventing Serious Facial Injury," *JAMA,* 1996, vol. 276, pp. 1974–75. The researchers conclude: "Helmets do not appear to offer any protection for the lower face."

14. National Safety Council.

15. Robert Berkow M.D., Mark H. Beers M.D., and Andrew J. Fletcher editors, *The Merck Manual of Medical Information* (Whitehouse Station, N.J., Merck and Co. Inc., 1997), p. 357.

16. Ibid., p. 359.

17. Richard Cherry, *EMT-Basic Exam Review* (Upper Saddle River, N.J.: Prentice Hall, 1999), p. 195.

18. This quote taken very much out of context from Paine's essay "Old Testament Prophecies of Jesus Christ Proven False (Part 2)," which can be found in Daniel Wheeler, ed., *Life and Writings of Thomas Paine* (New York: Vincent Parke and Company, 1908). The complete quote goes like this: "When a book, as is the case with the Old and New Testament, is ushered into the world under the title of being the WORD OF GOD, it ought to be examined with the utmost strictness, in order to

know if it has a well founded claim to that title or not, and whether we are or are not imposed upon: for no poison is so dangerous as that which poisons the physic, so no falsehood is so fatal as that which is made an article of faith." Obviously, Paine wasn't referring to bicycle helmets, but it works for that, too.

19. Estimations of helmet use among the general cycling population vary wildly. The other day, I went out to make my own informal survey. I rode around for hours counting helmeted and nonhelmeted riders, and I found that seventy-seven of the first one hundred I counted were wearing helmets. Most of these riders were among the more gung ho recreational cyclists in an area where cyclists like to take themselves seriously and spend a lot of money on equipment (Denver, Colorado), which accounts for the high percentage of helmet wearers. Nationwide among adult cycling enthusiasts, 60 to 80 percent helmet use is a safe estimate. The estimate is similarly high for young children. Commuter cyclists seem to hover at around 40 percent.

20. The latest of the Seattle studies is summarized in Thompson, Nunn, Thompson, and Rivara, "Effectiveness of Bicycle Safety Helmets in Preventing Head Injuries: A Case Control Study," JAMA, 1996, vol. 276, pp. 1968–73.

21. Ibid. It was one of the very interesting results of this study that helmet wearers were found to be far more well-off than their bareheaded counterparts.

22. National Highway Traffic Safety Administration, "2002 Annual Assessment of Motor Vehicle Crashes." www-nrd.nhtsa.dot.gov/2002annual_assessment/non-occupants.htm.

23. Bruce Robinson, "Is There Any Reliable Evidence That Australian Helmet Legislation Works?" *Proceedings of Velo Australia,* Fremantle, Australia, October 30, 1996.

24. Paul Scuffham and John Langley, "Trends in Cycle Injuries in New Zealand Under Voluntary Helmet Use," *Accident Analysis and Prevention,* vol. 29, no. 1, 1997.

25. According to Failure Analysis Associates, Incorporated. "Comparative Risk of Different Activities," *Design News,* October 4, 1993.

26. "Helmet Help Ahead," *Consumer Reports,* July 2002, pp. 22–24. The article mentions that some helmet models are effective at speeds close to 20 mph.

27. Conversations with Robert R., spring 2003.

28. Wording taken directly from the Web site of Giro Sport Design (www.giro.com).

CHAPTER FIVE: *Air Pollution and the Urban Cyclist*

1. Flink, *The Automobile Age,* p. 136. Jacobs, *The Death and Life of Great American Cities,* p. 341. Jacobs cites a 1958 *Architectural Review* article by H. B. Creswell.

2. Stephen Blewett and Mary Embree, *What's in the Air* (Ventura, Calif.: Seaview Publishing, 1998), p. 103.

3. Dietrich Schwela and Olivier Zali, eds., *Urban Traffic Pollution* (London: E & FN Spon, 1998), pp. 151–52. For a pointed discussion of the long, painful process of Washington's push for environmental regulations on automobiles, and the industry's gambits in response, see Jack Doyle, *Taken for a Ride* (New York: Four Walls Eight Windows, 2000).

4. Many municipalities are switching their diesel-fueled fleets to "Biodiesel," a 20 percent vegetable oil mixture made from genetically modified soybeans. Engineering students at the University of Colorado in Boulder are proving that buses can be run on a mixture including 100 percent recycled cooking oil, with no retrofitting of conventional diesel engines. Engines burning these new diesel formulations will still pollute far more than regular gasoline engines. Katy Human, "Running on Vegetable Oil," *Boulder Daily Camera,* March 16, 2003.

5. M. P. Walsh writes that "in 1990 there were 50 million more cars on USA highways than there were in 1970." Walsh, in Schwela and Zali, eds., *Urban Traffic Pollution,* p. 156. Roland Huang of the Union of Concerned Scientists estimates that "Americans collectively drive twice as much as they did" in the 1960s. Huang, "Benefits of Electric Vehicles," on the Union of Concerned Scientists Web site www.ucsusa.org.

6. Schwela and Zali, eds., *Urban Traffic Pollution,* pp. 92–96.

7. One of the only available studies that specifically attempted to quantify bicyclists' exposure to pollutants measured their CO exposure in Southampton, England, in 1991, between 7.9 and 13 parts-per-million. Ibid., p. 96.

8. Ibid., pp. 45–46.

9. "In summary, in spite of decades of laboratory, clinical and epidemiological research, the human health effects of NO_2 exposure have not been fully characterized," writes Isabelle Romieu. Ibid., p. 13.

10. Blewett and Embree, *What's in the Air,* p. 82. The authors quote a strongly worded EPA warning on ozone.

11. Schwela and Zali, eds., *Urban Traffic Pollution,* pp. 14–23.

12. Ibid., p. 161.

13. Ibid., pp. 23–33.

14. "Latex Particles From Tires: Are They a Health Hazard," *Journal of Allergy and Clinical Immunology,* September 2000, part one, vol. 106, no. 3, p. 573. Hugh Westrop, "Breathing Lessons," *Current Science,* April 20, 2001.

15. Ann Watson, Richard Bates, and Donald Kennedy, eds., *Air Pollution, the Automobile, and Public Health* (Washington, D.C.: National Academy Press, 1988), p. 325.

16. Ibid., p. 326.

17. Information for this paragraph was compiled from a comprehensive survey, by P. G. Flachsbart, of more than ninety different scientific studies: P. G. Flachsbart, "Exposure to Exhaust and Evaporative Emissions From Motor Vehicles," in Schwela and Zali, eds., *Urban Traffic Pollution,* pp. 89–126.

CHAPTER SIX: *Punctures and Flat Tires*

1. Written correspondence between the author and Jobst Brandt, June 1, 2003. It should be noted that Brandt's estimate of ten revolutions is on the high end, especially for tire wipers using the shoe method, who can reach the front tire almost immediately.

2. Charles Cohen, "All That Glitters Is Not Road," *City Paper* (Baltimore), March 1–March 7, 2000.

3. Technical information on Puncture Vine is derived from multiple sources, such as the University of California Statewide Integrated Pest Management Program.

4. Brilliant, *The Great Car Craze,* pp. 126–27. The irony is not lost on Brilliant: "The remarkable thing was that the Puncture Vine had not been at all common in California until the advent of the Mass Automobile."

CHAPTER SEVEN: *Equipment*

1. For instance, Forester's *Effective Cycling,* Edmund Burke's *Serious Cycling,* and Lennard Zinn's books on maintenance, to name just a few.

2. "Helmet Help Ahead," *Consumer Reports,* July 2002, pp. 22–24.

3. Smith, *A Social History of the Bicycle,* p. 19.

bibliography

Allen, Frederick Lewis. *The Big Change.* New York: Bantam Books, 1952.

Allen, John. *Street Smarts.* Emmaus, Pa.: Rodale Press, 1988.

Berkow, Robert, M.D., Mark H. Beers M.D., and Andrew J. Fletcher editors, *The Merck Manual of Medical Information.* Whitehouse Station, N.J.: Merck and Co. Inc., 1997

Blake, Peter. *The Master Builders.* New York: Alfred A. Knopf, 1960.

Blewett, Stephen, and Mary Embree. *What's in the Air.* Ventura, Calif.: Seaview Publishing, 1998.

Bottles, Scott. *L.A. and the Automobile.* Berkely: University of California Press, 1987.

Brandt, Jobst. *The Bicycle Wheel.* Menlo Park: Avocet, 1981.

Brilliant, Ashleigh. *The Great Car Craze.* Santa Barbara: Woodbridge Press, 1989.

Burke, Ed. *Serious Cycling.* Champaign, Ill.: Human Kinetics, 2002.

Campbell, Colin. *The Coming Oil Crisis.* Brentwood: Multi-Science Publishing Company, 1997.

Cherry, Richard. *EMT-Basic Exam Review.* Upper Saddle River, N.J.: Prentice Hall, 1999.

Davis, Mike. *City of Quartz: Excavating the Future in Los Angeles.* New York: Vintage, 1992.

Dodge, Pryor. *The Bicycle.* Paris: Flammerion, 1996.

Doyle, Jack. *Taken for a Ride.* New York: Four Walls Eight Windows, 2000.

Flink, James. *The Automobile Age.* Cambridge: MIT Press, 1988.

Ford, Larry. *The Spaces Between Buildings.* Baltimore: Johns Hopkins University Press, 2000.

Forester, John. *Bicycle Transportation: A Handbook for Cycling Transportation Engineers.* Cambridge: MIT Press, 1994.

———. *Effective Cycling.* Cambridge: MIT Press, 1984.

Garreau, Joel. *Edge City.* New York: Doubleday, 1991.

Gleick, James. *Chaos.* New York: Penguin, 1987.

Hugo-Brunt, Michael. *The History of City Planning*. Montreal: Harvest House, Ltd., 1972.

Jackson, Kenneth. *Crabgrass Frontier*. New York: Oxford University Press, 1985.

Jacobs, Jane. *The Death and Life of Great American Cities*. New York: Random House, 1961.

Johnson, Steven. *Emergence*. New York: Scribner and Sons, 2001.

Koolhaas, Rem. *S, M, L, XL*. New York: The Monacelli Press, 1994.

———. *The Lang Emergency*. New York: The Atlantic Monthly Press, 2005.

Kunstler, James Howard. *The City in Mind: Meditations on the Urban Condition*. New York: Free Press, 2001.

———. *Geography of Nowhere*. New York: Simon and Schuster, 1993.

Lacey, Robert. *Ford: The Men and the Machine*. Boston: Little, Brown and Company, 1986.

Le Corbusier. *The City of Tomorrow and Its Planning*. London: J. Rodker, 1929.

Marshall, Alex. *How Cities Work*. Austin: University of Texas Press, 2001.

McGurn, James. *On Your Bicycle: An Illustrated History of Cycling*. New York: Facts On File Publications, 1987.

McShane, Clay. *Down the Asphalt Path*. New York: Columbia University Press, 1995.

Mumford, Lewis. *The City in History*. New York: Harcourt, Brace and World, 1968.

Nye, Peter. *Hearts of Lions*. New York: W. W. Norton & Company, 1988.

Rae, John B. *The Road and the Car in American Life*. Cambridge: MIT Press, 1971.

Reti, Ladislau, ed. *The Unknown Leonardo*. New York: McGraw-Hill Book Company, 1974.

Robinson, Bruce. "Is There Any Reliable Evidence That Australian Helmet Legislation Works?" *Proceedings of Velo Australia*. Fremantle, Australia, October 30, 1996.

Rowland Whitt, Frank, and David Wilson. *Bicycling Science*. Cambridge: MIT Press, 1982.

Safdie, Moshe. *The City After the Automobile*. New York: Harper-Collins, 1997.

Schwela, Dietrich, and Olivier Zali, eds. *Urban Traffic Pollution*. London: E & FN Spon, 1998.

Scuffham, Paul, and John Langley. "Trends in Cycle Injuries in New Zealand Under Voluntary Helmet Use." In *Accident Analysis and Prevention*. Vol. 29, no. 1 (1997).

Smith, Robert. *A Social History of the Bicycle*. New York: McGraw-Hill, 1972.

Thompson, D. C., F. P. Rivara, and R. S. Thompson. "Effectiveness of Bicycle Safety Helmets in Preventing Head Injuries: A Case Control Study." In *JAMA*. Vol. 276, (1996): pp. 1968–73.

Walden, Russell, ed. *The Open Hand: Essays on Le Corbusier*. Cambridge: MIT Press, 1977.

Watson, Ann, Richard Bates, and Donald Kennedy, eds. *Air Pollution, the Automobile, and Public Health*. Washington, D.C.: National Academy Press, 1988.

Wilson, James Q., ed. *The Metropolitan Enigma*. New York: Doubleday, 1968.

Yang, Nai C. *Design of Functional Pavements*. New York: McGraw-Hill, 1972.

Yoder, E. J. *Principles of Pavement Design*. New York: John Wiley and Sons, 1959.

Zinn, Lennard. *Zinn and the Art of Road Bike Maintenance*. Boulder: Velo Press, 2000.

Bibliography

index

A

accidents. *See also* injuries
    anticipating driver pullout, 88
    bike-on-bike, 154–55
    bike paths and, 135, 136, 141–142
    blame for, 67–69
    carelessness causing, 63
    common causes, 161–62
    drivetrain failures causing, 175
    experience reducing, 164–65
    falling techniques for, 171–73
    learning from, 165–66
    look-backs and, 105–6
    night riding and, 149–53
    rear-end, 106, 123, 163
    responsibility for, 67–69
    route choice and, 75
    vigilance against. *See* vigilance
accident statistics, 158–63
    accident causes, 161–62
    experience and, 164–65
    fatalities, 162–63
    quagmire, 158–60
air pollution
    breathing strategies, 193–96
    carbon monoxide, 190–91
    good news about, 188–90
    health benefits and, 196–97
    high, avoiding, 195–96
    historical perspective, 186–88
    hydrocarbons, 191
    masks for, 196
    nitrogen oxides, 191
    ozone, 192
    particulate matter, 192–93
    pollutants/effects, 190–93
Armstrong, Lance, 132
asphalt, 42–43
    composition, 43

"glassphalt", 207–8
    waves, 49
automated highways, 32–33
    automobiles
    congestion by, 31–33
    early racing, 16, 17–19
    enclosure of, 33–34
    evolution of, 20–22
    mass production of, 20–21
    origin of, 14–15
    road rage and, 34–35
    streetcars and, 24, 26–28
    suburbs and, 24–26

B

backpacks, 234, 235
bags, packs, panniers, 234–36
balancing, track stands, 125–28
bicycle history. *See also* nineteenth
    century bikes
    automobile origin and, 14–15
    chain-drive origin, 3, 9
    continuum, 2–3
    fake gas tanks, 22
    Leonardo da Vinci and, 3–4
    modern boom, 22–23
    racing, 15–16, 22–23
bike-bike wrecks, 154–55
bike choice, 221–23
bike fit, 225–27
bike lanes
    history of, 134–38
    legal protection of, 138–39
    pros/cons of, 138–40
bike paths
    accidents on, 135, 136, 141–42
    danger of, 75, 134–35, 136–37
    Door Zone and, 138
    first in world, 11

history of, 134–38
pedestrians on, 141–42
pros/cons of, 134–38, 139–40
riding on, 134–35, 141–42
route choice and, 75
side paths, 75, 134–35, 136–37, 138, 140
sidewalks and, 143–47
surfaces, 42–43
blame, responsibility vs., 66–69
blowouts, 214–15
boneshakers, 6, 7, 8
Bott's Dots, 44, 50
braking
front-brake modulation, 234
Lance Armstrong example, 132
panic stops, 130–33
breathing strategies, 193–96
broken glass, 204–5
buffer zone, 77–78
bunny hop, 53, 56, 58
Burke, Ed, 164

C
carbon monoxide, 190–91
car doors, 116–18
catalytic converters, 188
chain-drive origin, 3–4, 9
chain lubrication, 237
chumps of the road, 12–13
cities
congestion in, 31–33
as emerging systems, 34
freeways and, 28–30
ongoing challenges with, 35–37
suburbs and, 24–26
today, 35–37
transportation history, 23–28
twentieth century, 28–33
urban rail systems, 24, 27–28
clothing, 167, 232–34
Codex Madrid, 4
collarbone injuries, 168–70
concrete. See Portland cement concrete (PCC)

concussions, 174
Coney Island bikeway, 11
congestion
bicycle efficiency in, 33
car-curbing legislation and, 32
inevitability of, 31–33
positioning in, 121–23
Consumer Products Safety Commission (CPSC), 177, 179–80
control joints, 47–48
Cooper, Tom, 16, 18
corner cutters, 104–5
cornering, 128–29
countersteer, 128
crash helmets
characteristics of, 179–81
controversy of, 176–79
design intent of, 179–81
disclaimer on, 176
facial injuries and, 173–74
head injuries and, 163, 173–74, 174–75
torsion injuries from, 181–82
verdict on, 182–83
wearing, 175, 182–83
crashing technique, 171–73. See also accidents
crossing accidents, 161
crossing freeways, 75
crowned streets, 52
curbs, 57–59

D
danger
of bike paths, 73, 134–35, 136–37
reality of, 69–71
vigilance and, 69–71
da Vinci, Leonardo
bicycle design, 3–4
Codex Madrid, 4
deaths, 162–63
default position, 77
deicer, 54
destination positioning, 97, 100
Door Zone (DZ), 76, 116–18, 138

drainage, 51–53
    crowned streets and, 52
    grates, 52–53
Drais de Saverbrun, Baron Karl, 5–6
draisienne, 5
driver arms, 121
drivetrain
    failures causing accidents, 175
    maintenance, 236–37

E

elevated bicycle highway, 11–12
enclosure, 33–34
engine-running check, 120
equipment, 217–37
    bags, packs, panniers, 234–36
    bike choice, 221–23
    bike fit and, 225–27
    clothing, 167, 232–34
    crash helmets. *See* crash helmets
    cult of, 218–21
    drivetrain maintenance, 236–37
    tools, 227–30
    track bikes, 223–25
evasive moves
    Fake Right Turn, 89
    for Gap Effect, 89–91, 120
    repositioning stopped bike, 101
    turn-and-stop curlicue, 88
experience, 164–65
eye contact, 86–89

F

facial injuries, 173–74
fake gas tanks, 22
Fake Right Turn, 89
falling technique, 171–73
fatalities, 162–63
Figurative Stops, 94
filtering, 100
fitting bike, 225–27
flat tires
    blowouts, 214–15
    broken glass causing, 204–5
    "glassphalt" and, 207–8

    goathead thorns causing, 208, 209, 211–12
    pinch flats, 213–14
    random items causing, 212–13
    repair equipment, 200
    repairing, 201–4
    tire wiping to avoid, 204–7
    tribulus terrestris plant causing, 208–11
Flink, James, 14
Ford, Henry, 14, 20–21, 23
Ford-Cooper racers, 16, 17
Forester, John, 63, 139
former bicycle manufacturers, 14–15
four-way stops, 92–93
freeways, 28–30, 75
front-brake modulation, 234
front-hub cranks, 7–8

G

Gap Effect, 89–91, 120
gas taxes, 28
General Motors, 26–27
glass, broken, 204–5
"glassphalt," 207–8
goathead thorns, 208–12
gravel, 54
green light cautions, 84–86
gutter riding, 113–15

H

hand signals, 112–13
head injuries, 163, 173–74, 174–75
    See also crash helmets
headphones, 108
head scanning, 119
head-watching, 120
hearing sounds, 108, 123
heavy traffic positioning, 121–23
helmets. *See* crash helmets
hematomas, 175
highways
    automated, 33
    limited-access freeways, 28–30, 75

high-wheelers, 7–9
history. *See* bicycle history; nineteenth
    century bikes
hopping. *See* jumping
horsecars, 24
hydrocarbons, 191

I

ice, 54
individualized transport, 14
injuries
    broken appendages, 176
    cleaning, 168
    collarbone, 168–70
    crash helmets and. *See* crash
        helmets
    facial, 173–74
    fatality statistics, 162–63
    head, 163, 173–74, 174–75
    leg/knee, 176
    night riding and, 149–53
    psychogenic shock and, 169
    rib cage, 175
    road rash, 166–68
    "soft," 176
    torsion, 181–82
instinct, 109–11
intersections. *See also* stop signs; traffic
    lights
    bike lanes and, 135
    corner cutters at, 104–5
    eye contact and, 86–89
    Gap Effect and, 89–91, 120
    momentum and, 93–95
    pedestrian-like crossing
        at, 103
    positioning for, 77
intracranial bleeding, 175
invisible cyclists, 79–80, 151–53

J

Jacobs, Jane, 34
Jeanneret, Charles Edouard. *See* Le
    Corbusier
Johnson, Steven, 34

jumping
    curbs, 57–59
    grates, 53

K

Kiser, Earl, 19
knee injuries, 175–76
Koolhass, Rem, 32

L

lane markers, 49–50
lane ownership myth, 81–84
lateral moves, 79
League of American Bicyclists
    (LAB), 63
League of American Wheelmen
    (LAW), 11, 63
Le Corbusier, 28, 30, 56
ledges, 46
left turns, 77, 103
leg injuries, 176
limited-access freeways, 28–30, 75
longitudinal cracks/seams, 47–48
look-backs
    complementary techniques to,
        107–11
    dangers of, 105–6
    secret of, 106
looking forward, 106
low-speed balance, 125–28
lubrication, 237

M

Marinoni, Augusto, 3
match sprint, 125–26
messenger bags, 234–36
metal, wet, 50
Michaux, Pierre and Ernest, 6–7
mirrors, 108
Model T Fords, 20–21
momentum, 93–95
mountain bikes, 22–23
MTBE (methyl tertiary butyl
    ether), 189
multiple cyclists, 153–55

N

National System of Interstate and
    Defense Highways, 30
night riding, 149–53
    invisible style for, 151–53
    lights/flashers and, 149–50, 152
    potholes and, 45–47, 51–52
nineteenth century bikes, 4–13
    boneshakers (velocipedes), 6, 7, 8
    contemptuous attitudes toward,
        12–13
    cost, 13
    craze of, 10–12
    Drais and, 5–6
    front-hub cranks, 7–8
    high-wheelers, 7–9
    J. K. Starley and, 9
    Michaux influence on, 6–7
    pneumatic tires and, 10–11
    rear-wheel-drive system, 6
    Safety Bikes, 8, 9
    women on, 11
nitrogen oxides, 191

O

oil sludge, 54
Oldfield, Barney, 16, 17–19
one-way streets, 74
oxygenated fuels, 189
ozone, 192

P

panic stops, 130–33
panniers, 235
parked vehicles
    bank robbery story, 118–19
    Door Zone and, 76, 116–18
    reading, 118–21
particulate matter, 192–93
paths. See bike paths
pavement. See surfaces
pedestrians
    from behind parked vehicles, 118
    on bike paths, 141–42
    crossing intersections with, 103

green light cautions, 84–86
    rolling stops and, 93
Pedretti, Carlo, 4
pinch flats, 213–14
pioneers, 37
plazas, 56–57
pneumatic tires, 10–11
Portland cement concrete (PCC), 47–48
    control joints, 47–48
    ledges, 48
    longitudinal cracks/seams, 47–48
    rigidity of, 42–43
    wet, 54
positioning. See road position/location;
    spacing; traffic lights; turns
potholes, 45–47, 152–53
psychogenic shock, 169
punctures. See flat tires

R

raccoon eyes, 175
racing
    automobiles, 16, 17–19
    bicycles, 15–16, 22–23, 125–26
    match sprint, 125–26
railroad tracks, 53–54
reaction time, 133
reading parked vehicles, 118–22
rear-end collisions, 106, 123, 163
red lights, running, 101–102
responsibility
    for accidents, 67–69
    blame vs., 66–69
    for personal safety, 66–69
    quote on, 62
    surface hazards and, 43–44
reverse lights, 121
rib cage injuries, 175
riding with others, 153–55
right turns, 97–100
road position/location, 76–79
    basic guidelines, 76–77
    buffer zone, 77–78
    default, 77
    flexibility and, 78

in heavy traffic, 121–23
lane ownership and, 81–84
space and. *See* spacing
for traffic lights. *See* traffic lights
visibility and. *See* visibility
road rage, 34
road rash, 166–68
Rohe, Mies van der, 56
rolling stops, 93
route choice, 72–76
    assessing options, 73–75
    bike paths and, 75
    gutter riding and, 113–15
    least hassles, 72
    most direct, 72
    objectives, 73
    one-way streets, 74
    riding repeatedly, 76
    varying, 76
rumble strips, 50

S

safety
    Door Zone and, 76, 116–18
    equipment. *See* crash helmets
    feeling for, 76
    instinct and, 109–11
    invisible cyclists and, 79–80, 151–53
    multiple cyclists and, 153–55
    riding position/location and, 76–79
    straight-line riding and, 123–25
    vigilance for, 69–71
Safety Bikes, 8, 9
Seagram Building, 56
seeing, without looking, 107–9, 120
shock, psychogenic, 169
side paths, 75, 134–35, 136–137, 138, 140
sidewalks, 143–47
snow, 54
sounds, hearing, 107–9, 120
spacing
    buffer zone, 77–78
    Gap Effect and, 89–91, 120
    increasing speed and, 78

lane ownership and, 81–84
visibility vs., 80–81
speed
    buffer zone and, 77–78
    momentum and, 93–95
    slow, track stands for, 125–28
    spacing and, 78
Starley, John Kemp, 9
statistics. *See* accident statistics
steering exercise, 127–28
stopping
    distance, 130
    panic stops, 130–33
stop signs
    corner cutters at, 104–5
    eye contact and, 86–89
    Fake Right Turns at, 89
    Figurative Stops at, 94
    four-way, 92–93
    momentum and, 93–95
    red lights as, 101–2
    rolling through, 92–93
straight-line riding, 123–25
streetcars, 24, 26–28
street design
    Le Corbusier and, 28–30
    limited-access freeways and, 28–30
suburbs, 24–26
surface hazards, 43–59
    control joints, 47–48
    cracks, 47–48
    curbs, 57–59
    drainage, 51–53
    grates, 52–53
    lane markers, 49–50
    potholes, 45–47, 152–53
    railroad tracks, 53–54
    seams, 47–48
    toppings, 54–55
    waves, 49
    wet metal, 50
surfaces
    asphalt, 42–43, 207–8
    gutter riding and, 113–15
    pavement types, 42–43

PCC, 42–43, 47–48
of plazas, 56–57

T

tail lights, parked cars and, 120
thorns, 208–12
tires
    flat. *See* flat tires
    as movement indicators, 120
    pneumatic, 10–11
tire wiping, 204–7
tools, 227–30
toppings, 54–55
torsion injuries, 181–82
track bikes, 223–25
track stands, 125–28
traffic lights, 95–102
    destination positioning at, 97, 100
    evolution of, 95–96
    filtering at, 100
    Gap Effect and, 89–91, 120
    green light cautions, 84–86
    left turns at, 75, 95, 96, 103
    not blocking right on red, 100
    pedestrian-like crossing at, 103
    running red lights, 101–2
    technology controlling, 96–97
    timing, cautions, 97
    waiting/positioning at, 97–101
tribulus terrestris plant, 208–11
turning, 128–29
turns
    accident statistic, 161
    hand signals, 112–13
    left-hand, 77, 103
    at traffic lights, 97, 100
    vehicle turn signals and, 111–12
turn signals, 111–12

U

urban rail systems, 24, 26–28

V

vehicular-cycling principle, 62–66
    abusing, 63
    adapting, effectively, 64–66
    origin, 63
    vulnerabilities of, 63–64
velocipedes. *See* boneshakers
vigilance, 69–71
    anticipating driver pullout,
        118–21
    instinct and, 109–11
    preparation and, 70
    road position/location and, 76–79
    vehicle turn signals and, 111–12
visibility
    eye contact and, 86–89
    invisibility vs., 79–80
    night riding and, 149–53
    on side paths, 135
    space vs., 80–81

W

water, on street, 54
waves, 49
wet surfaces
    leaves, 54
    metal, 50
    PCC, 54
winter riding, 54–55
Winton, Alexander, 16, 18
wrenches, 228–30

About
the Author

Robert Hurst is a veteran bicycle messenger and all-around urban cyclist who has cycled more than 150,000 miles and 15,000 hours in heavy traffic. In this time, he has completed something like 80,000 deliveries. Robert is also the author of *Mountain Biking Colorado's San Juan Mountains: Durango and Telluride* (FalconGuides) and *Road Biking Colorado's Front Range* (FalconGuides).